The Motor Racing Story

BY THE SAME AUTHOR
Fast and Furious

RICHARD GARRETT

The Motor Racing Story

SOUTH BRUNSWICK AND NEW YORK:
A. S. BARNES AND CO.

THE MOTOR RACING STORY. © Richard Garrett 1969. First American edition published 1970 by A. S. Barnes and Co., Inc., Cranbury, New Jersey 08512.

Library of Congress Catalogue Card Number: 78-114990

ISBN 0-498-07667-9
Printed in the United States of America

For Anne

Contents

Transatlantic Trackscape

Introduction

Part One   Before the dust settled

1	Teuf, Teuf	3
2	There's a long, long road	21
3	Who were these men?	38
4	A pretty little place called Brooklands	47
5	For the good of the breed	57
6	Pride (plus a lot of prejudice)	66

Part Two   Thunder at noon

7	When the troops came marching home	77

8 Trial by distance	89
9 When in Rome (or Brescia, or Monza, or even Sicily)...	97
10 Into the 'thirties	106
11 Meanwhile—back at the factory	119
12 Interlude on sand and salt	131
13 Children of the Gods	139

Part Three *Towards the present*

14 Where do we go from here?	153
15 Le Mans super spectacular	162
16 Green over red	171
17 Fast, faster, fastest	183
18 For the time being	188

Illustrations

Between pages xvi and xvii

Race-maker in trouble
Log cabin grandstand
Barney Oldfield
Moody Monster
The Greatest Show on Earth
Wine for Victory
The Way of a Conqueror

Between pages 36 and 37

The car that won the Paris–Rouen race of 1895
The other competitors for the 1895 race
S. F. Edge in his Napier at the start of the 1902 Gordon Bennett race
The Napier of Lieutenant-Colonel Mark Mayhew
The first woman racing driver, Mme du Gast
The first Targa Florio (1906)
The Kaiser at the Kaiserpreis
Baron de Caters
Charles Jarrott
Louis Renault
Felice Nazzaro
Leon Théry
Camille Jenatzy
Jenatzy's 'Jamais Contente'
Henry Ford's car called the '999'
The first Grand Prix at Le Mans in 1906
The first Tourist Trophy race on the Isle of Man in 1905
The 1908 French Grand Prix at Dieppe

Illustrations

Between pages 84 and 85

The 1922 French Grand Prix at Strasbourg
Henry Segrave after winning the 1923 French Grand Prix
A 2-litre Sunbeam at the 1922 French Grand Prix
The start of a three-lap cyclecar race at Brooklands
Count Louis Zborowski
'The Bentley Boys'
Two of the 4½-litre conquerors
Count Masetti in the 1922 Targa Florio
An E.R.A. in Ulster for the TT
The 1929 Tourist Trophy race near Belfast
Building George Eyston's 'Thunderbolt'
Malcolm Campbell demonstrates one of the Bluebirds
Tarzo Nuvolari
Campari
Nuvolari at the wheel of an 8-cylinder Alfa Romeo
The Mercedes team of 1938
Visitors to Mercedes
Ferdinand Porsche
The Auto-Union with Rosemeyer driving

Between pages 132 and 133

Farina winning the 1950 British Grand Prix
Stirling Moss winning the 1957 European Grand Prix
Mike Hawthorn
Fangio
Two rear-engined Coopers
Stirling Moss in a Cooper-B.R.M. at Aintree
Levegh in his Mercedes at Le Mans
Levegh is killed at Le Mans
Stirling Moss
Juan Manuel Fangio
Alberto Ascari
Jim Clark
The sprint start at Le Mans
Gurney, Surtees and Ginther
'Spirit of America'
Craig Breedlove crashes
Jim Hall's Chaparral at the 1967 Le Mans
Graham Hill in his Lotus-Ford at the 1968 British Grand Prix

The author wishes to thank the following for providing photographs: The Mathieson Collection, Montagu Motor Museum, *Radio Times*-Hulton, Shell, BP, Daimler-Benz and Porsche.

Introduction to the American Edition: Transatlantic Trackscape

James Gordon Bennett was one of the great American eccentrics. One evening, the story goes, he was entertaining a large party on board his yacht off Monte Carlo. Presently, some of the guests decided the time had come to return to their hotels on shore. They went up on deck and saw, to their considerable dismay, that the vessel was some way out to sea. On a sudden whim, Gordon Bennett had instructed his captain to up-anchor and steam southeastwards. The fun-loving assembly spent a somewhat uncomfortable night on the ocean; and it was not until well into the following morning, that the ship returned to Monte Carlo and they were released from their floating prison.

As a newspaperman (he was proprietor of the *New York Herald*), Gordon Bennett's original turn of mind had plenty of opportunities in which to indulge its fancies. He realised, as any circulation-builder must, the importance of stunts, scoops and spectacles. After he took up residence in Paris, he became aware of the growing interest in motor racing. They say that the French gave birth to the sport. If this is so, at least one American was waiting in the maternity ward to slap the lusty infant into life. Not only did James Gordon Bennett help to finance the Paris-Rouen road race of 1895, but he also instituted his own series of events, the Gordon Bennett Races, which were held in an atmosphere of sometimes furious argument and always furious excitement, between 1900 and 1905.

Another wealthy American who supported the Paris-Rouen race was W. K. Vanderbilt. Unlike Gordon Bennett, Vanderbilt was an extremely talented driver. On two occasions, in 1902 and 1904, he held the World Land Speed Record. On the first, driving a 60 h.p. Mors which had been built for road racing, his speed was 76.08 m.p.h. On the second, he took a racing Mercedes "Ninety" to Daytona Beach in Florida, where he put up an average speed of 92.03 m.p.h. Neither of Vanderbilt's records endured for very long, but at least he had the credit for being the first man to break the magic number at Daytona. Twenty years later, this stretch of seashore became the most popular place for these ventures—until the speeds outstripped the capacity of the sands, and the venue moved to Bonneville Salt Flats in Utah.

Like Gordon Bennett, Vanderbilt also established his own series of races. They were indeed to North America what Gordon Bennett's were to Europe, and they were surrounded by no less controversy and drama.

They were originally designed to be run on public roads in Nassau County, Long Island. The first took place in 1904, and was won by a driver named George Heath at the wheel of a huge Panhard. Vanderbilt is said to have observed afterwards that it "was a good, clean contest—full of interest."

It was certainly interesting, though its goodness and its cleanliness may have been open to doubt. For one thing, the local farmers, resenting the intrusion of the loud-sounding juggernauts and the crowds which poured out of New York City to follow their fortunes, did all they could to sabotage the event. They put nails and other obstructions on to the road, and the result was a fearful Armageddon of crashed cars and broken bodies.

Nevertheless, the races were held for two more years under these conditions. Eventually, however, something had to be done about what was becoming known as "the annual Long Island blood bath". In Europe, the carnage which occurred in the 1903 Paris-Madrid Race had caused motor racing to be confined to closed circuits. In 1908, Vanderbilt built a closed circuit on private land. It was called the Long Island Motor Parkway. Races for his cup were held there in 1908, 1909, 1910. By all accounts, the carnage and the casualties were only marginally reduced.

When the English circuit at Brooklands was completed in 1907, a party of Americans is said to have studied it, and to have built a rough replica at a place in Hoosier Country named Indianapolis. In fact, the idea for the speedway occurred when four businessmen were motoring in a car of unspecified make, but which kept on breaking down. At some point in the trip, one of them observed that there ought to be a special place for the proper testing and development of automobiles, so that the public would not be subjected to so much unreliability and inconvenience.

One of the men, Carl G. Fisher, had made a trip to Europe some years earlier (he, possibly, was the student of Brooklands) and had conceived an ambition to build a racing track. Now, his companions told him, was surely the time to do something about it.

Presently, they found an old farm on the edge of the town, which was placed conveniently close to the highway and the railroad. The farmer was asking $80,000 for his land. But, said a real estate man who was in the party, he would probably take $300 an acre. Eventually, with five stockholders each holding 50,000 dollars' worth of shares, the land was purchased and a 2.5-mile oval track was built.

Initially, it had a gravel surface, and it was inaugurated with three days of racing in August 1909. These were sprint events, and they were marked by an unacceptably high rate of accidents. The toll, indeed, was such that the management became convinced that a dirt track would not do. In one of the most remarkable construction operations ever carried out, the track was resurfaced with 3,200,000 bricks (hence, presumably, the Indianapolis nickname of "the Brickyard"). The work was completed in time for a series of sprint races scheduled for December 18 of that year. Unfortunately, the weather was less cooperative than the local labourers. On the appointed day, the thermometer registered 32°F., which was totally unsuitable for racing—brick surface, or no brick surface. The event had to be postponed until May of the following year.

In 1935, part of the track was resurfaced with asphalt. Nowadays, it is all asphalt except for a 36-inch strip of the original bricks across the starting line. The speedway covers 539 acres, and the track consists of four turns, each of them ¼-mile long, linked by ⅛-mile straights. The corners are banked at 9°12 minutes.

After the second World War, Brooklands was never reopened as a circuit. The aircraft industry had established itself there since the early days of flying. Its buildings had grown and grown until they virtually gobbled the place up. At about this time, it looked as if Indianapolis might be condemned to a similar fate. The threat came not from the aviation industry, but from four years of neglect. When, shortly after the end of the war, Wilbur Shaw (he who was the first man to win the Indianapolis "500" for two years running, and won it three times in all) visited the Brickyard to test some tyres for Firestone, he was appalled at the appearance of the place.

There were large cracks in the track, which had to be patched up before Shaw could carry out his tests. Weeds were growing through bricks on the main straight, and the old wooden grandstands looked as if, given a healthy puff of wind, they would tumble over. Captain Eddie Rickenbacker, who had been president of the speedway ever since he had bought it in 1927, was clearly not interested in undertaking the extremely expensive reconstruction programme needed to restore it. Consequently, Shaw launched a one man save-the-speedway campaign. He eventually succeeded in interesting a wealthy local industrialist, and the work began. Among the improvements were large concrete grandstands and the scoreboard tower, which was completed in 1959.

Wilbur Shaw served as president and general manager to the speedway until his tragic death in an air crash on October 30, 1954.

The first Indianapolis "500" race took place on May 30, 1911, and this classic has been held on Memorial Day ever since. The price of general admission was $1.00. At 6:30 A.M. an aerial bomb exploded, the gates were opened and the crowd surged in. Something like 80,000 people were present to watch a lineup of 40 cars. Each driver went round for one lap solo, while a commentator introduced him to the spectators. The competitors then returned to the starting line and waited. Presently another aerial bomb exploded. This was the signal to start the engines. Travelling at 40 m.p.h., and driving in tight formation, they set off on the pace lap. As the pace car crossed the line, it peeled off onto the pit apron. The starter swept the air with his red flag to show that the track ahead was clear and, with a roar that sounded like the anger of the gods, the pack took off on its 500-mile journey. The race was won by Ray Harroun in a Marmon Wasp at an average speed of 74.69 m.p.h.

The story of Indianapolis has been beautifully told by Al Bloemker in his book *500 Miles to Go*. In 1913, the race was seriously invaded by foreigners for the first time, and was won by a Frenchman named Jules Goux in a Peugeot. Goux spoke no English. When he was asked to say a few words after his victory, he announced: *"Sans le bon vin, je n'aurais pas été en état d'être vainqueur"*.* All of which was no doubt perfectly true; for, during pit-stops at which his Peugeot's wheels were changed, he consumed no fewer than four bottles of champagne.

Nowadays, all top drivers are paid starting money. When, in 1916, Ralph de Palma (who had won the race in the previous year) put in a claim for "appearance money", and threatened to boycott the race if he did not receive it, the organisers tersely told him that he could "stay at home and rot". By de Palma's own estimate, he was motor racing's biggest single-seater attraction. Nevertheless, on this occasion, he stayed at home (he did not rot, but he never won the "500" again).

The first driver to complete the race at an average speed of over 100 m.p.h. was Billy Arnold who, in 1930, averaged 100.448 in his Miller Hartz Special; and 1965 was the year in which it was won for the first time by a British driver driving an all-British car. The driver was Jim Clark and the car was a Lotus-Ford ("Ford" in this case meaning Ford U.K. as opposed to Ford U.S.A.).

In 1959, the first United States Grand Prix was held. The venue was at Sebring. In the following year, it was transferred to Riverside Speedway, and in 1961 it moved to its present home at Watkins Glen in upstate New York. With such a well established classic as the Indianapolis "500" already on the American calendar, it may seem strange that it was necessary to produce a new event to appear on the list of *grandes epreuves* which count for the winning of World Championship points. This was due to the nature

---

* Without good wine, I could not have been the winner.

of the race and, particularly, to the circuit. The grand prix events grew out of the old road races, whilst the Brickyard is essentially an oval saucer in which the cars circulate in an anti-clockwise direction. This had produced a special breed of "Indi" car, with a bigger engine than that permitted by the Fédération Internationale Automobile's regulations governing grand prix racing. Furthermore, since the driver spends most of his time in the race turning left, the body is offset on the chassis to provide better handling. On the European grand prix circuits, an "Indi" car would be virtually undriveable.

Ironically enough, since the United States Grand Prix was founded, it has never yet been won by an American driver. However, there may perhaps be an element of compensation in the fact that when, in 1966, Graham Hill won at Indianapolis, and Jim Clark won at Watkins Glen, the 24-Hour Race at Le Mans was won by Chris Amon and Bruce McLaren driving a 7-litre Ford which had made the trip from Detroit. When, in the following year, this event was won for a second time by Ford with A. J. Foyt and Dan Gurney driving, it was an all-American victory. If any further proof is needed of the equity which exists in the melting pot of results, there is Phil Hill's World Championship of 1961; or, with Phil Hill at the wheel, the victory of Jim Hall's Chaparral in the six-hour race at Brands Hatch, England, in 1967.

Dan Gurney, Phil Hill, and an occasional drive from Mario Andretti (who won at the Brickyard in 1969) are the only top American drivers to have been seen in Formula 1 races during recent years. The reason for this is largely economic. The prize money is so much better in America that a driver who is capable of winning races would do better to remain in the U.S.A. and build up a fortune. The somewhat parsimonious purses offered by European race organisers are hardly worth the fare across the Atlantic.

At least one breed of sports cars has been preserved thanks entirely to North American enterprise. This is the machine which, according to F.I.A. regulations, is classified under Group 7. It is basically a two-seater sports racing car, but it is a great many other things besides. Group 7 is the category in which anything, but *anything,* goes. There are no restrictions to curb the speed-seeking dreams of the designers. The result is an extremely potent, desperately athletic, brute of a car, which is tremendously exciting to watch.

RACE-MAKER IN TROUBLE
W. K. Vanderbilt changes a tyre. Lame car in the background is Vanderbilt's powerful racer, "Red Devil."

LOG CABIN GRANDSTAND
... is at the starting line of Vanderbilt's autocourse on Long Island.

BARNEY OLDFIELD
. . . ace driver.

MOODY MONSTER
A 16-litre Benz competing in one of the Vanderbilt Cup races. The machines were enormous—the conditions sometimes chaotic.

THE GREATEST SHOW ON EARTH
A poster advertises an event at the "Brickyard" in 1910. The first "500" race was to take place in the following year.

WINE FOR VICTORY
After winning the 1913 "500" at Indianapolis, Frenchman Jules Goux (seen here in his Peugeot) told reporters that copious glasses of champagne during the race had sped him to victory.

THE WAY OF A CONQUEROR
Arnold racing to victory in the 1930 Indianapolis "500" at the wheel of a Miller-Hartz special.

In Europe, Group 7 events were banned after the 1965 season. In North America, however, they flourish in the Can-Am series, which first came on to the calendar in 1966.

There are a number of peculiarly American types of motor sport, such as drag racing and stockcar events, of which one only finds rather pale reflections on the European side of the Atlantic. Certainly, as one might expect, the North American Continent provides the greatest variety of automobile racing to be found anywhere on earth. If one wishes to see the World Land Speed Record broken, one takes oneself to Bonneville to watch the fantastic runs of the jetcars, which owe their origins to the Californian dragsters. If one wishes to watch European-style sports car racing, one can go to the races at Sebring or Daytona, and watch Ferraris and Porsches going about their fast and capable business. Anyone whose Formula 1 appetite is not satisfied by one race a year at Watkins Glen can take a trip to Canada for the Canadian Grand Prix, or travel south into Mexico for the event at Mexico City. Since it is the final event in the World Championship series, it is sometimes the most exciting.

When I sat down to plan this book, I took a hurried look at the entire trackscape of motor racing. It is immense. To do anything like justice to it would require more than one volume. That is why, in *The Motor Racing Story*, I have concentrated largely on the European scene and contented myself with introducing the occasional sidelight from North America.

R. G.

Tunbridge Wells, England

Introduction

This isn't a complete history of motor racing. It couldn't possibly be. The sport has been in existence for nearly eighty years. During this period it has grown more branches than the average tree. To deal with them all between one set of covers would be quite out of the question.

Fortunately, motor racing has never been short of historians. In my research for this book I have consulted more volumes than can conveniently be listed here. Not unnaturally, perhaps, they have mostly been concerned with the results of races and the specifications of cars.

Drivers and entrants, on the whole, have received short shrift from history.

My intention has been to try to show a little of the sweat and toil which has gone into motor racing: the frustrations, the dramas, the comedy and the tragedy of it. As a writer, I have been impressed by the exquisite pattern of motor racing as a dramatic form. It has its beginnings, its middles and its ends. It is crammed with climaxes, and the personalities at the top are a little apart from the rest of the world—just as actors are.

It is a curiously unreal world and, if my research is accurate, it has always been like that. Above all things, it is seldom dull.

Nobody in his right mind would think of attempting a work such as this without consulting Gerald Rose's *A Record of Motor Racing* and I certainly haven't tried to do so without it. The source books, of course, are the old volumes of *The Autocar* and *Motor*, which reach right back into history. Wherever would one have been without them?

My thanks are also due to Mme Alice Caracciola, who was so helpful to me when I visited her in Lugano.

To Mr. Cecil Bianchi, Mr. Tony Brooks, Mr. S. C. H. Davis, Mr. Sidney Enever, Captain George Eyston, Mr. Alec Hounslow, Mr. Raymond Mays and Major Harold Parker—who are among the people who supplied me with first-hand accounts of events.

To the librarians at the Royal Automobile Club and the Veteran Car Club, for letting me camp out on their premises for days on end.

To the Shell International Petroleum Co. Ltd. for arranging a special showing of all their films on the history of motor racing, and for giving me copies of the scripts.

To Mr. Ken Tyrrell, who loaned me his copy of William Court's capacious *Power and Glory* (MacDonald) over a year ago, and still hasn't had it back.

To all the people who, during the course of my normal duties as a motoring journalist, fed me with information.

To Mr. William Boddy, Mr. W. F. Bradley, Mlle L'Ébe Bugatti, Mr. Rudolf Caracciola, Mr. W. O. Duncan, Mr. Selwyn F. Edge, Commendatore Enzo Ferrari, Mr. David Hodges, Mr. Richard Hough, Mr. Peter Hull, Mr. Charles Jarrott, Mr. Denis Jenkinson, Mr. Kent Karslake, M. Sain Loup, Mr. Peter Miller, Lord Montagu of Beaulieu, Mr. Arthur Owen, Mr. Lawrence Pomeroy, Mr. Roy Slater, and Mr. Rodney Walkerley, who have either written or edited books which I have consulted.

Finally, thank you for buying this copy of *The Motor Racing Story* (or for taking it out of the library—every little helps!). I hope you'll enjoy it.

R.G.

Tunbridge Wells, Kent
1969

'I will show you fear in a handful of dust'
　　　　　　　　　　　T. S. ELIOT *The Waste Land*

Part One
Before the dust settled

Part One
Before the first settler

1 Teuf Teuf[1]

When the Spirit of Internal Combustion tottered on to the roads in the late nineteenth century, different nations regarded it in different ways. The Germans considered it an opportunity to build engines. The French saw it as an occasion to manufacture cars. The British viewed it with intense suspicion.

One of the more articulate antagonists in England suggested that it 'barked like a dog and stank like a cat'. Pioneer motorists were sometimes horsewhipped by their opponents. When the Countess of Warwick arrived at a hunt in a motorised landaulette she was given a severe reprimand by the Master of Foxhounds. At least one newspaper, *The North British Daily Mail*, accused the automobile of being responsible for political disturbances in France. 'Remove the car', its editorial primly said, 'and the troubles will be at an end.'

When the Hon. John Scott-Montagu, M.P. (later 2nd Lord

[1] Being the French word for a veteran car. It is so excellently onomatopoeic that it ought to be used by the British to replace such descriptive nouns as 'veteran' and 'old crock'. It would, after all, be a fair swop for le weekend, le coming man, and all les other things.

Montagu of Beaulieu), tried to park in the palace yard at Westminster his way was barred by a policeman. It was not until he had complained to the Speaker of the House of Commons that his car was allowed in. Well after the so-called Emancipation Day rejoicings, a motorist in Sevenoaks was fined £5 plus £1 17s. costs for 'furiously driving a motor car to the common danger at a speed exceeding 12 m.p.h.' The prosecution alleged that he had been doing 40 m.p.h.; the defence protested that he had only been doing 9 m.p.h. Since it happened on the way up a stretch of fairly steep hill, one has to assume that the latter's estimate was more accurate.

This was just one of thousands such cases.

The law, of course, was an ass. Somebody or some*thing* had given birth to this monstrous new contraption. To begin with, no lawmaker seemed to be certain what, precisely, it was. Some members of the body politic closed their eyes tightly and hoped it would go away. Others, who were more dangerous, looked around for a few precedents. Unhappily, they found them.

There was nothing new about self-propelled vehicles in Britain. Quite apart from the railways, which were fondly considered to be the envy of the world, there were a number of steam vehicles on the roads. As early as 1827, a man named Gurney had been running a steam-driven stage-coach between London and Bath; and in 1834 Hancock was treating Londoners to the delights of a steam bus service. His coach, called 'Era', carried fourteen passengers at a time between Paddington, Regent's Park and the City. The fare was a penny each way. About 4,000 people made the trip.

Later on the traction engines arrived. Nobody seemed to regard them with excessive dislike. In any case, they were quickly surrounded by legislation, presumably to protect innocent citizens from them. All told, there were four Acts of Parliament involved. The one of 1865 insisted that each should have two men on board, with a third out in front carrying a red flag. It was amended in 1878, when the man in front no longer needed to take a flag with him. His job was to warn horse traffic of the approaching locomotive, and to help calm down the panic-stricken beasts when it came into view. This Act also laid down a couple of speed limits. In towns they were confined to 2 m.p.h.—in the country to 4 m.p.h. And that was what Emancipation Day was all about.

The Authorities had regarded the horseless carriage, autocar, automatic carriage, or whatever anyone cared to call it, and tried to find some sort of kinship between it and something that already existed. It was clearly not a horse, nor was it a bicycle. It had few of the features of a railway train, and not by the longest stretch of the imagination could you call it a ship. So what was left? Obviously—a traction engine. It was another locomotive on the highways, and was treated accordingly.

They dug out that fusty old Act of 1878 and clamped it on to the car. They said that a man must precede it wherever it went, and that it must never travel faster than 2 m.p.h. (in towns) and 4 m.p.h. (in the country). They also gave local authorities a certain amount of scope for making irksome byelaws. In short, they did their very best with existing material to legislate the thing out of existence.

Horses, of course, were always cropping up. Perhaps the pity of it was that nobody was able to ask for their opinion. King Edward VII may have come reasonably close to guessing it after a holiday on the Riviera, during which he had learned to drive. He was Prince of Wales at the time, and he was reputed to have said that in London traffic it was better to punish cars than horses. It was a sentiment with which the latter must have devoutly agreed. In the overcrowded streets of the metropolis their treatment was often little short of brutal. However, constitutional monarchy being what it is, His Royal Highness's opinions went unheeded.

A writer's vision of roads becoming monopolised by cars and bicycles, with horses freed from servitude and happily 'roaming the trackless plains', was dismissed as fantasy—possibly because Britain, already on the way to becoming overcrowded, was short of trackless plains.

There the luckless newcomer to the highway scene was—surrounded by bigotry, suspicion, primitive fear, and plain hatred. There were, fortunately, one or two individualists who took a somewhat different view. One of them was a baronet, who lived near Tunbridge Wells. His name was David Salomons.

Salomons was the nephew of a wealthy London banker. When the latter died after two marriages had failed to produce any sons or daughters, this young man inherited the greater part of his fortune. Thereafter, he seems to have lived life on two levels. One was as a pillar of society. He was a director of the South Eastern Railway, a member of the Kent County Council and Justice of the Peace—everything, indeed, that our Victorian ancestors, who had a great sense of position, could have asked of a baronet.

But then came his other side. He had always been an enthusiast for popular science, and, by giving lectures, he had done his best to *make* it popular. In a beautifully equipped workshop which was part of his Gothic (nineteenth-century version) mansion at Southborough in Kent, he *invented* things. Among his discoveries were an indicator for measuring the speed of revolving shafts, improvements to the electric-lamp bulb, a slide rule for photographic purposes, and an electric tricycle. The last of these, which was produced in 1875, was a failure—mainly because he was floored by the problem of recharging the batteries.

The motor car, of course, was just the kind of thing that David Salomons really enjoyed. He was a prolific writer, and he was soon battering the *Daily Telegraph* with letters on its behalf. In 1895 he promoted Britain's first motor show at Tunbridge Wells. With great daring he actually took some of the exhibits out on to the road. There were only two horseless carriages on show—the *pièce de résistance* was a petrol-driven fire engine, which was demonstrated with great aplomb by the local Volunteer Fire Brigade.

Thanks to David Salomons and his friends, other exhibitions followed. The most important took place at the Imperial Institute in 1896. It was visited by the Prince of Wales, who was driven around the exhibits by the Hon. Evelyn Ellis in a Canstatt-Daimler. Also present were members of the Houses of Lords and Commons, who were lavishly entertained. This was the sort of thing which latter-day public-relations men have learned to do instinctively, and it worked (up to a point, at any rate). The result was the passing of the somewhat euphemistically named 'Emancipation Act', which was, of course, nothing of the kind.

Nevertheless, *The Autocar*[1] saw fit to print an issue throughout in red ink to celebrate the occasion. Red was because, in *Autocar's* words, 'Today, November 14th, 1896, is a red-letter day, not only in the history of automobilism, but in that of England itself, for it marks the throwing open of the highways and byways of our beautiful country to those who elect to travel thereupon in carriages propelled by motors, instead of in horse-drawn vehicles or upon bicycles.'

Warming to its subject, the editorial continued: 'Yesterday we were criminals, if we ventured upon the Queen's highways, and our journeys were either taken surreptitiously, in fear and trembling, as trespassers upon forbidden ground, at the mercy of every officious country bumpkin in the uniform of the police force who sought to score points for promotion by securing a "case", or else we rode, where every other British subject enjoyed the right of

[1] The first issue was published in November 2nd, 1895.

way, only by favour of certain more enlightened authorities, who, to their credit be it said, elected to use common sense in the matter, and refused to be bound hand and foot by an illogical, stagnating, and misconstrued enactment.'

What, in fact, the 'red-letter day' was celebrating was that, henceforth, nobody need walk in front of cars. The speed limit was raised to 12 m.p.h. in towns and 14 m.p.h. in the country, and that was all. To be fair to the country bumpkins who wore the uniform of police, many of them turned a kindly blind eye to the very occasional vehicle which clattered by.

The actual Emancipation Day run, which was from the Hotel Metropole in London to the Hotel Metropole in Brighton, was something of a flop. The horseless carriages set off in fog. It was not supposed to be a race, but it became one—with Leon Bollée completing the 60-odd miles in 3 hours 44 minutes, 35 seconds, and Camille Bollée arriving about an hour later. Few of the vehicles finished. A parcels van, which was supposed to be serving as a breakdown truck, spent most of its time in a somewhat supine condition beside the road. It didn't reach Brighton until 3 a.m. on the following morning. As for the people who lined the route to watch the cars pass by—as evidence of mechanical reliability, they found the whole thing remarkably unimpressive.

Later, in 1901, Thomas Alva Edison was to observe that: 'The motor car ought to have been British. You invented it in the 1830's. You have roads only second to those of France. You have thousands of skilled mechanics in your midst, but you have lost your trade by the same kind of stupid legislation and prejudice that have put you back in many departments of the electrical field.'

There must have been many in Britain who, on that dark November day of 1896, thought similar things. In particular, there were forty members of the Motor Car Club who, earlier in the year, had taken advantage of an excursion to France arranged by the club. In return for £5 each (or four guineas, if they were prepared to travel second class) they had been to see the Paris–Marseilles–Paris motor race. This included not only the return fares but also hotel accommodation, trips round the car-makers' factories in Paris, the services of a courier, and even a guide-book.

No doubt it was heavily subsidised by that remarkable financier Harry Lawson (he either made or broke the fledgling British car industry—it depends on how you look at these things), who was then more or less running the Motor Car Club. Nevertheless, they had enjoyed the opportunity of actually witnessing a motor race, and that was something which nobody in England would be able to do for a good few years to come.

A race, if it is to be given that description, ought to consist of more than one competitor. Consequently, it is a little difficult to accept an effort of 1887 as the the world's first motor-sport event—though that is what its organisers, the French magazine *Vélocipède*, clearly intended it to be. It consisted of Count Albert de Dion circulating on a steam quadricycle round and round a covered course in Paris. For want of any opponent, he was riding all by himself.

This may not have been a very breathtaking spectacle, but it gives us an opportunity to bring the Count on to the stage. This great man was almost a show in himself. Although his ancestors were Belgian, one of them raised sixty ships for Napoleon's unaccomplished invasion of Britain. His father commanded a battalion in the Franco-Prussian War. The family had huge estates and, of course, masses of money.

In his teens, Albert de Dion revealed a technical bent. He built a small hydraulic hammer and was later despatched to Munich to learn German. He learned it, but, which was probably more important to the course of history, he also discovered how to build steam engines.

Presently he returned to Paris. He was large, flamboyant, with an elegantly waxed moustache, and a personality fit to topple the Eiffel Tower. At the gambling tables he won and lost thousands of pounds. He was a good shot, an excellent linguist (he spoke English fluently), and a quite remarkably *bon viveur*. Although robustly good-natured, he was quick to anger and fought at least one duel. Socially, he was greatly sought after—not only because of his rank and his very noble family but also because he was inclined to liven up even the most dreary dinner table.

On one occasion the Duc de Morny was proposing to hold a ball. He asked his friend de Dion to buy the favours for the cotillon. (In case you haven't been involved in one, I should, perhaps, explain that this is a dance which is named after the French word for 'petticoat'. Among its complicated collection of steps are times when partners are exchanged and small presents are given.) Anyway, de Dion had to purchase these favours, and off he set down the Boulevard des Italiens with his customary thick bankroll.

He hadn't gone very far when he was pulled up short by a fabulous sight in one of the shop windows. It was a small working model of a steam engine. The cylinder was made of glass, and you could watch the tiny piston being pushed up and down.

The Count strode inside. 'Who,' he demanded, 'made this mechanical gem?'

He was directed to a little firm named Bouton and Trépardoux at the east end of Paris. He drove over there in his luxurious carriage and pair, and presently was face to face with Bouton.

If de Dion was rather larger than life, Bouton was just the opposite. He regarded the world quietly over the top of a huge moustache. His voice was gentle and his movements careful.

De Dion came straight to the point. 'How much do you earn by making these machines?' he asked.

Bouton told him: 'On average seven to eight francs a day. We just about get an honest living from them, but sales are rare and the work is badly paid.'

'Right,' said de Dion, 'I'll pay you ten francs a day if you'll work exclusively for me.' They shook hands and that, for the moment was that.

The object at the back of de Dion's mind was to build a steam-engined carriage. First of all, however, they had to invent a suitable boiler. Once they'd got that right, they built a steam quadricycle—the very same, no doubt, as that on which the Count raced round the track in Paris that day in 1887.

Nothing ever goes entirely smoothly, even when you have all the wealth and power of the de Dions behind you. Before the new enterprise had gone very far the Count's father tried to slap a restraining injunction on him. There was a lot of talk about fortunes squandered at the gambling tables and similar excesses, but happily it petered out. This was possibly due to the fact that nearly everyone liked Albert de Dion. When, in 1891, he was elected deputy for Nantes, it was by a majority so large that it had never been equalled in French history.

In 1894 Trépardoux, who was Bouton's brother-in-law, was bought out. But by then the Count and his big-moustached accomplice were established as one of the first, and certainly one of the leading, car-makers in the world.

While gentlemen in England were still wondering what strange mechanical shape had come about and what dark tidings it was trying to tell them, the French were busy conceiving motor racing. Birth of a kind occurred one day in 1894, when the paper *Le Petit Journal* announced that it proposed to sponsor a *'Concours des Voitures sans Chevaux'*. It was to take place between Paris and Rouen, and entries were invited. Members of the paper's staff were to be the judges (they were later dismissed as a crowd of 'incompetents' by a writer named Giffart who did the organising), and the first prize would be awarded to the vehicle which, in the judges' opinions, was 'without danger, easily handled, and of low running cost'. There was no mention of speed—although, to qualify, an aspiring competitor had to cover 50 km in four hours (originally it had been three hours, but some of the candidates considered that an average speed of 10 m.p.h. was dangerously fast).

The list of entries closed on April 30th, 1894, and what a fantastic document it was! One hundred and two were received and they encompassed just about every form of motive power that man could make, or imagine making. There were vehicles propelled by petrol, by steam, and by electricity. But then there were such ingenious devices as compressed air, hydraulics, the weight of the passengers, a system of levers, high-pressure gas, gas and pendulum, a pendulum on its own, electro-pneumatic (whatever that was), a system of pedals, and so on. In the end, however, realism seems to have prevailed, for the only vehicles at the eliminating trials were driven either by petrol or else by steam. In the event, thirty-seven petrol vehicles and twenty-nine steamers turned up.

The date of the run had to be postponed twice. On the first Marioni—the proprietor of *Le Petit Journal*, who was presenting second, third, fourth, and fifth prizes (the paper itself was giving a first prize of £200)—had to be somewhere else on business. On the second, it transpired that not enough vehicles were ready. Eventually, it took place on July 22nd.

The idea was for the twenty-one vehicles which had qualified to assemble at the Porte Maillot in Paris between 7 a.m. and 7.45 a.m. This would give the people of Paris a fine opportunity to view the machines. At 8 a.m. they were scheduled to set off from the Boulevard Maillot, arrive at Mantes for lunch at about midday, and, with a bit of luck, reach Rouen at about 8 p.m. The weather was good, and everybody was very impressed and optimistic.

In due course, motor racing was to produce its so-called *formula libre*. For this event there was no formula at all—or, if there was, it was so free that it defied definition. De Dion was hedging his bets by entering both steam- and petrol-driven vehicles. Count Albert himself was at the controls of a lively little steam tractor which, possibly in deference to his status, was the first to set off.

There were touring cars by Peugeot and by Panhard and Lavassor, a whopping great eight-seater omnibus entered by a man named J. Scotte of Epernay, a pair of huge Serpollet steam delivery vans from the Le Blant brothers who owned a Parisian store called La Belle Jardinière, and other, less spectacular, machines.

One of the difficulties at the outset was finding enough drivers to go round. Maurice Le Blant, for example, had obviously no intention of letting his brother Etienne take the controls of his second great steamer. Everybody acknowledged that Etienne had excellent intentions. But, they said, he hadn't enough experience to be any good.

Alas—poor Etienne lost no time in showing them how right they were. The very act of trying to park in the Boulevard Maillot turned out to be too much for his limited experience. He ran the vehicle on to the footpath and demolished a bench.

Maurice Le Blant sought help. Surely there must be somebody who could put up a better performance than his unhappy brother? There wasn't. Etienne was forced to set off for Rouen. Not surprisingly, he never got there.

The cavalcade departed with de Dion's tractor in the lead, and the rest following at 30-second intervals. The Le Blants were having trouble already. They did not get off at a 30-second interval. It was quite some time after the last-but-two competitor had rattled away before they managed to coax their engines on to the highway which led to Rouen.

Naturally, there were some disappointments. One of the early starters succumbed when an axle was damaged by a rough section of road. However, the car behind it stopped and picked up the driver and his passengers. It was a nice piece of chivalry and characteristic of the event. All along the line those who were still in the running loaded their vehicles up with those who were not.

M. Scotte's omnibus dropped out when one of the boiler tubes burst—just as the stoker (*chauffeur* in French, if you want to see how *that* word originated) was seeing to the fire. The driver jumped clear before the vehicle stopped, and cut his hands and knees. Otherwise, there were no casualties.

As a matter of fact, this was not quite such an unhappy occurrence as it seemed to be at the time. When all was done, M. Scotte was awarded a consolation prize of £20 for owning the most deserving car that never reached Rouen.

All along the way, the route was lined with spectators. Some of them were terrified; most of them were ecstatic. Indeed, the crowds were so big that when the competitors stopped at Mantes for lunch, some of them never got anything to eat.

There was a princely reception awaiting at Rouen, with a specially erected triumphal arch, bouquets of flowers for the drivers, and food and wine galore. De Dion was the first to arrive, in spite of having taken a wrong turning at one stage and driven into a field of potatoes. His average speed for the trip was 11·6 m.p.h. Peugeots came second and third, with speeds of 11·5 and 11·1 m.p.h., and then came a brace of Panhard and Levassors. Panhard was driving the first (average speed: 10·7 m.p.h.), and Levassor the second (average speed: 10·2 m.p.h.).

It only remained to decide who should win first prize.

De Dion's steam tractor was praised for the vigorous way in which it tackled hills, but, by some devious logic, it was ruled out because it required a mechanic on board as well as a driver. This did not, however, disqualify the Count from winning the second prize (of £80).

The choice was now between Peugeot and Panhard and Levassor. At first the former was favoured because the steering seemed to be better, and it was more like an 'ordinary' [sic] car than the big-wheeled Panhard. But then Giffard pointed out that Panhards were made entirely at their own works in France, whilst Peugeots purchased their engines from the Panhard-Levassor plant and only fitted them to chassis. This being the case, Panhard and Levassor seemed to be the more deserving, and were awarded the £200 first prize.

Out of all this motley collection of early automobiliana only four failed to complete the course, and it was considered to be a great success. Somebody (probably de Dion) said: 'We must do something like this again.'

To make sure that something did happen, a committee was formed as soon as the event was over. The prime mover was Count de Dion with his friend the Baron de Zuylen de Nyevell backing him up. This was the beginning of the Automobile Club de France, the oldest of all the bodies which govern motor sport. All they needed now was another event. The officials on the Paris–Rouen run had made a complete mess of the timekeeping. Now it was to be done properly. It would be a genuine motor race.

In view of its early support, it was not surprising that they looked once more to the munificient French press to act as sponsor. They approached Giffard, who put the idea before his editor on *Le Petit Journal*. Much to Giffard's, and doubtless other people's, surprise, the editor suddenly got cold feet.

With considerable emotion he exclaimed: 'Racing? Never! When an event is a great proof of reliability, that is fine. But speed as an end in itself? That is impossible. What if there should be an accident? It would be disastrous. Think of all the ammunition it would give to *Le Petit Journal*'s political opponents!'

As is so often the case, politics won the day. There were to be no hand-outs from *Le Petit Journal*. If, however, the editor imagined that matters would rest there, he reckoned without de Dion. Soon that diehard automobilist was sending out invitations to a small dinner party at his house on the Quai D'Orsay. Giffard was there (defying his editor?), the Count de Chasseloup-Laubat, Peugeot, Serpollet, Levassor (Panhard busy back at the factory?), and others. Between them they formed a subcommittee of the newly formed club. The object was to organise a race for the following year (1895) and they decided that it should be from Paris to Bordeaux and back again.

The fact that this subcommittee was largely composed of constructors with a scattering of aristocrats gives an apt impression of motor racing as it was then, and as it was to be for the next ten years. The aristocrats did it for the sheer love of a new sport; the manufacturers did it because they had already cottoned on to the idea that racing successes would help to sell cars.

Perhaps in deference to the anxieties of *Le Petit Journal*'s editor, the sub-committee made it clear that this was not to be exclusively a test of speed. After all, speed and reliability were two things which had to go together. A car which was only fast wouldn't finish—and, therefore, couldn't win. Similarly, a car which was slow through faulty design certainly didn't deserve to win; and, equally certainly, it wouldn't. They even went so far as to stipulate that the first prize should not be given to a car with only two seats. There was no talk of 'improving the breed', but that was obviously what they were getting at. As it turned out, the fastest cars didn't even finish. They were the first to break down.

A sum of £2,800 was subscribed by way of prize money. Among those who sent cheques was James Gordon Bennett,[1] proprietor of the *New York Herald*, and his fellow American, W. K. Vanderbilt. The total amount was to be divided up among the winners on the basis of 50 per cent to the driver of the first car, 20 per cent to the second and 10 per cent to the third. Those who

---

[1] Gordon Bennett had shown his interest in the new sport in the previous year when he despatched a reporter on a bicycle to cover the Paris–Rouen run.

finished in fourth, fifth, sixth and seventh places were to receive 5 per cent each. Manufacturers could enter as many cars as they pleased—so long as they did not make them all of identical design. Drivers could be changed *en route*; but repairs, which could only be done with materials carried on the car, had to be supervised by race drivers.

Forty-six vehicles were entered for the race. Twenty-three of them were petrol-driven, thirteen were steamers, and two were powered by electricity. There were also eight tricycles and bicycles. It may have been because they were in a minority, but a member of the French Institute of Civil Engineers was moved to remark that 'motor cycles are never likely to be more than a curiosity'. Or had he just returned from a trip to England, where any self-propelled device was still regarded as a devilish oddity?

Complicated exercises in planning followed the publication of the rules. Panhard and Levassor, believing that their entries would perform best if only two drivers handled each car, stationed a team of reserves at a point along the route. The first team was supposed to drive from the start to this point, whereupon the second drivers would take over. They would travel the remaining distance to Bordeaux and so back to the change-over spot. The cars would then be returned to the original team, who would take them over the last leg back to Paris. Not the least of the plan's merits was that the drivers would be reasonably fresh when they sat down behind the controls.

In the event, Levassor, who piloted one of his firm's machines, chose to ignore his relief driver and went the entire distance on his own. The other drivers did what they were told.

The Peugeot tactics were based upon two men to a car. They also took the wise precaution of including a timetable of trains at stations near the chief controls. The driver who was about to take over rode as passenger on the preceding stage. This gave him some idea of the car's condition before he got to grips with the steering lever.

As in the Paris–Rouen run, there was the odd vehicle which bore little evidence of its kinship with the rest. In this case it was a seven-seater bus entered by Bollée. It travelled with every seat occupied.

And so, on June 11th, 1895, the twenty-two vehicles which actually made it forgathered at the Place de l'Etoile, proceeded over the pavé (which gave the competitors on two wheels a nasty jolting up) and came to Versailles, where the race was scheduled to start. The vehicles had previously undergone a form of scrutineering, and each had been rubber-stamped with the engineer's approval. Now they were ready to roll.

Strangely enough, the Bollée bus turned out to be more athletic than it looked. In one of the early stages it was lying second. But then came disaster. A big end became unhealthily hot. Bollée stopped and wrapped a pad of wet rags around it. All might still have been well if he'd remembered to remove them. Unfortunately in the business of restarting, he forgot. The rags were drawn into the machinery, put a con rod out of true and broke a cast-iron support. Still—Bollée was a trier! He managed to carry out emergency repairs and this was the only one of the six steam cars to cover the full distance to Bordeaux and back.

If anyone had really bad luck, it was undoubtedly Levassor. At night he was hunched over the steering wheel, thundering on flat out with shockingly inadequate lighting and averaging 15 m.p.h. Just after midday on the 13th, he was the first to cross the finishing line back at the Porte Maillot in Paris. He had driven for $48\frac{3}{4}$ hours (732 miles) on end in a car which had hardly given any trouble at all. But . . .

The regulations said that two-seater cars were not eligible, and Levassor's was precisely that. Consequently, Koechlin, with his much slower Peugeot, was acclaimed the official winner.[1]

France began as she wished to continue: by establishing something very much akin to a motor-racing monopoly. The laws in Britain ruled out any possibility of such a sport. Nor were the other European countries active—doubtless because the motor industry in France had grown up so much more quickly than anywhere else. It wasn't until the Gordon Bennett series excited the mechanical bile of Britain, Germany and Italy, that France had to battle for her position at the top.

It is not the purpose of this book to explore American motor racing in any detail, but it should go on record (and to America's credit) that the first race over there was scheduled to take place on November 2nd, 1895. The *Chicago Times-Herald* offered a prize of $5,000, and 100 cars were entered. However, only two were in a fit state to start on the appointed day, and it had to be postponed. Eventually, after the course had been reduced from

---

[1] One might have imagined that Levassor would have acquainted himself with this stipulation at the outset. In those days, however, there was an optimism among the competitors and an unpredictable quality to the rules which amounted almost to fantasy.

94 miles to 54 miles, six vehicles turned up. The day was cold, with slushy snow in the streets.

Four of the entrants were variations on the Benz theme: the remaining two were powered by electricity and were described, for no apparent reason (they both had more than two wheels), as motor cycles.

All except two vehicles were abandoned during the race, and it was left to a Benz to arrive home first at 8.53 p.m. through snow-clad, deserted streets.

By some extraordinary logic, both the finishers were afterwards disqualified, and the prizes seem to have been distributed at random to almost everybody.

Later, an event was put on in New York by the magazine *Cosmopolitan*. Six cars started, and only one finished. What it lacked in motor-racing appeal was, perhaps, made up for by a report published in one of the New York papers. It must surely be one of the most succinct accounts of these things ever printed. It went like this:

> Six horseless carriages, entered for a drive,
> Wheel came off one, and then there were five;
>
> Five horseless carriages, racing as before,
> Chain slipped on one, and then there were four;
>
> Four horseless carriages, speeding merrily,
> Bicycle ran into one, and then there were three;
>
> Three horseless carriages came to a hill,
> Hill stayed right where it was, so the drivers had to
>
> get off and push, and that was why the time between
> City Hall and Irvington for the prize of 3,000
> dollars offered by a magazine, was not what it might
> have been if there had not been any hill there.

Back to France. On Thursday, September 24th, 1896, twenty-four cars and four tricycles set off on what was to be by far the most ambitious race so far—and, for that matter, the most eventful. The idea, this time, was to go from Paris to Marseilles and back. Among the cars which tried to do it were representatives from Panhard and Levassor, de Dion and Bouton, Delahaye, Benz, Peugeot, Bollée, des Automobiles Michelin, Mors and Rochet and Schneider. It was, perhaps, significant that on this occasion only three of the entrants were driven by steam (the electric-car enthusiasts had, of course, long ago realised that you can't get a quart out of a pint battery and so, from the long-distance road-racing point of view, it was utterly out of the question).

In Britain, or so it is said, the peasants fumed and fretted whenever a horseless carriage clattered by. They feared for their cattle and their cats, their sheep and their horses and their dogs; and, above all, they disliked the dust. Oh yes—and the noise and the smell and everything about it (including the driver, who was clearly in the pay of Satan).

The French were different. They adored this new thing, which was so splendidly unlike any other thing. They invested it with beauty and glamour, and they considered the men who drove such contraptions to be almost godlike. Of course, like all gods, they had the power to terrify, but it was a delicious fear which excited them no end. And so, when there was a race, they all turned out, and some of them even paid tribute by throwing flowers into the cars. Certainly the cult of car worship, which in the last two decades or so has stricken the world, was already becoming manifest in late nineteenth-century France.

Even the town people adored, or else were profoundly curious about, the mechanical newcomers; and so it was that, when the Paris–Marseilles–Paris race started on this early autumn day, an almighty mass of sightseers was packed in the Avenue de Paris. It was this that caused the first disaster (albeit not a very big one).

It happened when Fisson (driving a Benz-engined Fisson) turned into the Avenue de Paris. A man was pushed, or ran, on to the roadway and Fisson's two-seater victoria struck him. The man fell down, and was pulled back on to the pavement unconscious. The crowd swayed round, craning a forest of necks; and then, groggily, the man got to his feet. It turned out that he was only bruised and shaken. There was a small delay, and then all the cars departed for Versailles.

The favourite was Number 5, driven by Levassor. Shortly after leaving Versailles, however, it ran into trouble. One of the tyres slipped off the rim. Levassor quickly put matters right, and drove off furiously trying to make up lost time. On the second day of the race he overtook just about everybody.

Meanwhile, the lead had passed to one of the steamers, which, appropriately enough, was going like an express train—until its pneumatic tyres more or less disintegrated. De Dion in his steam tractor was also going great guns (another de Dion and Bouton steam tractor fell out after its axle had seized through overheating).

Bollée, too, was going like the clappers on a two-seater voiturette tandem powered by a petrol engine. By the end of the first day he had a lead of 25 miles.

And then the wind got up. It happened during the first night, and a most fearful storm it was. Trees were uprooted. The roads became wet and muddy, and there were fears that the race might have to be abandoned. It wasn't, of course, but the wind showed no signs of letting up.

On the second day a Bollée stopped because one of its axles had seized. Soon afterwards some very unsporting rumours started to circulate. Somebody, they suggested, had got at the cars during the overnight halt and put emery into the bearings.

Bollée himself soldiered on until, in driving rain, he crashed into a tree. The carriage was smashed to pieces and its four occupants were thrown a distance of 20 yards. Nobody was hurt.

Other cars were literally blown over by the wind, and the exposed gearing of the light vehicles couldn't cope with the mud. But they struggled on through the second day, and hoped that the third would be better (it could hardly, they said, be worse).

It wasn't very much of an improvement. One of the cars hesitated about halfway up a hill. The passengers all got out and pushed. They reached the top when a great gust of wind smashed into the car and sent it flying down backwards. Its progress was eventually stopped by a tree.

A motor tricycle was upset by a dog. A Bollée tandem was charged by a bull and seriously damaged. A car was upset trying to avoid a wagon in Villefranche, and one of its four passengers had to be taken to hospital with a broken nose and a deep wound in his forehead.

Still, the leading Panhard reached Lyon that night having travelled at an average speed of nearly 19 m.p.h., which was a great deal faster than anyone had expected. Fourteen of the starters were still in the running, including three intrepid tricyclists—and what a terrible time they were having! One of them had had to pedal for 15 km after running out of petrol.

On the fourth day the weather was a little bit better, though the wind was still high. Emile Levassor tried to avoid a dog and collided with a tree. He wasn't injured, but he was tired and shaken, and he decided to retire. After all, he'd won a moral victory in the Paris–Bordeaux race; and he had other cars still running which were capable of upholding the Panhard and Levassor honour.

And on they went. At Marseilles over 50,000 people turned out to witness the great spectacle. On the way back there were more incidents. The Rochet and Schneider was charged by a bull and Schneider's leg was hurt. The motor cyclists were having a terrible time fighting the headwind. They were having to pedal for much of the way and were becoming very tired. The tricyclists complained that their machines were being nobbled. This time it was suspected that somebody was scattering nails about on the road and causing punctures. One of the Panhards collided with an ordinary carriage (the kind that used horses), and turned over. The Peugeot's burners kept on going out.

In spite of all these ordeals a surprisingly large proportion did get back to Paris—certainly many, many more than the single car which some prophet of doom had predicted would make it.

It was eleven o'clock on a Saturday morning. The scene was the Porte Maillot and there were tens of thousands of people on the streets, thirty private cars, and goodness knows how many cycles and tricycles. The first to arrive was a tricycle escorted by a large number of cyclists. Then came another tricycle. And then, at last, came the moment which everyone had been waiting for. Smothered in dust and flowers, its engine going very sweetly, a Panhard and Levassor arrived on the scene.

But this was Number 8. As it happened, neither this, nor the tricycles, nor anything else in the crowded street outside the Restaurant Gillet (where the control was), was the winner. The winner was the Panhard numbered 6, and where was that?

It was back at Versailles. Its steering had been damaged. The repair took 35 minutes, but nobody worried about that. It was easily the victor, having put up the best overall time, and it could well afford the delay. It had travelled 1,080 miles at an average speed of 16 m.p.h., which meant that for a lot of the journey it had been travelling at about 25 m.p.h.

The other Panhard came second, and a de Dion tricycle was third. Fifty-two vehicles had entered for the race. Thirty-two started. Thirteen reached Marseilles, nine finished. Oh yes—and fifteen dogs were killed.

The Autocar's correspondent returning from Paris after the race reported that: 'In France, the rule is simply this: the faster you go, the more interest you excite in the manly bosoms of the sergeants de ville. We went off down the Champs Élysées at a sharp clip—faster than 14 m.p.h.'

And in Britain, where Emancipation Day had not yet dawned, the sharpest permissible clip was still 4 m.p.h. (2 m.p.h. in towns).

2 There's a long, long road

Motor racing is something which those involved in it would like to be doing all the time. The post mortems on the Paris–Marseilles–Paris race were scarcely done, the cigar smoke had barely cleared away from the conference rooms, before the agile minds of the Automobile Club de France were planning something new. At first it might have seemed that this new sport was a seasonal thing. After all, what could you reasonably ask people to do in winter?

Somebody quickly answered this question by pointing out that the quality of winter usually depends on where you happen to be. The north of France was obviously no place to go motor racing, say, in mid-January, but what about the south? Didn't the better-heeled members of society flock down there—simply to get away from the cold weather?

What better idea, then, than to hold an event in which the cars raced from Marseilles to Nice, culminating in a hill climb at a place called La Turbie (it lies just behind Monte Carlo)?

As soon as the new contest was announced, the Editor of *La France Automobile* came out with a warning. Motor racing, he said, was getting out of hand. Manufacturers were concentrating on building hairy monsters with 8 h.p. engines which had only the most tenuous connection with the little 3 and 4½ h.p. touring cars which ordinary people used. Furthermore they were being driven by men who either could afford to or else were paid to devote nearly all their time to driving. The professional, heavily clad in fur coat and goggles, had already marched on to the scene.

Instead of improving the breed, racing seemed to be deserting it and starting something else. 'Don't,' this worthy man pleaded, 'kill the goose which laid the golden egg by discouraging the amateur.'

As a matter of fact, the amateur's goose had already been cooked —and, strangely enough, he had helped in the cooking of it. Since racing was still the virtual monopoly of France (with the possible exception of America, where a number of events had taken place), it had not yet developed into the orgy of national pride which it became later. Nevertheless, it was already an intensely competitive business between manufacturers. To be fair, they were using it to try out new ideas, which might, in spite of the editor of *La France Automobile*'s gloomy forecast, eventually benefit touring cars. But, which undoubtedly featured high on their list of priorities, they were also using it for publicity. After all, any car which won a race had to be the ultimate in speed and reliability. What better advertisement could there be than that? And, indeed, one of the features of the big races were miniature motor shows which were held before and after.

So far as the amateur was concerned, he was abetting this policy of building 'specials' by going out and ordering the very cars which were winning. You can just imagine him. There he'd be, struggling along with the back markers, and knowing that far, far better cars were racing to glory down the road. He wanted one of them, and the following year probably saw him at the controls of one. The snag, of course, was that, by then, the manufacturers had already made drastic changes to their top racing models. Once again, the unfortunate amateur found himself with out-of-date machinery.

The Marseilles–Nice race was very good fun. The drivers wore numbers on their right arms to show who they were. Masses of people lined the route, and saw that most of the entrants had already realised that performance is not simply a matter of horse power. The lighter the car, the more effective the engine becomes. Consequently, most of them had stripped their vehicles of cushions and mudguards.

There's a long, long road 23

At the rear, the seats were piled high with petrol cans, and to make sure that his own vehicle never wanted for fuel the Count de Dion followed the race on a tricycle. Strapped across his shoulders was a large gourd brim full with motor spirit.

There were two incidents. One was when a tricyclist came off and somehow managed to rip the seats out of his trousers and underpants without hurting himself. The other was when Charron was racing recklessly downhill to make up lost time. At the bottom there was a right-angle corner. He swung the steering lever of his Panhard over too smartly. The car skidded sideways and somersaulted. The lamps, mudguards and levers were smashed, and everything, including the mechanic, was slung out on to the highway. Almost miraculously, however, the car landed on all four wheels with Charron still in the driving seat.

After repairs and first aid it continued.

Motor racing had yet to claim its first victim. The first fatality of the new age probably occurred in Cambridge, Massachusetts, back in 1873 in circumstances which were, to say the least, unusual.

An elderly inventor, aged seventy-three, had built himself a steam tricycle. He took it to a bicycle racing track near Boston to try it out. He made the first run on his own and everything seemed to be going very well indeed. Then a professional cycle racer joined him, and the two set off to see who could go fastest. The steam tricycle was overhauling the man-propelled machine when at a speed of 30 m.p.h. its inventor/driver suddenly fell down dead. Afterwards, it transpired that he had been suffering from a heart disease. The excitement had been too much for this tender organ.

In Britain the first fatality occurred on February 25th, 1899, when a driver and his passenger died after a crash at Harrow, Middlesex.

Mayade, who won the Paris–Marseilles–Paris event, was killed shortly after the race, though not in a competition. He was driving to Biarritz with his wife and two friends when he had occasion to overtake a horse and cart. The animal shied and backed the cart into Mayade's car, which overturned. The occupants were hurled out. Mayade died almost immediately.

The first fatal accident in organised motor sport took place in a minor event at Perigueux on May 1st, 1898. It was a 90-mile race over hilly country, with men stationed with red flags at danger points. Before the last competitor had set off, a serious accident had already been reported. The Marquis de Montaignée, who was driving a large, heavy car, was overtaking a Benz-engined Parisienne. As he drew alongside, the Marquis gave a friendly wave. His car was fitted with tiller steering, which was a pig at the best of times, and deadly if one did not concentrate completely. This instant of inattention caused his car to swerve to the right and collide with the front of the Parisienne. The latter ran off the road, shot up a low bank and overturned. The driver jumped clear but the mechanic was pinned underneath.

Hearing the noise of the accident, the Marquis looked round.

Once again his car swerved violently. It careered up the bank, plunged into the field, and rolled over. He was badly injured and died within three hours—but not before he had been able to tell the officials that it was all his fault.

The Parisienne's mechanic died later.

Motor racing was assuming a pattern. Smaller events, such as the race at Perigueux, were creeping into the calendar. Nevertheless, the organising genii at the A.C.F. decided that there should be one great road race every year. Hitherto these had been confined to France. In 1898 they resolved to go international—doubtless with the idea of bringing their wares to the attention of export markets.

Amsterdam was selected as the target. Competitors would race all the way from Paris to the Dutch capital, and then back to Paris again. The regulations were published in a 115-page booklet. There were to be six stages—three each way—and those taking part would be divided into two categories. The first were the racers themselves (sixty-nine entries). The second were tourists (twenty-six entries), who wanted to motor along and watch the fun but didn't want to expose themselves to the hazards of travelling at excessive speeds.

There was no great drama in the race itself, though the preliminaries had enough for about a dozen events. They all hinged upon a point of law and an officious police engineer.

According to a law passed in 1893, all drivers had to have certificates of (one) *réception* and (two) *capacité*. The first had to show that the car was suitable for driving on public roads. The second had to record the fact that its driver was capable of handling it. Whilst everyone took the second one reasonably seriously, the first one was thought to be rather silly. Nobody really bothered about it.

During the count-down period for the Paris–Amsterdam–Paris race, however, the Prefect of Police in Paris suddenly decided to go by the book. From headquarters came the edict that any driver who didn't possess a certificate of *réception* must present his car at the prefecture for examination by a police engineer. The time specified was between 6 and 9 p.m. on the eve of the event.

A number of people duly turned up, and the police engineer began his examination. At 6.15, however, he put down his equipment and sauntered off for dinner. He did not return until 8.15. Possibly the meal had been a bad one, or he resented having his evening disrupted in this manner—whichever it was, he now began rejecting car after car completely out of hand.

The drivers asked him why, but the engineer, whose name was Bochet, refused to give any explanation.

This was too much! When an obsolete byelaw is enforced by an attitude which falls far short of courtesy, people are apt to rebel. The drivers did just that. They said 'Damn you', took their cars away, and decided to get on with the race no matter what the police rules might be.

But they reckoned without the persistence of Bochet, who seems to have been a very powerful police engineer. No sooner had the rebel motorists departed than he called out the army. A company of infantry was posted to a strategic point on one of the roads leading away from Paris, and a half squadron of Hussars was despatched to Champigny, where the start was to be. To make things even more uncomfortable for the rebels, two field guns had their sights trained on to the road—presumably with the object of mowing them down.

There was only one thing to do, and that was to start the race from somewhere outside Engineer Bochet's jurisdiction. Word was passed around to meet at Villiers in the department Seine-et-Oise, where the authorities were thought to be more friendly. Some of the cars went on trains, others were towed by horses. Forty-eight competitors arrived there.

But now came the second crisis. All the petrol supplies were back at Champigny, which was occupied by hostile forces. The organisers called for volunteers for a mission which was clearly fraught with danger. Amedée Bollée came forward. He set off on a horse-drawn cart and, some while later after goodness knows what clever tactics, returned with the motor spirit.

Victory seemed to be in sight. Bochet, however, had still one last, despairing card to play. Knowing that the race was to pass through Versailles, he proposed to set up an ambush there.

News of the engineer's intention leaked out. Hurriedly a new route was devised, which neatly sidestepped Versailles. Unfortunately this didn't please the town's racing enthusiasts. They had already put up a triumphal arch. Then they had taken it down. Now, hoping perhaps that the drivers would defy Bochet on ground of the latter's own choosing, they began to put it up again.

And what about the reception they'd planned? All that food and wine going to waste! By this time, however, the competitors, who had spent the better part of a night in a rain-drenched wood, were fed up. They didn't want to be received by anybody—whether in enmity by Bochet and his men, or in friendship by the people of Versailles. They refused to go anywhere near the place.

So far, all motor racing had taken place on public roads with cars which, albeit with increasing remoteness, were still identifiable as production cars. It was, perhaps, inevitable that one day somebody would have a go at establishing an absolute speed record.

The pioneers in this respect were a founder member of the A.C.F. named the Marquis de Chasseloup-Laubat and his younger brother, Count Gaston. The Marquis built the cars, and Gaston drove them.

For the first attempt on the flying kilometer they chose a stretch of dead straight road at Achères, some miles from Paris, in the mid-winter of 1898. The car was a somewhat cumbersome-looking electric vehicle which the Chasseloup-Laubats had christened Jeantaud.

It was a cold, wet day and the timekeepers had equipment which, at best, could be described as unsophisticated. Count Gaston sped over the appointed distance at what seemed to be the quite considerable speed of 39·24 m.p.h. The first World Land Speed Record (though it could only be considered for cars: railway trains went a good deal faster) had been established.

The news of the Chasseloup-Laubat record had scarcely been published before one of the most remarkable men in early motor racing was furiously unscrewing the cap of his fountain pen and issuing a challenge. This was a Belgian who had been trained as a civil engineer but was now devoting all his time to the manufacture of electric cars. His name was Camille Jenatzy. A few weeks before the original attack on the flying kilometer he had distinguised himself by putting up a quite remarkable performance (an all-electric 16 m.p.h.) on a hill-climb at Chanteloup.

Jenatzy's challenge, as was the custom with these things, had a time limit of one month attached to it. The Chasseloup-Laubats agreed, and January 17th, 1899, was selected as the day. The venue was to be, again, that stretch of road at Achères.

The Marquis and his brother were still using Jeantaud, whilst Jenatzy turned up in a way-out machine which looked rather like a cigar tube on wheels. Since range had no bearing on the matter, the electric motors were entirely suitable. All you had to do was to squeeze every drop of juice out of the battery, and no matter if it *was* exhausted at the end of the run.

As challenger, Jenatzy was entitled to make the first attempt. He hoisted the record up to 41·4 m.p.h. Count Gaston replied with 43·7 m.p.h., though he would probably have done a good deal better if his motor hadn't burnt out 200 yards from the finish.

Ten days later they tried again. This time Jenatzy did 49·92 m.p.h. Count Gaston did nothing at all, for his motor burnt out before he got under way.

Matters were now postponed until March 4th, when Count Gaston took the record up to 57·6 m.p.h. in a highly modified version of Jeantaud, which obviously owed a good deal to his rival's ideas on streamlining.[1] At the time, Jenatzy was busy installing bigger batteries and more powerful motors in his car, which he called by the very appropriate name of La Jamais Contente. With no brakes, smaller-than-usual wheels, and a highly individualistic shape, it was probably the first real racing 'freak'. Genealogically, it was more likely to be the begetter of a dragster than of a road- or circuit-racing car. Even though it never fulfilled Jenatzy's ambition of taking the record up to 100 m.p.h., it certainly travelled very quickly (for the time) indeed.

On April 1st they were back at Achères again. The road surface at the original starting line had been patched up with bitumen, which had made rather a bump. Consequently, they agreed to move it 200 yards further on. Jenatzy, ever impatient, climbed into his curious car and set off before the timekeepers had finished measuring out the new route. As he flashed by, one of them flicked his stop-watch on, but such haphazard business would never do—especially as record breaking had now come under the authority of the A.C.F. In any case, there were some doubts about whether he had covered the exact distance. The run was disallowed.

[1] The one thing they couldn't streamline was the driver, whose body stuck up from the waist above his bullet-like machine.

There was no more juice in the batteries for a second attempt. The car was towed away, and there things remained until April 29th. This time Jenatzy did 65·75 m.p.h. and thus became the first man to cross the mile-a-minute barrier. The Chasseloup-Laubats were convinced, and gave up the struggle.

The World Land Speed Record is a temporary affair which stands only until the next man breaks it. But Jenatzy's was to remain the all-time record for electric cars. When Serpollet set off the next wave of bids in 1902, and did 75·06 m.p.h., he used a steam car. After this, apart from a flash-in-the-pan effort by a Stanley steamer in 1906 (127·66 m.p.h.), the distinction of being the fastest thing on land remained with petrol-driven cars until the jet-engined runs of post-World War II days.

We now come to James Gordon Bennett, a tough, stocky newspaper proprietor with a large moustache and a homburg hat habitually perched on his head. He owned the *New York Herald* and the Commercial Cable Company. Even though somebody described him as 'the one man in the newspaper business not interested in making money' (possibly because he had once said of the *New York Herald*: 'This paper has only one reader, and I am the man'), he obviously had a very shrewd appreciation of the value of stunts and 'exclusives' as circulation-builders. It was he who in 1867 engaged H. M. Stanley to serve as war correspondent with the British forces in Abyssinia and who, two years later, sent this same journalist to search for Dr. Livingstone.

He had sponsored an Arctic expedition (an ill-fated one, as it happened: the ship foundered in pack ice), skippered the yacht *Dauntless* in the 1870 transatlantic race, but he had never driven a car. As a matter of fact, he didn't like them very much. Furthermore, he never, once, went to watch the European motor races which bore his name—nor, indeed, did he care much about being associated with them. Although the world resolutely called them the 'Gordon Bennett Cup Races', his own paper always referred to the trophy as the 'Coupe Internationale'. Gordon Bennett himself is said to have preferred the words 'Columbia Cup', though nobody seems to know why.[1]

[1] In America there was the Vanderbilt Cup, presented by W. K. Vanderbilt (himself a racing driver), and run on similar lines to the Gordon Bennett series in Europe. European manufacturers used these events as a useful opportunity to generate export sales. Panhard and Darracqs were among the marques which won Vanderbilt Cup races.

In 1887 he arrived in Paris to set up a Continental edition of the *New York Herald*. As already mentioned, he sent a reporter off on a bicycle to cover the Paris–Rouen run of 1894 and he was one of the subscribers to the Paris–Bordeaux race of 1895. Quite clearly he realised that, whether he liked it or not, the motor car was something which had to be taken into account. From the very earliest days, the French press had played an important part in sponsoring races, presumably because they felt it would help their circulations and advertising. Was Gordon Bennett after similar rewards? One might have imagined so, if the trophy had been called the 'New York Herald Cup', or even if he had acknowledged the title 'Gordon Bennett Cup'. In his attempts at dissociation there was a certain coyness. Since Gordon Bennett was a very un-coy man, it may be that his donation to the up-and-coming sport really was an act of disinterested benevolence.

At any rate, he presented the A.C.F. with a huge trophy, which depicted the Goddess of Speed at the wheel of a racing Panhard, with the Goddess of Victory riding mechanic. It certainly wasn't a cup—more of a statue, really—and it was manufactured at doubtless great cost by a firm of Paris silversmiths.

The rules of the new competition were published in November, 1899. The important thing was that they attempted to break the French monopoly by turning motor racing into an international sport. All foreign automobile clubs[1] which were recognised by the A.C.F. were allowed to compete, and each could enter a team of three cars. The cars had to be wholly constructed in the competitors' own countries: they had to weigh at least 400 kilos and, in addition to this, they had to carry a driver and a mechanic, seated side by side, whose combined weight was at least 70 kilos. If it wasn't, the difference had to be made up with ballast.

The race itself had to be between 550 and 650 km long. It was to be an annual event, which would take place in the country of whichever nation was holding the cup at the time. The first race, naturally, would be held in France.

All told there were twenty-two articles in the original rules, to which a couple more were added after the always vociferous *La France Automobile* had asked who was going to pay the cost of organising the events.

The first Gordon Bennett Race was very nearly a complete fiasco. It may be tempting to imagine that, whilst in Britain road racing along French lines was totally out of the question, in France

[1] This was another important thing: it was to be a contest of clubs rather than of manufacturers or individual drivers.

everything was going along just beautifully. One may be imagining that, with the exception of Police Engineer Bochet, the authorities were solidly behind the sport. That, alas, is not entirely true. Indeed, the first problem confronting the original Gordon Bennett Cup Race was whether it could take place in France at all. There was some talk of having to switch the location to Italy.

One cause of official antagonism was an unfortunate episode which had occurred in a race for motor tricycles between Paris and Roubaix. The Deputy for the Department of the Seine had decided to drive out with his wife to watch the event. M. and Mme Darracq were invited to accompany them.

What seemed to be a good vantage point was a right-hand bend at a village called Croix des Noailles. There was an inviting stretch of grass beside the road, and the distinguished visitors joined a mass of cyclists who had congregated to watch the racers rush through.

The trouble came when one of the competitors, taking the bend very fast, went a little bit wide of the mark. The rider behind him tried to slip through on the inside, but misjudged it. The two machines collided, crashed over the bicycles which were lining the road, and hurtled into the crowd. One of the riders fractured his collar-bone: the other seems to have got away scot free. Unfortunately, the same cannot be said of the Deputy's party. Mme Deputy and one of the Darracqs both sustained broken legs.

Now if you want motor racing—or, for that matter, any other sport—to succeed, the one thing you mustn't do is to injure a V.I.P. Within two days of the crash, the Prefect of Seine-et-Oise had forbidden all motor racing in his territory. *Le Velo*, which had sponsored the race, and all the competitors were prosecuted and fined. And, as a final gesture, the Secretary to the Minister of the Interior telegraphed all prefects elsewhere in France, telling them to forbid motor racing.

All this took place while preparations for the Gordon Bennett Race were in progress. There was, of course, an outcry. Motoring journals called it an autocratic suppression of a national industry, a curb on the flourishing engineering trade, and something which would cause France to lose her superiority over other nations.

The A.C.F. did the best thing possible, which was nothing. Without joining in the general clamour, it quietly waited for the fever of official indignation to die down. The trouble now was that nobody would say anything *definite*. There might be a race, and then, on the other hand, there might not be. And even if it did take place it would certainly be at very short notice.

For this reason, in spite of its much vaunted internationalism, only two foreign competitors were able to take part. One was Jenatzy (nothing could stop *him*). The other was an American named Winton, who had built a number of so-called 'motor wagons', and had issued a challenge to Charron after the latter's victory in the Paris–Bordeaux race of 1899. According to Winton's terms, it was to be run over a distance of 1,000 miles. Charron accepted and promptly deposited 20,000 francs at the *New York Herald* office. However, nothing ever came of it.

Jenatzy, who was very excitable, was more frenzied than ever. His car had been impounded by the Customs, and he had to make do with a stripped-down touring car with tyres of somewhat doubtful Belgian origin. There might have been one German competitor, namely Eugen, but he refused to start on the grounds that the rear tyres on his Benz were unreliable.

In the end, only five competitors turned up for the race, which was between Paris and Lyons. Panhards driven by Charron and Girardot came first and second. Nobody else finished.

The Gordon Bennett race of 1902 might have been described as Motor Racing's Big Surprise. Improbably enough, it was won by an Englishman driving an English car. The man was S. F. Edge. The car was a Napier, which was sometimes known, perhaps unfairly, as a 'Panhard in disguise'.

Edge, who was born in Australia, came to Britain when he was still a youngster, and was educated at a school in South London. He worked part-time for Harry Lawson, when the latter was still trying to monopolise the British motor industry, and simultaneously carried out the duties of London manager for the Dunlop Tyre Company. He was not an engineer, but he was a quite remarkable commercial opportunist.

Early on he had distinguished himself as a tricycle racer. Whenever he, Charles Jarrot (more about him shortly), and a man named Charles Ridgeway were competing on the wooden cycle track at Herne Hill, or else on the Tower Athletic Grounds at New Brighton (where the London Motor Club held its 'First Grand International Motor Cycling Tournament'), they could always be relied upon to pull in the crowds. Edge was a cautious driver with a considerable knack of getting himself out of trouble. Furthermore, nearly everything he did was for a commercial purpose. In the case of the 1902 Gordon Bennett race it was to sell Napier cars.

The Panhard influence was easy enough to trace, for it was the purchase of a 6 h.p. Panhard and Levassor which brought Edge and that brilliant engineer Montagu Napier together. Edge bought the car and asked Napier to improve it.

Napier began by converting it from tiller to wheel steering and fitting pneumatic tyres. Then, his interest kindled, he asked Edge whether he might build a new engine for it. Since this was what the latter, in a somewhat devious way, had been after all the time, he agreed with alacrity.

Out of this grew the Napier car with its strong and not surprising Panhard influence. From the motor-racing point of view this was not a bad thing, for Panhards had always been extremely successful. It was, indeed, this firm's practice of always painting its cars blue that led France to adopt this as its national colour for the Gordon Bennett races.

Britain, incidentally, chose green out of deference to Ireland, where the Gordon Bennett race of 1903 was held. There was, however, an interesting prelude to this. In the long-distance road race between Paris and Berlin of 1901, Charles Jarrott, an Englishman, was assigned to drive a Clement. Since no one else would have it, the number 13 was allotted to him. However, to make up for this, his car was painted green, which the French regard as a lucky colour. Jarrott seems to have been quite pleased by the compromise. He described it as 'a beautiful rich, dark colour, which gave it such a handsome appearance'.[1]

However—back to the Gordon Bennett race of 1902 and Edge's victory. It had been decided to run the race between Paris and Innsbruck at the same time as the big road race of the year, which was from Paris to Vienna.

Afterwards, Edge, with commendable candour, told people that: 'We have won the Gordon Bennett Cup through others breaking down.' This was certainly true, though Edge himself experienced his fair share of troubles.

To begin with, he took a wrong turning in Paris and went up a *cul de sac*. What made this so difficult was the fact that his car was not fitted with a reversing gear. Then he was stopped by a

---

[1] Is thirteen unlucky? Jarrott finished eighth in the race, but had five punctures. Afterwards his hands are said to have been in a bad state through changing tyres. But this was no worse fortune than a lot of drivers suffered before the Rudge-Whitworth detachable wire wheel transformed the roadside scene.

couple of talkative policemen on bicycles, who wanted to see his passport. This delay took up four minutes. When, at last, he got out on to the open road, he began to have trouble with the coil, and presently he was running on only two out of four cylinders. This was put right, but there were more snags lying in wait at Belford, where the competitors were due to spend the night. A consignment of tyres had failed to turn up at the station.

The next train was due in at 2.30 a.m. and everything depended on its punctuality. If it was late, Edge would probably be delayed in starting. It was punctual, but then the station authorities became difficult. The tyres had been booked through to Innsbruck. They couldn't be taken off the train.

While his companion argued with the station master, Edge quietly took the tyres out of their box and fled with them. They got away on time.

In Switzerland matters improved when the Panhard representatives mistook the Napier for one of their own cars. They fed Edge and his mechanic on champagne and sponge cakes, gave them free petrol, and even poured water over their tyres to cool them down.

Then came the challenge. The big obstacle of the race was the lofty Arlburg pass. Edge said afterwards, 'But really there was nothing the matter with that unless one chose to fail to take a corner.' In fact, they had experienced far worse trouble on the way up to it. At one point the car was slammed by a hefty gust of wind. It flew off at a bend and ended up in a field. Until he got out to examine things Edge thought that his race was over. However, the damage turned out to be nothing more serious than a fractured connection to the water tank. It was quickly mended and off they went once more—up to the Arlburg, which, as Edge said, gave no trouble.

As they approached Innsbruck on the far side, they saw René de Knyff's car parked by the roadside. Thinking that de Knyff had won, Edge leaned out to congratulate him. But then, shortly afterwards in a village, Jarrott came running up. 'You've won the Cup!' he cried. 'You've only ten kilometers to go.' It transpired that the Arlburg had been too much for de Knyff's Panhard. With the leader out of the way, Edge drove on to a comfortable victory. His average speed for the race was 31·8 m.p.h.[1]

[1] Doubtless owing to the trip over the Alps, this was relatively slow. Girardot's average speed when he won the previous year's race from Paris to Bordeaux in a Panhard had been 37 m.p.h., whilst in the Irish event of 1903 Jenatzy's average speed was 49·2 m.p.h.

Edge's victory meant that the 1903 Gordon Bennett Race would be held somewhere in Britain. But before then the motor-racing world was to be shocked by the horrors of the A.C.F.-sponsored Paris–Madrid road race. It was, if you discount an event which took place between St. Petersburg and Moscow in 1908, the last of the big road races until the first Mille Miglia in 1927. It was also the most terrible. Perhaps the most remarkable thing is that it was ever held.

You must understand: by 1903, the racing car had grown up. From being a somewhat tentative engineering experiment, it had become a juggernaut. It was powered by an enormous engine, bolted on to a chassis and with a body which could only be described as nominal.

And yet a flock of these monsters was to be released upon public highways, watched by crowds who were only dimly aware of what racing-car speeds meant, and with totally inadequate policing and supervision. Nobody with any imagination could have doubted that a catastrophe would occur. The only question could be—when?

In all fairness, the French authorities clearly didn't wish the race to take place. Right until May of 1903 there was uncertainty about it. Shortly before the end of that month Count Zborowski had been killed in his giant Mercedes on the hill-climb at La Tourbie. This, it seemed, must surely affect the government's attitude to the Paris–Madrid event. But the government did nothing. And said nothing. It was, perhaps, better that a racing driver should be killed than that a Deputy's wife should be injured.

Nevertheless, the uncertainty persisted. The man who probably made up the French government's mind for it was the King of Spain. He made it perfectly clear that he had no objection to the race coming through his country: indeed, he welcomed it. This was hardly surprising. The monarch was known to be a great car enthusiast, particularly of fast cars travelling at high speeds. He was, if we are to believe the account of one of his passengers, a somewhat terrifying driver.

As for so many of the early races, the first leg was to take the cars along the unusually good road to Bordeaux. To ensure the maximum number of spectators, the start was scheduled to take place at Versailles at 3 a.m. on a Sunday morning.[1]

Through Saturday evening the racing cars rumbled out of their

---

[1] It may sound an improbable hour at which to expect large crowds, but, as things turned out, the A.C.F. were depressingly right.

depots in Paris and over the roads to Versailles. Around the starting point there were already masses of people. The scene was gaily illuminated by scores of Chinese lanterns, which were all the rage in Paris at that time. There were cyclists, wagonettes parked all over the place, carriages and cars. The Society for Health Beverages was selling soup at three sous a cup. A small dog, apparently somebody's mascot, was wearing goggles. There were piles of tyres near trucks parked under the trees. And all the time the angry snorts of racing car engines as they fought their way through the crowds.

Mme du Gast, heavily corseted, was to drive a 30 h.p. de Dietrich. She was the only woman competitor. Now she was trying on a helmet made out of zinc. Louis Renault was wearing a black leather jacket. He was busy—trying to be in about a dozen places at once. His brother, Marcel, was depressed. Some said that he had experienced a premonition. They even drew attention to a strike which had occurred at the Renault plant some weeks earlier. They said that Marcel had welcomed it: that it gave him an excuse for not getting his car ready.

If any of this were true there was ample reason for it. Possibly Marcel realised what everyone else should have understood: that power had conquered weight too convincingly, that there were too many fast cars and far too few precautions.

In the meanwhile he cut a somewhat sombre figure with his thick black beard and deerstalker cap as he sat there and brooded.

Charles Jarrott from England, who had won the previous year's Circuit des Ardennes race, was trying to become accustomed to the controls of his brand-new de Dietrich. The car was fresh from the factory, and hadn't even been run in. Furthermore, it differed in several particulars from any car he had ever driven before. As winner of the previous year's main event, it was Jarrott's privilege to set off first. It was possibly one which he would cheerfully have forgone.

As the hours went by, the atmosphere became a curious mixture of gaiety from the crowd and absorbed tension from the drivers and their mechanics. At three o'clock it was still too dark to start. By 3.30 the sky was beginning to light up. At 3.45 Jarrott was sent on his way.

Cecil Bianchi, who was his mechanic, remembers it well. 'The biggest trouble', he recalls, 'is that the crowd hadn't the least idea what motor car speed was. The road from the start was fairly straight for three or four miles, but it was packed solid with people. When we eventually started, you could see this crowd dividing up. Some went to one side of the road, and some to the other. It was a ghastly sight.'

Along the route to Bordeaux there was only a mere scattering of soldiers to control the crowds. Cattle and dogs wandered about on the highway. People packed it, and only cleared away when the cars drew near. Even the level crossings were unpredictable. Some were open, and some were closed.

And the cars sped on, each one enveloped in a hateful cloud of dust. A fragment of stone shattered Marcel Renault's goggles. The dust got into his eyes, and they became inflamed.

Lorraine Barrow had been ill when he set out. A dog ran into the road, and he swerved to avoid it. The car went out of control and crashed into a tree at 80 m.p.h. His mechanic, Pierre Rodez, was killed on the spot. Barrow was hurled into a ditch 10 yards away as the car telescoped to half its length. He was dead within three days—from pneumonia.

Jenatzy's big grey Mercedes came to a halt. A fly had got into the radiator.

Marcel Renault, now tired and his eyes hurting more than ever, went out to overtake Leon Théry. He could hardly see what he was doing for the dust which was all around. He obviously didn't see the drain at the side of the road. The wheels hit it: the car spun round twice, turned over three times, and ended up some distance down the road—facing Paris. His mechanic was thrown clear. Marcel was trapped underneath.

Maurice Farnham came up, stopped his car, and went over to haul Marcel clear of the wreck. He was taken to a farmhouse. Before the day was over, Marcel Renault was dead.

Leslie Porter, in a Wolseley, came unexpectedly upon a level crossing which had been deserted by its flagman. He took it too fast, tried to steer into a field, but collided with the wall of a house. His mechanic was flung against the wall and killed outright. And then the car caught fire.

Tourant braked violently as he tried to avoid a child who had strayed into the road. His car spun, shot into the crowd, and killed his mechanic and a soldier.

Stead tried to overtake Salleron, and the two cars collided. Stead's overturned and he was trapped beneath it. Fortunately, the redoubtable Mme du Gast was coming up behind. She stopped and, with the help of her mechanic, dragged him out. Then she busied herself with first aid.

And so the grisly tale of the Paris–Madrid race unfolded. Down in Bordeaux it was extremely hot and most of the local police

EARLY IN THE MORNING
... of motorsport. RIGHT *The car with which Emile Levassor won the Paris–Rouen race of 1895. The drawings across the centre of this page show some of the other competitors—including the steambus for which J. Scotte received what they were too polite to call a booby prize* BELOW *S. F. Edge and his thunderous Napier at the start of the 1902 Gordon Bennett race— which he won*

IT WAS ALL A HORRIBLE MISTAKE
LEFT *The 35 h.p. Napier of Lieutenant-Colonel Mark Mayhew after weighing-in on the eve of the 1903 Paris–Madrid fiasco*

BELOW *Probably the first woman* ***racing*** *driver, Mme du Gast set off on the road to Madrid in a De Dietrich. Later, she abandoned the race and looked after the injured*

PETTICOAT MECHANIC AND IMPERIAL POMP
ABOVE *In the first Targa Florio (1906) Mme Le Blon rode beside her husband—as mechanic*
BELOW *Kaiser Bill's batman called His Imperial Majesty at 4 a.m. to get him to the Kaiserpreis on time*

THE HEROES
Baron de Caters—a man of chivalry

Charles Jarrott—in Britain, he led the way

Louis Renault—a car for the people?

Felice Nazzaro—the master of a new art

Leon Théry—they called him 'The Stop-watch'

Camille Jenatzy—a pact with the devil?

UP TO THE LIMITS

ABOVE *Jenatzy's 'Jamais Contente'*. It went like the bomb it resembled until the batteries ran out. BELOW *Even Henry Ford had a go at the land speed record. His car was called the '999'*—seen here with Barney Oldfield (Ford's sometime racing driver) at the controls, and H.F. in attendance

THE FIRST GRAND PRIX
... *was at Le Mans in 1906. Among those taking part were* RIGHT *F. Szisz who won it in a Renault;* CENTRE *Villemain in a Clément-Bayard; and others* BELOW *seen here lining up for the start*

WEIGHTS AND PRESSURES

ABOVE *A competitor weighing in for the first Tourist Trophy race on the Isle of Man in 1905.* BELOW *Lautenschlager took plenty of exercise changing rims on his Mercedes during the 1908 French Grand Prix at Dieppe. Still, it was worth the trouble: he won the event*

were in bad tempers. Jarrott was the first to arrive, wondering why only one car had overtaken him. It was Werner in a Mercedes. About 750 yards further on, Werner's back axle broke. The wheels shot off to either side of the road, and the Mercedes slithered into the side. Thereafter, Jarrott was on his own.

Louis Renault arrived next, having made the fastest time. In his lightweight car he had confounded the theory that 'competitions, like wars, are won by higher capacities' or (as the Americans say) 'there's no substitute for litres'. Now he was in a state of exhaustion. As soon as he heard the news of Marcel's accident he announced the withdrawal of all his cars from the race. This was a somewhat empty gesture. Apart from his own, there was none left in it.

As soon as the French authorities learned the sickening story of the race, they put a ban on all further motor racing on French territory. The Spanish government reacted with similar alacrity by withdrawing permission for the cars to travel through Spain. The race, which should never have taken place, was over. As for the cars, they suffered the final indignity of being towed to Bordeaux station by horses—and despatched back to Paris by train.

3 Who were these men?

Some died in their beds, some perished violently. Some were noblemen, some were businessmen, and some were mechanics. All were possessed of amazing powers of physical endurance and courage. Many, but by no means all, were rich.

These were the first racing drivers. In France, to begin with, they were mostly members of the aristocracy or else car-makers. Panhard and his partner Levassor had been manufacturing woodworking machinery before they began to build automobiles. Leon Bollée, who was born at Le Mans, constructed a calculating machine when he was only nineteen years old. Henry Farman never made cars, but he was one of the earliest aircraft builders. On January 3rd, 1908, he became the first man in the world to fly one kilometer around a measured course. The machine was of his own making.

They travelled, they raced, sometimes they invented, often they acted as salesmen. Serpollet accompanied the Shah of Persia on his first car ride. Later, in Germany, he picked up Edward VII at Homburg and drove him ten kilometers to keep an appointment with Grand Duke Michael of Russia (the Grand Duke had made his first trip in a horseless carriage two years earlier—on a steam tram somewhere in the Caucasus).

And then there were the Renault brothers: Louis the extrovert and Marcel (several years older than he) seemingly the introvert. Louis, who, when he wasn't wearing a moustache, looked rather like Humphrey Bogart, was brilliant, charming and ruthless. Marcel was softer, more gentle. Until the Paris–Madrid disaster proved so convincingly otherwise, he was considered to be a lucky driver.

Possibly the Renaults, particularly Louis, had something in common with Henry Ford. They watched the juvenile automobile industry concentrating its efforts on cars which were ever bigger and more expensive. But, reasoned Louis Renault, if motoring was to become popular the vehicles would have to be lighter and cheaper. There were many who believed that a *reliable* light car was an impossibility. Renault proved that it was not.

'The reliability of a vehicle,' he would say, 'depends upon the strength of its weakest part.' It may not have been a very original observation, but it was surprising how many manufacturers ignored it.

The early sport glittered with titles. There was the Chevalier René de Knyff, the Marquis de Chasseloup-Laubat, Baron de Caters, the Marquis de Montaignée, Count Zborowski, Baron de Zuylen (who became president of the A.C.F.), Count de Dion, and so on.

These were men of chivalry. When, in the Paris–Bordeaux race of 1895, René de Knyff found Charron stranded dejectedly by the roadside he stopped, asked him what the trouble was, and encouraged him to snap out of his gloom and continue.

During the Gordon Bennett Race, which took place in Ireland in 1903, the steering failed on Charles Jarrott's car, which shot off the road and overturned. Jarrott and Bianchi, his mechanic, were injured. De Caters, who was following them, stopped immediately and walked over to see whether he could help.

'My sister's somewhere in the grandstand,' Jarrott told him. 'Would you tell her we're all right?'

De Caters carried out this mission, and then got on with the race.

They were usually kind to beginners. René de Knyff—large, heavily bearded, and always looking rather sullen when he raced—was very good in this respect. He knew the roads of France intimately. He also had a wealth of information about the art of good living. He said that at Chalons sur Marne one should opt for the red champagne. At Turin he knew of a shop where a special (and, presumably, superior) type of cigar could be obtained, and if you were in Vienna with him he would insist that you drink a particular Rhine wine and ignore the local stuff.

The Chevalier always went racing in a yachting cap, which was blown off before he had gone very far. His creed was to finish at all costs on the supposition that nobody else would (it seldom worked out that way). To keep fit he played racquets at the covered-in courts in the Tuileries, went pigeon shooting and enjoyed cycling.

Count Eliot Zborowski, who was also a well-known steeplechase rider, drove a Mercedes, and he really pushed it. When he stopped at a control, however, he seemed to relax completely. He would pull up in the shadiest spot and nonchalantly light a cigarette. He was always immaculately turned out.

One of Zborowski's ambitions was to win a big road race. He very nearly fulfilled it in the Paris–Vienna event. There was little doubt in his own mind (and, in all fairness, in the minds of a number of other people) that there had been a mistake by the timekeepers. Certainly he regarded himself as the moral victor, and was very angry about the official result.

This, according to one theory, was the cause of his death in the following year on the La Turbie hill-climb. Zborowski had a spanking great new Mercedes, and, in a mood of patrician fury, he was determined to win. Never had he been in such a reckless mood: he set the car at the hill and really let it rip. At the first sharp corner he appeared to make no effort to slacken off his speed—with the inevitable result. The car went out of control, struck some rocks, and Zborowski was killed instantly.

S. C. H. Davis poses the interesting idea that one of his cufflinks jammed the throttle. If this is true they were very unlucky links, for his son was wearing them when, years later, he was killed at Monza.

Cecil Bianchi, who knew Zborowski, is inclined to shake his head and say: 'He had it coming to him. He was that sort of a man.'

By no means all the drivers had titles. There was Charron, for example, who had originally been famous as a racing cyclist. He was short and dapper and very charming. In a car he performed with considerable panache, though he was often unlucky. The fact that he was also a mass of nerves probably did little to help. At times he was liable to be plunged into profound gloom.

Possibly the most colourful of all the early drivers was the Belgian ace Camille Jenatzy. He had red hair, a red beard, and usually wore a villainous-looking fur coat. In the first race on the Circuit des Ardennes he was involved in a most fearful crash. When the dust had settled, the engine and part of the frame of his car were seen to be on one side of the road. The back axle and rear wheels were several hundred yards away on the other.

It seemed impossible that anybody could have survived such a shunt. And then, to the amazement of the spectators, there Jenatzy was—his face covered with blood, being driven back to the nearest control in a small car. 'This man,' they said, 'must surely have a pact with the devil.' And so, for ever afterwards, Jenatzy was known as the Red Devil.

He was a furious driver, who trembled with rage if anyone got in his way. His skids were the most hair-raising of them all. People said that nobody could take such risks and survive. Unfortunately, he was more spectacular than successful. His only important victory was when he and his giant Mercedes won the Irish Gordon Bennett Race of 1903.

But this was certainly not for want of trying. After his fashion he was a perfectionist. For example, when attempting to repeat his Irish victory in the German Gordon Bennett Race of the following year he got up very early each morning and practised for two months on end.[1] As ill luck (for Jenatzy) would have it, Théry's Brasier went more sweetly and smoothly than the Mercedes in the race, and he had to be content with second place. Théry, incidentally, made lap after lap with such unfaltering regularity that henceforth he was nicknamed 'The Chronometer'.

It was, perhaps, inevitable that a man of Jenatzy's temperament should be killed in action of some kind. It happened during a wild-boar hunt in the Ardennes, and there are two versions of what occurred. Jacques Ickx says that, as night fell, Jenatzy left his hiding place before the signal which marked the end of the hunt. Mistaking him for an animal in the half-light, Madoux, who was director of the daily newspaper *L'Étoile Belge*, shot at him and fatally wounded him.

According to Bianchi, however, Jenatzy was always a great practical joker. On the first day of the hunt they had been unlucky and had returned to base without any dead boars. On the following morning, just to liven things up a bit, Jenatzy had got down into the undergrowth and given a very passable imitation of a wild

[1] Even the Kaiser got up early on the day of the race. His Imperial Majesty was at the circuit—which was decorated to give a very passable imitation of ancient Rome, with even the inscription on the post office in Latin—at 6 a.m.

pig. Alas, it was altogether too convincing. Somebody took a shot in the direction of the rumpus, and hit Jenatzy.

Whichever the case, he was taken back and placed in his beloved big Mercedes, where he died soon afterwards.

The two great pioneers of motor racing from England were Charles Jarrot and S. F. Edge. Jarrott had studied law and afterwards went to work in the motor trade. For a time, he was employed by Harry Lawson. Later, he started his own business —importing cars from abroad.

When, in 1905, the police-trap menace in Britain became really vicious (one bench raised £1,000 in fines during a single year), he and his friend William Letts operated a private warning system on the Brighton road. This was really the beginning of the Automobile Association, of which, years later, Jarrott became chairman.

According to Cecil Bianchi, who was his racing mechanic: 'Jarrott was a man who really enjoyed life. He was very sporting: he'd been a good boxer and an excellent shot. He was a man who really *entered into* a meeting. Everyone liked him. He had a most charming personality; and, of course, as the ace driver of his day, he had lots of fans. He was a big fellow. He stood about six feet tall and must have weighed fourteen or fifteen stone. I never had any worries at all when driving with Jarrott—he inspired such confidence. I never thought he drove too fast.'

Edge and Jarrott had worked together, raced de Dion motor tricycles together, and, since they were both prolific writers, had frequently disagreed together in the columns of national and motoring papers. Jarrott once castigated Edge for driving cautiously. Edge criticised Jarrott for importing foreign cars to Britain. Jarrott was against the six-cylinder engine in which Edge had such faith. It was a great game.

Edge's letters must presumably have been typed—otherwise no editor would have been able to read them. His handwriting was atrocious. Jarrott recalled receiving the following telegram from him at Aix-la-Chapelle at the end of the first day of the Paris–Berlin race:

'Broken back cring/Trying to get repailed/admire club officiciers and ottner internoit'

With the help of *The Times* correspondent he eventually decided that what Edge's impossible writing had been trying to tell the telegraph operator was:

'Broken back spring/Trying to get repaired/Advise club officers and others interested'

As a matter of fact, the repair was not effected, and Edge was out of the race.

Edge was a man of enormous self-confidence who, in the words of a contemporary, 'in the first place, made sure you knew he was S. F. Edge. He was domineering, there was no question of that. On the other hand, one can forgive him, as he was a very good businessman.'

He was also a very good driver. One of his more impressive feats was on the 1,000-mile trial in Britain back in 1900. He was driving an unfinished Napier which, to all intents and purposes, had no brakes. On changing gear when going uphill near Kendal, the clutch slipped and the car began to roll backwards. His two companions jumped for their lives, but Edge remained in his seat. With enormous skill he managed to steer backwards down to the bottom. Neither he nor his car was hurt.

When the Italians began to take an interest in motor racing two firms were initially involved. One was Itala, the other Fiat (initials standing for Fabbrica Italiana Automobili Torinto. Torinto was said to have been added as an afterthought, when F.I.A. appeared to be too unpronounceable). With them came a new generation of drivers. These were men such as Felice Nazzaro, who was the son of a Turin coal merchant, joined the Fiat plant and later started a firm on his own. Nazzaro was extremely handsome and very well liked. His admirers said that he handled a racing car as delicately as a musician might handle a violin. Similarly Lancia (another Fiat graduate who eventually went off on his own), who was said to detect a false note in his engine as unerringly as he might pick one out in a performance of a work by Wagner (his favourite composer). And then there was Cagno, who had been personal chauffeur to the Queen Mother of Italy. Of him they said that he respectfully touched his cap to other competitors as he overtook them.

Among the largely unsung heroes of early motor sport were the racing mechanics. Some of them (such as Cecil Bianchi, who drove a Wolseley for England in the fifth and last Gordon Bennett Race of 1905) graduated into the driving seat. A number were killed or injured in races—perched, as they precariously were, on the floor beside their drivers.

One has to remember that in those days a driver seldom used the same car twice. Innovations were coming thick and fast. All too often the first time that he and his mechanic knew about them was on the day before an event. For example, a car which went racing in 1903 probably had a wooden frame, automatic valves, a tube radiator, a quadrant change-speed lever, and only the most rudimentary bearings in the wheels and gearbox. By the following year, the new racing model might quite possibly have advanced to a state in which it had a pressed steel frame, mechanical inlet valves, a honeycomb radiator, a gate gear change, and ball bearings in the wheels and gearbox.

It was the mechanic's job to find out, by hook or by crook, what these changes were. Let Cecil Bianchi tell it:

'All this was very difficult', he says. 'We very seldom saw the car more than a day or so before the race, and we never had a car of orthodox design.

'From the time the race started, everything depended on you. You had to diagnose your own troubles. The tools you took with you included such things as hack saws, a breast drill with drills up to three-eights, yards of strong cord, insulating tape, nuts and bolts, short lengths of pipe, and three or four yards of rubber tubing.

'We never dared start without a canvas bucket and about ten yards of rope. After about 150 miles, the water might start to boil—possibly because there was a leak in the hose joint. Then you'd have to stop at the nearest brook, fill up the canvas bucket and top up.

'You never used to worry, because you had a subconscious knowledge that you weren't the only one. The other bloke down the road would be having just the same things to cope with.'

On the Paris–Madrid run he and Jarrott took five spare inner tubes with them and two spare covers. The tank of the car had room for about 40 gallons of petrol. But because there were no supplies available along the entire route from Paris to Bordeaux they also carried two 5-litre cans of motor spirit.

After 46 miles of this race Bianchi recalls: 'The engine started to puff and then it stopped. I got out and found that some muck in the tank had clogged the pipe. I blew it clear, and then put my hand into the tank and tried to clear that out.

'After 150 miles, we suddenly began to run on only three cylinders. When I got the bonnet up, it looked as if the whole engine was covered with confetti. What had happened was that a spark plug had broken.'

In spite of the fact that a seat was provided for the mechanic, he usually travelled on the floorboards. Throughout the race he was extremely busy, for his duties included:

1. Responsibility for the kit of tools and getting as much information as possible about the car.

2. Advising the driver if anything was happening behind—like, for instance, somebody trying to overtake. The din of the engine made any kind of verbal communication impossible, and so it all had to be done by signals.

3. Carrying out manually all the lubrication operations which, nowadays, are done automatically. Between his legs, there was usually a two-gallon tank in which the oil was stored. There were two pumps on it. One was for the engine crankcase, and the other for the gearbox. From time to time he had to look at the exhaust. If it was clear he had to work the crankcase pump, until a slight blue tinge appeared. And, in addition to this, he also had to make sure that all the grease cups were topped up and the caps screwed down.

4. At every stop, he had to check that the wheel bearings weren't running hot.

5. Keep an eye open for any bolts which were working loose.

6. Do anything else which needed to be done—such as changing tyres.

'Still,' Bianchi says, 'it was jolly good fun. These people nowadays just don't know about it! They simply get into a car and steer it. If anything goes wrong, somebody else puts it right. A little thing, like a throttle control breaking, puts them out of a race.

'In those days you had the feeling when you were racing that you were doing something for the future. Ninety per cent of the innovations in one year's racing car appeared in production cars the next. It was very satisfactory.'

If a mechanic's lot was a tough one, the driver's was not much better. The cars were extremely uncomfortable; and, says Bianchi, 'Driving used almost to tear your arms out of your shoulders, you were counteracting so many undesirable things at one time. Of course, there were no such things as shock-absorbers or wheel balancing. All you used to see were your front wheels bouncing about.'

I once asked him whether the mechanic had to hang out over the side in an attempt to create some sort of stability on corners. 'Well,' he said, 'mechanics leaning out looked good, but it didn't do much good if you got into a spin. If it was a soft surface you just spun and came to rest. But if you encountered some solid object, such as a cobblestone or some projection you couldn't see, then over you went!'

There was, of course, also the problem of dust. As the years went by, the racing authorities made some effort to counteract this, though the cure turned out to be a good deal worse than the illness.

Initially, they used a substance called Westrumite, which was a mixture of petroleum and ammonia. It was, however, rather expensive and was eventually replaced by a cheaper product called Pulveranto. This and all similar remedies were sources of terrible eye inflammation. At least one story is told of a mechanic being led away from the track with his eyes in bandages.

In his *The Gordon Bennett Races* Lord Montagu recalls that Jenatzy's winnings from the Irish race were reckoned at £8,000. In addition to this, Bianchi—who is the last survivor of this great era (he is now a very young eighty-two and living in happy retirement at Wolverhampton)—says: 'Although there was no actual professionalism, the tyre, plug and oil companies used to give very handsome little presents. Yes—even in those days.'

Little presents, thousands of pounds—whichever it happened to be, those early drivers and their mechanics more than earned them.

4 A pretty little place called Brooklands

Edge's victory in the Gordon Bennett Race of 1902 had put the Automobile Club of Great Britain[1] in a curiously difficult position. As the winning club, its right—and, indeed, its duty—was to act as host for the following year. But where could the race be run in the United Kingdom?

Good roads seem to one of the rewards of militarism. Hitler built autobahnen so that he could move soldiers about quickly. Napoleon had similar ideas, when he caused those long, straight, highways to be constructed in France. The Romans, admittedly, did the same sort of thing in Britain, but all that was rather a long time ago. Whatever fine roads this country had once enjoyed had been allowed to perish from sheer neglect, as everything was staked on building canals and then railways.

There were certainly no long straight stretches such as the run from Paris to Bordeaux. And, in any case, the country was much too overcrowded.

When races went through towns on the Continent, a strict ritual was observed. On reaching the outskirts, the driver stopped

[1] *Royal* Automobile Club after Edward VII had given his O.K. in 1907.

at a control. A card recording his time of arrival was slipped into a sealed box on the side of the vehicle. He was then escorted by a cyclist through the centre at a speed which never exceeded 7 m.p.h. On the far side there was another control, where the time was again recorded and put into the box. After that he could drive off at full blast.

If you had to carry out such a procedure for every town and village in England the race would never get going properly. Furthermore, there was the country's by now traditional opposition to road racing, and it wasn't even worth wondering whether the Old Women of Westminster would allow such a thing to take place.

Fortunately, there is a stretch of water named the Irish Sea, and the land on the far side of it was sparsely populated. It was also somewhat undernourished financially. Here, possibly, might lie the answer to the Automobile Club's dilemma.

After a reconnaissance the club tentatively mapped out a course which took in most of County Kildare and spilt over into other counties to the south. The drivers were shown round it, and they said it seemed suitable. The local authorities were extremely enthusiastic, for they scented a big influx of money, and the Irish M.P.s were equally keen. The benefit, as they saw it, seems to have been improved roads. A petition was sent to Parliament, which didn't mind very much *what* went on in Ireland, and the resulting Bill got through its third reading on March 24th, 1903.

Later the Isle of Man performed a similar service. But both places only partly solved the problem of motor racing in Britain. To get to them you had to cross the sea, which meant much more than a day excursion for most people. What was needed was somewhere within reasonable reach of London, which could serve two purposes. One was racing: the other was to provide the motor industry with a test track. In 1903 the passing of the first Motor Car Act (which at last took heed of the fact that it wasn't really a locomotive) raised the speed limit to 20 m.p.h., but the age of traps began in earnest. The previous limit, perhaps because it was so obviously ridiculous, had not been enforced very vigorously. Now the police got down to the job with a zeal which suggested trying to make up for lost time.

What with antiquated roads and pettifogging laws, a car manufacturer found it hard to put a new model through its paces, unless he indulged in the costly business of taking it to the Continent. It was all very well for the French—they had all the facilities that anyone could wish for. And as for the Italians, there was plenty they could do up in the mountains. No wonder Britain was lagging behind in the sales race.

The man who came to the rescue was a wealthy Surrey landowner named H. F. Locke King. Locke King had built the Mena House Hotel in Cairo and a golf course at Byfleet. He owned a large Itala affectionately called Bambo, and in which he and his wife made extensive tours of the Continent. His land, which had been in the Locke King family for several generations, included swampy meadows, pine-clad hills, rough fields, woodland and several poultry farms. One boundary was a railway embankment, and the name of the place was Brooklands (doubtless because a brook went thought it).

Locke King, who smoked a pipe and was married to a lady who became a Dame of the British Empire, had the very adventurous idea that a racing circuit might be built within his domain. He canvassed around for opinions. Charles Jarrott said that he'd like to see a very large track which permitted high speeds in safety. S. F. Edge, doing his part in the Edge-Jarrott double act, said that he thought it should be a small track. If it was to become popular, he argued, the cars ought to be visible for most of a lap. In the end, it was decided to construct a large, roughly oval, circuit, nearly three miles long. It was to be built from concrete, and the two curved ends were to be steeply banked. This ingenious idea, which came from Colonel Holden, R.E., who drew up the plans, was to assist the drivers. If they took the correct line, the Colonel said, the cars would get round the curves at speeds of up to 120 m.p.h. without any need to be steered. This, of course, was due to centrifugal force.

Work on building the track began in September, 1906. In December of that year the Automobile Club of Great Britain issued a special permit allowing racing to take place at Brooklands. By June the following year, the circuit was complete. It had cost the better part of £250,000 to build, and had employed 2,000 workmen. Two farmhouses had to be demolished to make way for it. During the course of excavations Roman coins and pottery shards dating back 1,600 years were discovered.

So there was Brooklands: hated by its neighbours, loved by motor-racing men, the Mecca of British motor sport for the next thirty-three years. Its turnstiles were equipped to let 30,000 people pass by—an estimate which, at the time, was regarded as somewhat optimistic. Soon after it had been completed, a party of Americans came over. They made a minute examination of the track, and then went home. Presently, they presented the United

States with a rough, rather less ambitious, copy at a place called Indianapolis. The first Indianapolis '500' Race was held in 1911. Brooklands also helped to inspire the French circuit at Montlhery several years later.

It has been rightly said that the French invented motor racing. The way the English went on about it, one might have imagined that they had invented horses.

When they devised those early motor races it was almost as if they were trying to emulate the ways of Kempton Park or Ascot. Perhaps they imagined that, by doing so, they would make the new sport respectable. Or was it, simply, that this was the only way in which they knew *how* to organise this sort of thing? At all events, the drivers were made to wear smocks, each in his own colours, just like jockeys. The language was as close to the turf as anyone could make it. For example, the values of the prizes were expressed in sovereigns. There were rewards with such names as 'selling plates', and the president of the Brooklands Automobile Racing Club, which administered the circuit, was none other than Lord Lonsdale —a decidedly horsy man. Hugh Allen of the Jockey Club was the starter.

For the early events, it was forbidden to paint numbers on the cars, and you had to identify which was which by the colours of their drivers' smocks (this aping of equestrian attire persisted until 1914). There were bookies in attendance, and the race results were run up on telegraph boards, just as in horse racing.

Possibly taking their inspiration from the Roman chariot races, where they did it this way, the events were run anti-clockwise, and were a good deal shorter than those events which had been taking place in France.

The first meeting to be held at Brooklands was on Saturday, July 6th, 1907. Over 13,500 people turned up—500 of them in cars, the rest in special trains from Waterloo. Afterwards there was a good deal of criticism. Most of the complaints were about the sort of thing one stoically puts up with nowadays. In those halcyon days of the early twentieth century such things as queues and traffic jams and excessively crowded restaurants were largely unknown to the upper and middle classes. This initial meeting gave them a foretaste of life as it would eventually become, and they didn't like it. It was, for example, almost impossible to get any kind of service in the refreshment places. There were large traffic jams along the roads leading to the circuit; and touts outside were selling sixpenny official race cards for one shilling by gumming a label over the price.

Prices of admission were £1, 5s., and 2s. 6d. plus an extra 10s. if you wanted to take your car inside. These were considered to be too high for the facilities provided, and one critic said that in his opinion Brooklands had been opened a year too soon.

A point on which the authorities had certainly come adrift was failure to print any pass-out checks. If, for example, you were in the enclosure and you wanted to get something from your car, you were doomed. You either had to pay the price of admission all over again, or else stay outside. One spectator complained that he lost his wife, his car, and his chauffeur. As he was in the £1 enclosure, he'd have to pay another £1 to look for them.

The Autocar summed up a good many people's feelings by observing that: 'We must confess we should have no keen desire to attend many meetings unless we were confident that the management would steadily improve as meeting after meeting is held.' In this case Brooklands may have been the victim of all the publicity which had attended its construction. No circuit could have lived up to it. When all was ready it was, perhaps, an anticlimax. People expected too much.

The racing itself was quite good fun, with some interesting mechanical innovations—such as Newton injecting oxygen into his fuel when he needed to put on a spurt. There was also a somewhat spectacularly stripped-down Daimler used by Keating. It was a standard 45 h.p. production model, with the body and just about everything else removed. The driver sat on a bit of carpet tied to the petrol tank. As a back support, he used a broad leather belt which went round his waist, and was strapped to the dashboard. This, apparently, was the only competing car that had been in daily use. It was lying second in its race when the petrol supply choked.

And *The Autocar* pointed out: 'Several drivers went out without any mechanic or other passengers. This was bad practice, as it necessitated the driver looking behind to see his position with regard to other runners before entering the straight, whereas a second man can always count and check laps and note positions, if he does nothing else.'

The age of the rear-view mirror had obviously not yet arrived.

About a week before the first meeting was held there, Brooklands was used by S. F. Edge for one of the great publicity stunts of the period. His object was to motor non-stop for twenty-four hours in a 60 h.p. six-cylinder Napier, and to average 60 m.p.h. If he pulled it off it would be the greatest distance ever travelled by a man in one day. In the opinion of most people he wouldn't do it. One popular theory was that the tyres would melt (which they nearly did). Others said that the car wouldn't stand it, and a minority group advanced the interesting notion that some time after the 18th hour Edge would lose his reason.

The general climate of opinion, then, was pessimistic. About the only person, other than Edge, who considered that the attempt had a chance of succeeding was Charles Jarrott, who went along and watched.

An open-air garage was built at the top of the finishing straight. There was a tent for the drivers; two small cranes, which weren't used; stacks of Dunlop tyres mounted on detachable Rudge-Whitworth wire wheels; and (in the words of one reporter) 'enough Shell petrol to fill a small lake'. There were also six spare cars, though they were never needed.

To keep him company, two more Napiers were to be driven more or less alongside him. One of the cars was painted white, the other red.[1] Four Napier test drivers (one of them, Newton, was soon to make a name for himself as a racing driver) were to take three-hour spells at the wheel. Edge's car was slightly the faster of the three, and it was equipped with an adjustable glass screen of his own design. In the event of heavy rain it could be lowered. Much of his freshness after the run was attributed to this device.

The other cars were fitted with small fixed screens made out of gauze.

One of the problems was that of lighting. The Blériot lamps with which the Napiers were equipped were obviously hopelessly inadequate. Consequently some sort of track lighting was needed. The difficulty was solved by acquiring 352 red storm lanterns, which were set out on the circuit at the rate of one to every 10 yards, making a lap distance of 2 miles 61 chains 16 feet 2 inches. To complete the full distance, Edge had to travel on the outside of them, while Automobile Club officials cruised round on the inside—making sure that he did.

To provide additional illumination, Wells flares (suitably screened) were set up along the top of the banking; and, on the smaller of the two curves, fairy lights were used.

Four minutes before 6 p.m. on the afternoon of June 28th, Edge arrived in a two-seater car from his lodgings at the White Lion, Cobham. He looked very fit. His mechanic, Blackburn, was with him. The original idea had been that Blackburn should be

[1] Edge's own car was painted green.

relieved from time to time, but, in the event, he stuck it out to the bitter end. Although a place for food had been built into Edge's car it was never used. He decided to keep off solids for the whole trip.

At six o'clock, dead on time, Edge and his two companion cars drove off. It was chilly for June, though thankfully the rain kept away until the end. There was only a scattering of spectators present, and most of them melted away when told that they'd have to pay a sovereign per car plus 10s. for every passenger.

At first it looked as if the cars were not going fast enough. People had yet to get used to the effect of Brooklands in this respect. On the wide circuit everything seemed to travel a good deal more slowly than on a narrow road. But when, in the first hour, Edge covered 70 miles 130 yards, people became more optimistic.

After two hours he came in. The car needed water. Any misgivings that this might be the beginning of the end turned out to be groundless. The radiator wasn't topped up again for another eight hours.

The real menace was the effect of sustained high speed on the tyres—particularly the violent cornering. This became evident after 350 miles, when the troubles began. At one stage, despite the use of special security bolts, two tyres (one at the front and one at the back) actually came off. Edge had to motor for the rest of the lap on bare rims. All told, he made twelve stops to change tyres. During each of them he lay full length on the track to relax his muscles.

And so they motored through the night and throughout most of the next day. At 6 p.m., still looking fresh, Edge came in. Almost as if it had been prearranged, it began to rain in torrents.

In those 24 hours he had covered 1,581 miles 1,310 yards, averaging 65·8 m.p.h. His companion cars had averaged 64·12 m.p.h. and 63·3 m.p.h. All told twenty-six records were broken. The 24-hour one stood for eighteen years, until Gillett's A.C. broke it at Montlhery in 1924.

Commenting briefly that he now believed an average speed of 85 m.p.h. to be possible, Edge climbed into his two-seater, and drove back to the White Lion for a little rest.

Life at Brooklands was a mixture of stunts and straight racing. By September of 1907 the authorities had agreed that numbers could be painted on the cars, which made recognition easier—

although the drivers still had to wear their jockey smocks. Also in September of that year came the first handicap race. The object of handicapping was the very praiseworthy one of creating closer finishes. Previously, owing to the inequality of the cars, many of the races had become mere processions. However, the system doesn't appear to have been very satisfactory. Cecil Bianchi, who suffered under it, told me: 'The only way to win at Brooklands was by the smallest possible margin. Otherwise, you could bet your life you'd never win another race there. The system was completely unscientific—handicaps were merely what the judges thought they ought to be.'

If this was so, the judges must take full responsibility, for A. V. Ebblewhite, the Brooklands handicapper, was an enterprising man. It was he who persuaded the reluctant committee to let the drivers paint numbers on their cars.

Also in September, 1907, the first fatality occurred at the circuit. This occurred when Vincent Herman, driving a Minerva, failed to pull up after passing the finishing line. This brought him back on to the track. Travelling at considerable speed, he shot up on to the banking, where his right wheels went over the top. The car smartly spun round, went broadside back on to the track and toppled over just as a Napier was going by. The mechanic was thrown clear and injured. Herman was pinned underneath. He died a few hours afterwards.

One unsavoury aspect of the tragedy was a fight between officials and press photographers who were trying to force their way into the clubhouse, where the dying Herman lay on a stretcher.

There were races for ladies (in which Dame Ethel Locke King took part), races for officers of the Household Cavalry, stunts and challenges galore. A White steam car challenged an Aeriel-Simplex petrol car, and a quite remarkable effort was arranged to show the efficiency of the Cadillac spare parts service. Under R.A.C. supervision three cars did ten laps apiece. They were then taken away and locked up until the following Monday morning. Two mechanics, armed only with comparatively simple tool-kits, then descended upon them. With painstaking care they proceeded to dismantle each car into its 721 component parts (this included removing every possible nut and ball bearing).

Next day the Technical Committee of the R.A.C. examined the heap of parts, and selected items at random—to enable the mechanics to start rebuilding the vehicles. They also removed

A pretty little place called Brooklands 55

eighty-nine components, which were replaced by spares from the Cadillac depot in London.

When, at last, the three cars had been rebuilt, they all fired without any trouble at all, and straightaway set off round Brooklands for 500 miles at an average speed of 34 m.p.h. Between them, they actually covered 1,512 miles, used 51 gallons of petrol, and averaged 29·64 m.p.g.

The classic challenge of Brooklands occurred in 1908 when Edge pitted his giant 90 h.p. Napier, Samson, against a massive 18-litre[1] chain-driven Fiat named Mephistopheles. The match, which was to be run over six laps, took place on Whit Monday. Felice Nazzaro, the darling of the Italian motor-racing world, drove Mephistopheles (painted red) and Newton was at the wheel of Samson (painted green).

For a description of Nazzaro on this occasion, we cannot do better than quote *The Autocar* again. 'It would be difficult', that magazine's reporter wrote, 'to imagine anyone less like a professional race driver than Nazzaro. A *"roi de volant"*, as the French sporting papers love to describe this class of person, is always pictured as a kind of demon-faced individual who clings to his steering wheel with a horribly strained expression on his countenance. Nazzaro does not cling to his wheel, nor is his expression strained the least bit in the world. As a matter of fact, he is one of the nicest looking men I have seen for many a long day, and he handles his big machine with about as much effort as the average driver expends on a 6 h.p. runabout.'

In the Napier pits before the match, the activities seemed to be more than usually frenzied. By contrast, the Fiat team appeared to be calmly self-confident. The only crisis was when Nazzaro lost his black kid driving gloves. He refused to start without them, and the shops in Weybridge were ransacked until suitable replacements could be found. Shortly before zero hour, somebody came across the giant Fiat parked in the woods. Nazzaro was dozing peacefully in the driving seat.

Without a doubt, and in spite of any national pride, Mephistopheles was the favourite. The bookies were offering ten to one odds to anyone who cared to back the Napier, but nobody felt inclined to chance it.

And so they set off. For the first three laps the Napier led. Nazzaro seemed to find the track difficult. He was hugging the lower part of the banking at the curves, whilst Newton, who was used to the circuit, was letting his car take its natural position.

[1] The pistons were described as being 'as big as buckets'.

Presently, possibly through holding back and watching Newton, Nazzaro seemed to get the hang of things. He took a much better line on the curves and started to overhaul the Napier.

Unfortunately what might have been a very exciting finish was demolished when the Napier suddenly slowed down and then came to a grinding halt. A big end had seized and a con rod had bust—badly damaging the crankcase.

Nazzaro didn't seem to be aware that his opponent was no longer in the running. Much of the tread on his left-hand front tyre had been torn away and the canvas exposed, but he kept on motoring for the full six laps.

Afterwards an argument started which has never been resolved. According to the electric timing apparatus, Nazzaro's fastest lap was at 121·64 m.p.h. On the other hand, the official timekeepers hand-operated stop-watch put the speed at 107·98 m.p.h. Which was right? The only available evidence is that on the Thursday before the match the electric cables at Brooklands had been struck by lightning. Could this conceivably have damaged the timing apparatus? We shall never know, though one has—regretfully, perhaps—to place more reliance on the stop-watch.[1]

In any case, before the match was over, the big Fiat had been sold to Sir George Abercrombie, who proposed to use it for racing. The deal presumably paid the expenses of the trip from Italy and left enough over to start building another car.

---

[1] The crunch was that, at the end of 1907, Sir Algernon Guinness, Bt., had been timed at 115·4 m.p.h. in a 200 h.p. Darracq with a 22½-litre V8 engine. If Nazzaro really did do 121·64 m.p.h. it would have put up a new unofficial world record for petrol-driven cars—and made him the first to do two miles a minute in a car of this kind.

5 For the good of the breed

A heavyweight racing car was all engine. The designers devoted nearly all their inventiveness to making it go, with little over for the not altogether unimportant question of enabling it to stop. Where the engine led, good brakes surely ought to follow. Nor does undue thought seem to have been given to such matters as suspension and bodywork. The ideal, so far as the latter was concerned, was to have as little as possible: preferably none at all.

If this was going to assist the development of the ordinary touring car it would obviously be an odd sort of animal. It would be dangerous, uncomfortable, exorbitantly expensive to run, and almost impossible for the average person to drive.

Since the manufacturers were by now the mainstay of motor racing, and since the sport obviously provided invaluable opportunities for research, surely something was going rather wrong? There were plenty of people, among them the Automobile Club of Great Britain and the editors of the French motoring press, who said that it was.

The first attempt to tame racing was made in March, 1905. The French paper *L'Auto* announced that it proposed to provide a trophy called the 'Coupe des Voiturettes'. The climax would be a race over 250–300 km, and this was to be preceded by a six-day reliability trial. Each day the competitors would have to cover 200 km at a specified minimum speed.

Engine capacities of competing cars would be restricted to one litre. Chassis weights would be confined to between 350 and 500 kilos, and any car which didn't have an enclosed body would be penalised to the extent of 40 kilos (20 if it had a hood). The penalty was to be enforced by loading ballast into the car.

If *L'Auto* had expected the news to be greeted with excitement it must have been disappointed. The motor industry muttered a slightly bored 'Oh?', and went back to thinking about the row which was going on over next year's Gordon Bennett Race (see next chapter).

However, one mustn't underrate *L'Auto*'s tenacity. Presently, twenty-two entries were received, and thirteen cars actually turned up for the event, which was held in the Seine Valley at the end of November.

It was a disaster. Snow made the roads impossibly slippery, and the cars were skidding all over the place. A driver's only hope of success was to putter along and hope that nobody would overtake him. Twenty-five k.p.m. had been specified as the required speed —with no marks to be won or lost if it was exceeded. To maintain it meant motoring for eight hours a day over hazardous roads in conditions of extreme discomfort.

There were the customary skirmishes with walls and horses (two horses, one wall), but the de Dions went very nicely and it looked as if one of them would be the winner. But then, on the last day, some bright spark repeated a trick performed by another bright spark at the Circuit des Ardennes in 1903. He strewed a collection of large bent nails over the road.

The sabotage occurred on the highway between Poissy and Paris, and only one car seems to have got through unscathed.

Nevertheless, the race which was the event's climax was held at Chanteloup on the following day, and a single-cylinder de Dion put up the best time. But then the editor of *L'Auto* became worried.[1] In view of the business of the bent nails, ought not the results of the final day's trial to be cancelled? He put the question to the A.C.F.

One of the more charming features of this august body has always been its unpredictability. The sporting committee con-

---

[1] His name was Henri Desgrange. He had never learnt to drive a car: was said to be much more interested in cycling.

sidered the evidence, and presently gave a verdict which must have astonished even the editor of *L'Auto*. The whole thing, it said, must be cancelled—and more. De Dion and Vulpès (another marque which had done well) must each be fined the sum of 100 francs for advertising their successes. Furthermore—and goodness knows why, for it all seems very unjust—the firm of Lacoste and Battman, which had done well but not marvellously, was to be fined 1,000 francs for advertising *their* success *and* suspended for six months from taking part in contests. Eventually, after a protest, the suspension was cancelled, but the fine just about fixed Lacoste and Battman. Very little more was ever heard of them.

In the following year the rules were modified in recognition of the French tendency to turn everything into a race, and the event was held over a 200 km triangular course, which had to be travelled eight times a day in the so-called reliability run, and culminated in a seven-lap race.

To discover the origins of the Targa Florio we have to go to Sicily—to the large estate near Palermo of the Florio family. The Florios had blood connections with the Italian royal family, and once entertained the German emperor and empress at their house. They constructed railways, established steamer services to the mainland and America, built hotels on the island to attract tourists, and ran a large export business. Indeed, the current head of the household, Ignazio Florio, was reputed to have done more for the development of Sicily than any other man of his generation.

Ignazio had what must have been a rather tiresome, much younger, brother named Vicenzo. Their father had died shortly after Vicenzo's birth, and Ignazio had most of the responsibility for bringing the youngster up. He imported governesses from England and then tutors. Vicenzo developed into a cultured, strikingly handsome, young man with a rare taste for adventure.

At a comparatively early age he built a balloon, which he sent up unmanned. The flight seems to have been a success, for he then had the idea of making a bigger one and launching it with animals on board. This, presumably, was to be the experimental prelude to a flight by himself.

In spite of what anyone may say about Sicilians, the Florios were fond of their household pets. Consequently, the only suitable payload that Vicenzo could find for his contraption was rats. It might have had a happier ending if the lighter-than-air device hadn't connected with a church spire, which pierced the bag—after which it started to rain rats.

He travelled a good deal, took a keen interest in the 1,600-ton family steam yacht, which was being built on the Clyde,[1] and became an avid collector of bicycles. The pride of his collection was an all-aluminium Beeston Humber.

Presently the great day came in 1898, when Ignazio, who had been in Paris, brought back a de Dion-Bouton tricycle. He presented the machine to Vicenzo, who promptly went into raptures of delight, and quickly learnt how to drive it. On one of his earlier runs, a gang of Sicilian youths pelted him with overripe tomatoes. But Vicenzo was undaunted.

Since he was a keen sportsman, there seemed to be only one sensible thing to do with the machine—race it. The first event which he arranged was from Palermo to Mondello. Three competitors took part: a cyclist, a horse rider, and Vicenzo on the de Dion. The cyclist succumbed to cramp at the halfway mark. The de Dion overheated, and the horseman won. Still—everything has to begin somewhere. Vicenzo was now an automobile addict, and he began to collect cars with the same zeal that he had devoted to bicycles.

One of his earlier acquisitions was a Fiat. When Fiat delivered a custom-built car to an important client, they always sent an expert along with it, to explain how everything worked. In this case they sent a young engineer who was considered to be of unusual promise. His name was Felice Nazzaro.

Vicenzo and Nazzaro took to each other at once. The young Sicilian nobleman admired the way in which the Turin engineer treated the car—how he seemed to achieve a relationship with it that was rather like something between two human beings. Presently he said to Nazzaro: 'Why don't you stay here and help me look after my cars?' Nazzaro agreed and was signed on as Vicenzo's chauffeur.

He stayed for four years. Those were great times. The two young men raced together, talked together, and Nazzaro had a rare opportunity to examine all the very best European cars. He had only driven in one competition, and that was in a Fiat to win a bet for the Duke of Abruzzi. Vicenzo busied himself organising events in the park at Palermo, in which he, Nazzaro and their

---

[1] The Florios later sold it to Sir Thomas Lipton, who used it to ship his yacht *Shamrock* to the United States for one of the America Cup contests. In the First World War it served as a hospital ship and was eventually torpedoed in the Mediterranean.

friends took part. Possibly, during this period, Nazzaro began to discover the lurking brilliance which later was to make him one of the most famous drivers of the day.

As for Vicenzo, he was turning into a very competent performer. He had been going to take part in the Paris–Madrid race, but his brother put a veto on the idea. However, there were other events—such as the race at Brescia in which he was held up at a level crossing. As the train went by, he saw brother Ignazio looking down at him with undisguised disapproval from one of the carriage windows.

Vicenzo was grateful for the sport, and eager to put something back into it. In 1904 he presented the Coppa Florio which, also at Brescia, was first competed for in 1905. Later, on a trip to Paris, he met Desgrange of *L'Auto*. Said the latter: 'Why don't you organise a race in Sicily?'

There were many good reasons why not. For one thing, the island had no roads worthy of the name. For another, even the Florio power was not absolute. There were bandits in the hills and, of course, the Mafia had to be taken into consideration.

However, once Vicenzo got an idea into his head, there was no stopping him. He laid out a circuit of twisting road which at one point climbed to 3,670 feet. He ordered a solid gold plate (the 'targa') from a Parisian goldsmith. He even seems to have found a way of mollifying the bandits and the Mafia.

In 1906 the first Targa Florio race took place. The course was 90 miles long, and somebody estimated that there were 1,006 corners. This was clearly not an event for big bangers; and so, once again, the emphasis turned to touring cars. The rules were that they all had to be standard production cars, and that no chassis should cost more than 20,000 francs. A minimum weight limit of 1,300 kilos was also imposed.

The definition of a standard car was accepted as being one which was manufactured in a series with at least nine others.

Ten entries were received for the race, which was won by Cagno in an Itala. Le Blon, who drove a Hotchkiss, took his wife along as mechanic, and two competitors lost time by mistakenly pouring water into their petrol tanks. There were few spectators.

In the following year the Targa Florio was won by Vicenzo's old friend Felice Nazzaro.

The aristocracy's enthusiasm for motor cars came right from the top. In the early twentieth century there was scarcely a reigning monarch who wasn't enraptured with man's latest creation. They all had their collections of cars, and the Kaiser was no exception. Although, when he went to watch the Gordon Bennett Race at the Taunus Circuit near Hamburg, he didn't have the pleasure of seeing a German car win, he must have enjoyed his day out. At all events, His Imperial Majesty presented a cup for a touring-car race to take place in 1907. It was to be known as the Kaiserpreis.

The competing cars had to observe a maximum engine capacity of 8 litres, the minimum weight permitted was 1,715 kilos, the gearboxes had to include reverse, the exhaust had to be expelled horizontally, and there were all sorts of statistics about the required dimensions of the chassis. The object, quite definitely, was to eliminate *anything* which might be regarded as a racing car pure and simple.

Two eliminating trials were held on a 73-mile circuit. The first twenty in each competed in the final. The trials were of two laps each—the final, of four. Ninety-two entries were received.

The event started at the unearthly hour of 4 a.m. (the Kaiser seems to have been a fanatic about early rising), and was won by Nazzaro in a Fiat. Winning things was getting quite a habit with this young Italian, who, by introducing what W. F. Bradley has described as 'the "gentlemanly" type of driving', revolutionised the attitude to driving a racing car. But, then, 1907 was Nazzaro's big year. In it he won the French Grand Prix, the Kaiserpreis, and the Targa Florio—three out of his seven big victories between 1906 and 1923.

And so to the Isle of Man. Like Ireland, it has always been blessedly immune from the more fiddling aspects of British legislation. To close a road in Great Britain requires an Act of Parliament, and nobody could seriously imagine that such an act would be passed on behalf of motor racing in England. On the island, however, there is an institution known as the Tynwald Court, which is never too busy to consider amending the local Highway Act—especially if it's likely to do the tourist trade a bit of good. This, indeed, is hardly surprising. If you took the visitors away from the island there wouldn't be a great deal of prosperity left.

The origin of motor racing on the Isle of Man was the Gordon Bennett Races. Every year the Automobile Club of Great Britain had to select a three-car team to take part. The best way of doing

For the good of the breed

this was obviously to run an eliminating trial, in which the best performers would be earmarked to represent the club. The first time the island was used for this purpose was 1904. Each driver had to complete five laps of a 50-mile course, which started at Douglas in the north, went down to Castletown in the south, and more or less circumscribed the island. Afterwards they had to carry out stopping and restarting tests on a steep hill.

It was a more than adequate trial of strength for both cars and drivers. The roads were dusty, ill made and steeply cambered. There were broad grass verges and deep ditches. Furthermore, for part of its length, the route ran over the mountains.

Meanwhile, the pundits at the Automobile Club had become worried about the turn motor racing was taking in Europe. Like so many other responsible people, they believed that it was creating a new breed of monsters—instead of directly benefiting the development of the kind of car which ordinary motorists could buy.

Having discovered this remarkable gold-mine of racing opportunity on the Isle of Man, the Automobile Club decided to do something about it. And so, in 1905, they invented a race which they called the Tourist Trophy. It was to be a contest not only of speed but also of fuel consumption.

A weight limit of 1,600 lb was put on the chassis, but this didn't deter Mercedes, Mors, Fiat, or Leon Bollée—all of whom produced heavyweights—from entering. Every chassis had to carry a minimum load of 950 lb and the wheelbase of every car had to be at least 7 ft 6 in.

It was quite amazing what human ingenuity could get up to in attempts to reduce weight. In his book on the T.T. races Richard Hough tells of how rags were used for axle caps, leaves were taken out of springs, and collapsible cardboard bonnets and steps were used.

Fuel consumption regulations, which were almost the *raison d'être* for the first three T.T.s, insisted that petrol was to be used at the maximum rate of 25 m.p.g. (just before the race it was changed to 22·54 m.p.g.) on what was somewhat flatteringly described as 'a dry average road'. Once again ingenuity got to work. Some competitors even tried to install hidden pipes leading from concealed tanks, which sounds reprehensibly like cheating.

The bodies of the cars had to be removable for weighing-in, and every entry had to have the maker's selling price marked on its chassis. This, presumably, was to ensure that they really were production cars.

Once again, the course circumscribed the island. The rules

stated that, in villages or at any place marked by a red flag, no overtaking could take place unless the driver was 'in difficulties, or unless a car was going so slow as to hinder others' (which seems a rather odd way of putting it). Blue flags were used to warn drivers of the imminence of red ones, and to warn them of approaching corners. There were Automobile Club observers cruising round the course in a brand-new 30 h.p. Rolls-Royce, which had been loaned to the club for the occasion by the Hon. C. S. Rolls.

The first T.T. race set the pattern for all the other ones. It was relaxed, friendly, enormously good fun and with something interesting continually taking place—or seeming to be about to take place. Pretty well every British car maker of any repute contributed something to the entry list of fifty-eight, though the very regulations which were designed to make this a race for touring cars seemed to be defeating their own ends. Because of the stringent rules about weight and fuel consumption, there was hardly a model present which hadn't been modified out of all recognition. This was mostly to keep the weight down, though special tanks were also fitted, to ensure that the last drop of fuel went where it belonged—into the carburettor.

Enormous publicity heralded the event, which completely disrupted the life of the island. The visitors, of course, loved it. It was an opportunity to look at lots of fascinating motor cars and to see some very exciting driving. The practice times were the big topic of discussion, and some of the competitors made most elaborate preparations.

C. S. Rolls, for example, filled several notebooks with observations about road conditions, and even went so far as to make a catalogue of posters to remind him where to change gear. Tom Thorneycroft was observed measuring gradients with a pocket handkerchief. One just couldn't be too careful.

The main cause of accidents was this business of petrol consumption. It obviously helped if you coasted downhill—which is not an exercise to be recommended at high speeds. Still, it was very tempting to make the most of those five miles which descended from Snaefell, even if it did entail the risk of bashing into a house or a wall, or (as very nearly happened once) a herd of cattle.

Perhaps the most remarkable example of pitwork in the race was when Hadley went up a bank in his Wolseley—where, to add to the confusion, it was struck by Thorneycroft's car. The shunt didn't do very much damage, but the trip up the bank bent the front axle. It was removed and taken to a blacksmith about a mile away, who obligingly straightened it out. Once it had been reassembled, Hadley went back into the race. It was won by J. P. Napier in an 18 h.p. Arrol-Johnston at an average speed of 33·8 m.p.h.

The T.T. course was modified in varying degrees until 1909, when it settled down as the standard circuit which has been used ever since (though, since 1922, only by motor cycles. After that year there was a long gap until in 1928 the Tourist Trophy car races were resumed on the Ards circuit in Northern Ireland.)

In 1907 the cars were divided into two classes, heavy and light. They ran simultaneously in torrential rain, which reduced the winner's average speed to 28 m.p.h. In the following year the organisers abandoned all pretences about sticking to touring cars and the R.A.C. (as it had now become) introduced its horse-power formula. Since it resulted in most of the engines having a bore of four inches, it became known as the 'Four Inch Formula'. Less respectfully, the trophy was dubbed the 'Four Inch Trophy'. The whole thing seems to have filled people with a great many misgivings. While the craze for nicknames was in full spate, the scene of the races was called the 'Isle of Manslaughter'.

After that year the T.T. was dropped until 1914, when an engine limit of 3,310 c.c. was imposed plus a weight limit of 21½ cwt. The *Daily Telegraph* provided prizes of £1,000 for the winning driver and £250 for second place. There was also a £300 team prize. Sunbeams were the favourites, and it was one of these cars which won (with Lee Guinness at the wheel). W. O. Bentley was there with a most beautifully prepared car named a Doriot, Flandrin and Parant.[1] The race again took place in heavy rain, with gale-force winds sweeping the mountain. A singularly vile dust-layer manufactured from calcium chloride was used, which was excruciatingly painful if it got into the eyes.

And there things had to remain until 1922. The R.A.C. had been working out plans for the 1915 event a few weeks before war broke out. They were published in *The Autocar* in the issue which appeared on the Saturday after August 4th. But by then most people had stopped thinking about motor racing, and several of the men who had performed on the T.T. circuit in 1914 were dead in Flanders before the year was out. Among them was Bentley's mechanic, Leroux.

---

[1] *The Autocar* suggested that the initials stood for 'Deserves First Place'.

6 Pride (plus a lot of prejudice)

The French had never liked the Gordon Bennett Races. They considered them to be unfair. Here was this great nation, the world's leading motor builder, expected to compete on equal terms with other countries whose production figures were, by comparison, insignificant. At the end of 1904 France could boast (which it unashamedly did) of ten automobile manufacturers which, between them, could turn out twenty-nine highly competitive models. In spite of this, under the Gordon Bennett rules, French entries were restricted to three cars—when, as they saw it, they should have been given an overwhelming numerical superiority. It was enough to send the tricolour down to half-mast.

At first, the A.C.F. had carried out its part as organiser of the races somewhat grudgingly. The fact that French cars and drivers won the first two races may have helped to restore national pride; but then came 1902 and a British victory, and after that 1903 and a German triumph. This, in the opinion of the French motor industry, was not at all how things should have been.

Admittedly Théry beat the Germans on their own ground in

the Gordon Bennett Race of 1904;[1] but by now things had gone too far. At the Paris motor show of that year a deputation from the industry lobbied members of the A.C.F. They asked that the 1905 Gordon Bennett Race should be held simultaneously with another event—to be called the Grand Prix de l'Automobile Club de France. A system of proportionate representation would be used for the latter, which meant that France would stand an overwhelming chance of victory—if only by sheer weight of numbers. After that there'd be no further truck with the Gordon Bennett affair unless the rules were severely modified.

Simplicity of thought is a rare and beautiful thing. It is certainly not always present in the minds of those who think up motor races. The A.C.F. agreed to the French manufacturers' request, which is more than could be said of any other motor sport organisation.

On June 20th, 1904, after the German Gordon Bennett Race, an historic meeting had taken place at Hamburg. The six national automobile clubs, which had been concerned with these events, decided to co-ordinate their efforts. Soon afterwards, seven more clubs joined the alliance, which became known as the Association Internationale des Automobiles Clubs Reconnus (in 1946, it changed its name to Fédération Internationale Automobile). The A.C.F. had no sooner announced its support for the French constructors' ideas, when all its fellow members of the A.I.A.C.R. turned upon it.

The rows began immediately. Some people said that running two races simultaneously would lead to another Paris–Madrid bloodbath. The English were particularly vociferous about the injustice of it, and the Germans threatened to withdraw from the Gordon Bennett Race altogether. As for the French, they now said that, even if they won the 1905 Gordon Bennett event, they'd never stage another.

Strangely enough, the A.C.F. hierarchy was a little puzzled by the hostile foreign attitudes, and couldn't understand what all the fuss was about. Its members were not so surprised. They criticised the club and the industry for alienating the sympathies of foreign clubs; for causing the A.C.F. to lose prestige as the leading controlling body of motor sport; and for giving the motor industry too much protection.

[1] It certainly wasn't for want of trying on the Germans' part. Although confined, like everyone else, to three cars, they sent three more Mercedes over to Vienna, whence they were entered for the race under the Austrian flag.

As if heedless of the storm which was raging, the A.C.F. announced that the first fifteen in the French Gordon Bennett eliminating trials would represent France in the Grand Prix, and that the first three would be the country's Gordon Bennett team. Germany and Britain would be confined to six entries each in the Grand Prix: Austria, Italy, Switzerland, America and Belgium would be allowed to enter three cars apiece. *L'Auto*, ever ready to hand out prize money, offered 100,000 francs (£4,000) to the winner.

More protests poured in, and things were beginning to get out of hand. In an attempt to bring back some sort of sanity, a meeting was held in Paris during February, 1905. Delegates from all the clubs concerned were invited to attend. When it was over they had at least agreed upon one thing: to hold the two races separately. Shortly afterwards, the A.C.F. decided to abandon the Grand Prix idea for the time being.

But this didn't mean a reprieve for the Gordon Bennett series. In this respect France stuck to her guns. If a French driver won the race the A.C.F. wouldn't invite challengers; and, if some other country won it, it wouldn't be challenging the winning club.

For a very short time things were back to normal—or almost. The Gordon Bennett Race was held at the mountainous Auvergne circuit, which was one of the most difficult. Nevertheless, the authorities certainly didn't propose to repeat the mistakes of Paris–Madrid. £3,300 was spent on covering the route with an expensive dust-laying preparation. Three wooden bridges were erected so that cars could go over the railway lines, and be independent of level crossings and passing trains. All the towns and villages were barricaded off, so that no spectators would be able to stray on to the track. There was also a system of telephone cables, designed to link up the three spacing controls with the starting line. It might have worked very well had not a party of local peasants stolen most of the cable on the eve of the race. As it was, there were no communications and out on the more distant parts of the circuit nobody knew very much about what was going on.

The idea of the spacing controls was to stop the cars from bunching up too much. If there were any signs of this happening, such as one driver too close on the tail of another, the rear car would be stopped and compelled to wait for four minutes before starting off again.

At the eliminating trials there were two accidents. On the second lap Henry Farman skidded on the edge of a ravine. He

Pride (*plus a lot of prejudice*) 69

and his mechanic were mercifully thrown up into the branches of a tree. The car was less fortunate. It went over the side and crashed to its destruction many feet below.

On the third lap Girardot's two front tyres came off simultaneously. The car hit a telegraph pole and then went into a ditch. Girardot and his mechanic were flung out and injured.

The race, which was run over four laps, began at 6 a.m. on July 5th with the cars being sent off at 5-minute intervals. Among the British entry (two Wolseleys and a Napier) was a six-cylinder giant belonging to S. F. Edge, which had captured half a dozen world records at Daytona Beach in Florida, and sounds suspiciously like Samson, which battled against Nazzaro's Mephistopheles at Brooklands. The attack on the records reads like a typical Edge piece of grand scale sales promotion. It was doubtless intended as a fanfare to usher in the six-cylinder era at Napier's. In the Gordon Bennett Race the big brute only finished eighth and was beaten by one of the Wolseleys.

A last echo of the age of steam was present in the form of a Locomobile from America, but that didn't finish at all. It was still on its second lap a quarter of an hour after the race had been won.

The winner was Théry in a Brasier, who thus repeated his victory of the previous year. Nazzaro in a Fiat came second, and another Fiat with Cagno at the wheel was third. The last car to come in arrived at four o'clock on the following morning, with its mechanic covered from head to foot in oil. They believed in sticking it out to the bitter end, and then beyond, in those days.

And that was the end of the Gordon Bennett Races. Thereafter the newspaper proprietor turned his attention to aviation. He was said to have been somewhat sickened by the commercialism of car racing. Ever an optimist, he hoped that ethics in the sky might be better, and accordingly presented 25,000 francs for the Gordon Bennett Aeronautical Cup. The award was to be for balloon racing, which must have been very peaceful after the angry and acrimonious sounds of car racing. In 1909 he presented another trophy—this time for heavier-than-air machines. It was known as the Gordon Bennett Aviation Cup.

Meanwhile the A.C.F. was busy hatching out its plans for a Grand Prix race, which was scheduled to take place in the summer of 1906. A triangular circuit was mapped out in the Le Mans area. It consisted of three long, straight, roads connected by very tight corners. The idea was to make it the toughest possible test of men and machines. A race distance of 770 miles was to be spread out over two days, with no neutralisation periods for passing through towns.

The snag in this last respect was the village of St. Calais, which was situated on one of the corners. The road there was so bad that it looked as if some sort of neutralisation would have to take place. However, the inhabitants of St. Calais solved the matter themselves. They didn't want to miss out on all the visitors which the race was expected to attract and so, at their own expense, they built a wooden track joining the two arms of the circuit. The track went through a field, and missed the village altogether.

Another stretch of wooden road was built in the Forest of Vibraye, where the going was particularly bad.

The Germans had taught people a thing or two when, at the Taunus circuit, they built a tunnel for pedestrians under the track. The French did exactly the same thing at Pont-de-Gennes on the Le Mans circuit. They also erected large grandstands with pits opposite them, and even tarred the road in front to keep the dust down.

So far as the cars were concerned, the only regulation was a weight limit of 1,000 kilos, which followed the Gordon Bennett ruling. Once they'd started, the drivers and their mechanics had to do all the work themselves. Previously, they had been allowed assistance when changing tyres.

During the night between the two days' racing, the cars had to be locked up in a specially constructed parking area, which was heavily fenced in. A two-million candlepower searchlight roamed over the vehicles, and Prince d'Armberg, Count R. de Vogué, and Sr. Quinonés de Léon (all of them on the sporting committee, but in no way connected with the trade) sat up all night on guard.

There was no lack of entries. Renault, Clément-Bayard, Fiat, Hotchkiss, Brasier, Panhard, Darracq, Mercedes, de Dietrich, and Itala were all fielding three-car teams. A Gobron-Brillié driven by Rigolly added a nice touch of history. It had been built in 1903 and had been racing ever since (a fact which, in those days, made it old).

The start was at 6 a.m. The cars set off at 1½-minute intervals. Before the race was very old, Le Blon (remember him and his wife in the first Targa Florio?) ran out of road on the wooden track at St. Calais and buckled the right-hand rear wheel of his Hotchkiss. Using spokes from his other wheels, and borrowing a few from Shepard[1] and Salleron, who were the other two Hotchkiss drivers, he laboriously rebuilt it. The job took three hours, but Le Blon stuck at it. Possibly he borrowed too many spokes from Shepard, for the latter's car succumbed to the same trouble on the following day.

With these long, long straights this was primarily a test of sustained high speed—and tyres. It was a scorchingly hot day (one eyewitness described it as 'nearly tropical'), and the tyres were taking most fearful punishment. During the course of the first day alone Rougier changed no fewer than fourteen. The Fiats, the Italas, and the Renaults were best off in this respect. Their wheels were fitted with detachable rims. You only had to undo eight holding nuts, and the whole operation could be carried out in two minutes. Other manufacturers either said that the system hadn't been tested enough—or else, like Panhard, knew that those extra 9 kgm per wheel would bring the car too close to the weight limit.

One driver (Weillschott) became so exhausted that he couldn't keep his car on the wooden road at Vibraye. The dust, and the liquid which was supposed to keep it down, tortured the drivers' eyes. Edmond, who was driving a Darracq, had to give up on the last lap of the first day. He couldn't see the road any more.

Just after 11.45 a.m. Szisz—the Hungarian mechanic who had travelled with Louis Renault in the Paris–Madrid race, and was now driving a Renault—shot past the grandstand on his final lap. He was leading by 25 minutes, and had completed the day's run in 5 hours 45 minutes 30·4 seconds.

The system of starting the next day was ingenious. The cars were dragged out of the *parc fermé* by horses and taken to the line. Two mechanics were allowed to start the engines. After that the rules were as for the previous day.

But the clever thing was that each driver was sent off at whatever hour, minute and second was the time of his previous day's run. In other words, Szisz departed at 5.45–30·4 a.m., Clement at 6.11–40·6 a.m., Nazzaro at 6.26–53 a.m., and so on. At any given moment, a competitors' race time would be precisely that shown on the clock.

On the second day there were still seventeen cars in the race. All of them got away without any bother, which was more than most people had expected.

If any driver wished, he could appoint a substitute for the second

[1] A young American amateur taking part in his first race. He did very well, finishing fourth at the end of the first day.

day. Jenatzy was the only one who took advantage of this. Lancia had intended to, but his understudy never turned up. Consequently, he was compelled to motor in his ordinary clothes. There was no time to change.

The high speeds of the previous day had torn up the roads. The corners were a treacherous mess of loose pebbles, but no great dramas occurred. Szisz broke a rear spring on the penultimate lap, but it didn't matter much. He was so far ahead that nobody could catch him. He motored home and finished at 12.15 p.m. His average speed for the race was 63 m.p.h. Nazzaro arrived in his Fiat at 12.45 p.m. and Clément (Clément-Bayard) 3 minutes after that.

As a spectacle, the race must have been quite impressive. It was, however, something from which any feeling of sportsmanship was almost entirely missing. Furthermore, it was mainly a trial of strength between Renault and Fiat. Already, the big guns of commerce were turning motor racing into an unhealthy mixture of politics, money, and brute mechanical strength. Professionalism was well dug in; and, in any case, the entry fee of £200 per car which the A.C.F. levied for this race, was scarcely likely to encourage the amateur.

The French Grand Prix of the following year was held at Dieppe and was won by Nazzaro in a Fiat. In the year after that it again took place at Dieppe, and Lautenschlager (a former Daimler employee from a village near Stuttgart, who had risen to the position of foreman in the driving department) won it in a Mercedes. It may, then, not come as any great surprise to read that there was no Grand Prix in 1909, 1910, nor in 1911. Once again the intrigues of politics were at work.

In 1907 and 1908 the A.C.F. had been playing around with the regulations. In the former year it imposed a fuel limit of 9·4 m.p.g.: in the latter it laid down a maximum piston area of 117 square inches and a minimum weight of 1,150 kilos. Neither of these measures, however, pleased the French car industry.

They were now in a position in which the racing car had become a freak—and a very expensive one, at that. These big, over-engined monstrosities were completely out of touch with consumer requirements, and the consumer was beginning to be a problem. At last the supply of vehicles to the market was beginning to exceed the market's demand for them.

Not that the French industrialists wished to quit motor racing altogether. All they wanted was a cheaper version of the sport; something more in tune with production models; and something which would guarantee them success against the Fiats and Mercedes, which were such a thorn in their flesh. Accordingly, they formed a pact among themselves to give up Grand Prix racing for a period of years. Anyone who broke it was liable to a fine of £4,000. Having come to this agreement, they concentrated on voiturette racing.

The A.C.F. chose courses and organised Grand Prix races in 1909, 1910, and 1911, but nobody showed any interest in them (only eight entries were received for the 1909 event, and it certainly wasn't worth holding a race just for them).

And so, for a while, motor-racing initiative passed to Britain, where Brooklands was becoming popular, and America, where the Indianapolis speedway was nearing completion. In France all efforts were concentrated on the Coupe des Voiturettes, which had now become known as the Coupe de l'Auto.

In 1912, however, it began all over again. The French Grand Prix re-started (although, of course, it had never officially come to an end) and was run in conjuction with the Coupe de l'Auto. A width-of-car limit of 175 cm (69 in.) was imposed. The race was again run at Dieppe, and was won by a Peugeot.

Next year they introduced some very complicated regulations about fuel consumption (maximum: 14·2 m.p.g.) and some no less tricky ones about weight. The race was run at Amiens, and Peugeot, though with a different driver, repeated its success. Finally, in 1914, they limited engine capacities to 4·5 litres, kept to the 1913 weight limit, prohibited doped fuel and superchargers, held the race at Lyons, and watched Lautenschlager win it in a Mercedes.

Looking back on this section, I have to admit that the early history of the car, and of motor racing, doesn't appear particularly commendable. In Britain it brought out the worst reactionary attitudes; in France it degenerated into jungle warfare attended by feverish nationalism; even the German slate wasn't entirely clean (for instance, that dodge of sending Mercedes cars to Vienna just before the 1904 Gordon Bennett Race).

Perhaps there were better things to come. For the moment we must pause to allow the First World War to take place. This in itself was rather like motor racing at the time, for it was a matter of brave men risking their lives, and sometimes losing them, in pursuit of the devious purposes of their employers.

'The true artist will let his wife starve, his children go barefoot, his mother drudge for his living at seventy, sooner than work at anything but his art'.
GEORGE BERNARD SHAW *Man and Superman*

Part Two

Thunder at noon

7 When the troops came marching home

The wind blew the smell of cordite away from the battlefields and the troops came home. This was peace, and in peace you sometimes have an option about dying. You may also, with tolerable luck, be able to do the things you enjoy.

In Europe enthusiasts had to wait until 1921 for the first post-war Grand Prix. The roads of France were in an appalling condition, and a great deal of work was necessary before they could even be restored to the somewhat arguable standards of 1914.[1]

On the far side of the Atlantic things were better, and the speedway at Indianapolis was blessedly intact. Seven months after the Armistice the first post-war '500' race was held there. There were some very nasty crashes, and three drivers were killed. The event was won by an American driver, Howdy Wilcox, at the wheel of a Peugeot. The car had been stored up at the circuit during the war years. Another French firm, Ballot, had hopefully invested $120,000 on building and preparing entries. The money was to little avail. The cars did disappointingly badly.

[1] It took longer for the French to overcome their bitterness and allow German cars to take part in their races.

Among those who watched the race was the war leader Marshal Foch, who was seen talking earnestly to Louis Chevrolet.

Nothing could hold back the French enthusiasm for the sport. Since they couldn't go road racing in Grand Prix cars, they contained their impatience by racing cycle cars.

Back in Britain there were hill-climbs and Brooklands. The former were extremely spectacular. The cars were so large that they seemed to fill every square inch of the track. Strangely enough, and in spite of the official British mistrust of motor sport, the events were allowed to take place on public roads.

Having been hounded by the law, derided by the body politic, and fettered by ridiculous speed limits, the car had at last been given its freedom. The abolition of speed limits was supposed to be some sort of reward for helping to win the war (women were given the vote for a similar reason).

Technically, then, and assuming that the local police force took a similarly liberal view, there was no reason why sportsmen should not take their cars uphill at any speed they chose. Of course, it was necessary to keep away other traffic while the contest was taking place. The constabularies were usually reasonably obliging in this respect, and used to close the roads.

But there was also the question of spectators. They were among the hill-climber's greater perils, for they often stood alarmingly close to the track. On a very much smaller scale the situation was somewhat reminiscent of the Paris–Madrid race. Inevitably, there would one day be a crash in which somebody, other than a driver or his mechanic, would get hurt.

It happened at an event in Essex. Among the competitors was a young Oxford undergraduate named Francis Giveen, who had recently bought Raymond Mays's famous $1\frac{1}{2}$-litre Brescia Bugatti, Cordon Bleu (named after the well-known make of brandy). Giveen was optimistic, as all young people should be. After a few lessons from Mays he considered himself ready to compete.

In spite of numerous warnings, including several fatherly chats from Mays, he was full of confidence as he set off from the starting line. Everything went just fine until he reached the first right-hand bend. And then—well, goodness knows exactly what happened. Instead of making any attempt to take it, the car went straight ahead. It shot over the verge, jumped a small sand pit, knocked over and injured a number of onlookers and then, quite remarkably, regained the course. By some miracle or other, Giveen actually got to the top of the hill. Mays, who was one of the first to rush up to him, found the young driver in a daze. He remembered nothing about his antics at the first bend, and merely mumbled: 'Have I broken the record for the course?'

Clearly, such a disastrous thing could not be allowed to happen again. The R.A.C. stepped in and enforced much more stringent controls on hill-climbs. Furthermore, the law hastily adjusted itself, and gave out that never again would these events be allowed to take place on public roads.

Brooklands was still there. The bumps in the concrete were, admittedly, bumpier than ever. A bridge where the banking crossed the River Wey had subsided, making a substantial hump which caused a good many cars to become airborne.

From the earliest days the racing circuit had lived side by side with an aerodrome. The latter was a growing cancer that eventually proved to be the track's undoing. By 1919 little sheds had already become big sheds. It needed another war for the aircraft industry to take the circuit over completely. In the meanwhile the hangers provided a further discomfort for the drivers. Pockets of wind ricocheted off them, which was not a very pleasant experience if you happened to be passing at high speed.

And, of course, as the years went by, the performances of the cars outstripped the track. The banking had been built to accommodate speeds of up to 120 m.p.h. When Raymond Mays went round in his 2-litre E.R.A. at an International Trophy meeting in the mid-thirties, he was doing at least 150 m.p.h. 'You had to make almost crablike progress,' he recalls, 'otherwise you'd run out of banking. The job was just to keep the car on the track.'

After the war there was a switch in production car-building emphasis. To own a vehicle in the pre-war days you needed a certain indifference to the discomforts of rain and tempest, a fairly substantial mechanical ability (or else a mechanic), and a good deal of money.

In America Henry Ford had already invented the Model 'T', and thereby shown that it was possible to produce a car for the masses. In England a number of manufacturers were thinking much the same thing. To succeed they would have to devise machines which were lighter, cheaper and much more easy to maintain and run.

If motor racing was going to help develop this particular breed it would have to take a careful look at itself. All those huge engines, which seemed big enough to drive army tanks, were unrealistic. There would have to be events for 1100 and 1500 c.c. units.

Members of the Junior Car Club (now the British Automobile Racing Club), which had been formed with assistance from the motoring press, were only too well aware of this. They devised a race for two classes: cycle cars (1100 c.c.) and light cars (1500 c.c.). It had to be held at Brooklands for the very good reason that there wasn't anywhere else. The problem was, as S. C. H. Davis recalls: 'Would the R.A.C. and Brooklands have fits?'

At this stage in history it is difficult to imagine why the management at Brooklands might have had 'fits'. The truth, however, is that they were mainly concerned with making the circuit popular with spectators. To get the biggest 'gates', these gentlemen imagined, you had to obtain the largest cars. As they saw things, it was the thrill of watching these Titans racing round that attracted people.

However, the Junior Car Club was in for a pleasant surprise. When it proposed its idea for a 200-mile race on the lines already indicated, the R.A.C. agreed, and so the Brooklands '200 Mile Race' came about. There was wave upon wave of starters, and considerable ingenuity with regard to engines. The regulations put a limit on the bores. The wily entrants soon got the hang of this, and saw that it could be countered by making the stroke much longer. Before very long, there were, for example, 2-litre engines fully conforming with regulations which were supposed to keep the limit down to $1\frac{1}{2}$ litres.

In those days, of course, any talk about 'formula' meant only one thing: The Formula, which controlled Grand Prix racing. At Brooklands and the Tourist Trophy races small cars mixed it with big cars. Everything was governed by a system of handicapping, which was not always popular, but which seems to have worked. It may have been tough on the star drivers, who often started after everyone else, and were faced with the difficult task of catching up and overtaking the rest of the field. But it also produced some very piquant situations—such as when, in the 1930 500-mile race, S. C. H. Davis, at the wheel of a little orange supercharged Austin Seven, finished in front of the big Bentleys (when the first 500-mile race was organised by the B.R.D.C. in the previous year, Jack Barclay and F. C. Clement won it in a thunderous $4\frac{1}{4}$-litre Bentley).

Racing circuits nowadays display plentiful signs headlined 'Motor Racing is Dangerous', which point out that anyone who watches it does so at his or her own peril, and so on. This came about after an unfortunate episode in an event known as the Brooklands Double-Twelve Hours, which the Junior Car Club organised for a number of years. It was Britain's answer to the Le Mans 24-Hour Race.

Right from the start, and understandably, the neighbours of

Brooklands had been a great deal less than happy about the circuit. They had, after all, paid tolerably large sums of money to live in what they fondly imagined would be the peace of the Surrey countryside. Motor racing is very unpeaceful and one of the worst features is the noise.

The circuit management had made a play of coming to terms with local residents by insisting that any car which competed must be fitted with a 'Brooklands silencer' and a fish-tail exhaust. In fact, this did little to quell the din, although a number of drivers claimed that it robbed their engines of some power.

What, obviously, would have been quite intolerable was an event in which cars raced for the full twenty-four hours. The French might condone and even applaud such an occasion, but Surrey householders liked their standard eight-hour sleep each night throughout the year.

Consequently, for this event, they borrowed an idea from the French Grand Prix of 1906. The cars raced for twelve hours, and were then locked up. On the following morning they were unleashed to put in another dozen hours on the track.

At 6.56 p.m., towards the end of the first day's racing in the 1930 Double-Twelve Hours, a mass of cars was coming out of the finishing straight, taking the left-hand sweep as wide as possible, before roaring up to the banking *en route* for the Railway Straight. It was a situation which looked extremely dangerous, for the cars were always packed very tightly together on this part of the course. However, this had been happening every lap for over eleven hours, and nothing had gone wrong. It seemed to have become a routine.

And then, suddenly, in the midst of the pack, a large 3-litre Talbot (driven by Rabagliati) appeared to brake and swerve violently to the right. Another Talbot (Hebeler's) caught its rear wheels. Rabagliati's car was flung broadside across the track. It plunged through the iron railings and into the crowd. The mechanic was killed instantly and Rabagliati was gravely injured. Hebeler's front axle was completely torn off: his car crashed upside down on the track in a cloud of dust and sand. He and his mechanic escaped.

The Talbot drivers were notoriously hairy performers, and it may have been inevitable that a shunt like this should have happened one day. The really disastrous thing was that twelve of the spectators were seriously injured and two of them were killed.

Afterwards one of the injured spectators brought an action against the drivers and the club. At its first hearing the case went in his favour. However, the other parties appealed, and the decision was reversed. All concerned were exonerated from blame, but ever since the organisers of motor-racing meetings have very prudently displayed their warning notices.

During the between-war years three nations enjoyed the supremacy of Grand Prix racing: France, Italy and Germany. For most of the time, Britain stood aloof. Her car-makers, if one were to judge by appearances, were completely indifferent to the glory and engineering prestige which such successes might help to build.

In the 1930's Raymond Mays and Humphrey Cook made a valiant attempt to bring the U.K. on to the scene when they built the E.R.A. But this was a relatively light car, powered at the most by a 2-litre engine, and it was patently no match for the fearsome beasts of Alfa Romeo, Mercedes and Auto-Union. At its best it was a brave gesture—though one must also credit it as the beginning of a train of thought by Mays, which eventually produced the B.R.M.

Much earlier on, however, there had been a valiant attempt to bring Britain on to the scene when Louis Coatalen, the chief designer of Sunbeam, produced a Grand Prix car. Quite how Coatalen managed to persuade his board to approve the project is something of a mystery. It was so unlike the British car-maker's contemporary thinking. There is, indeed, one theory which suggests that the Sunbeam directors never quite realised what had happened.

By the time the Automobile Club de France was ready to put on the 1921 French Grand Prix, Coatalen was equipped to compete in it. He had a team of three cars and three drivers.

For a good many months before this the designer had been under fire from a fair-haired young man wearing an Old Etonian tie, with blue eyes and a sincere, eager, expression on his face. It seemed that the young man wanted to become a professional racing driver, and that he wished to join the Sunbeam team.

His name was Major Henry O'Neal de Hane Segrave. During the war he had served in the Royal Flying Corps until, shot down by German anti-aircraft fire, he crashed and injured one of his ankles. After that, he was sent to Washington as an attaché with the British Air Mission.

During his stay in America he had become friendly with the brother of a racing driver. One day the driver took him down to a track on Long Island and gave him a drive. He lapped at 82 m.p.h. and was afterwards rewarded with an engraved plaque.

Much more important than the plaque was the effect of the episode on the rest of Segrave's life. This, he told himself, was what everything was about. Other people might go about their lives and make their livings in one way or another, and good luck to them one and all. For H. O'N. de H. Segrave there was only one occupation worth following: motor racing.

Soon after his return to Britain, he approached Coatalen for the first time. Coatalen said no—he wasn't in the market for inexperienced racing drivers. Segrave went back to London and bought an interest in a Knightsbridge garage. The important thing about this firm, one has to imagine, was not so much the state of its accounts as the fact that it owned a couple of 1914 racing Opels.[1] He bought one of them.

On Whit Monday, 1920, he raced it for the first time at Brooklands. At 100 m.p.h. a tyre came off. By a fantastic feat of control he kept the car on the track and brought it into the pits undamaged. Three-quarters of an hour later he let it loose in another event. This time the tyres stayed on and he won.

The moment Coatalen announced his team for the 1921 French G.P., Segrave motored up to the Sunbeam factory. This time, there was a head-on confrontation. Once again, Coatalen's first word was 'No', but Segrave was not fobbed off so easily. Eventually, after several minutes of very hard talking indeed, he extracted a promise from The Patron (as they called Coatalen). O.K.—he could have the fourth car, but under the strict understanding that if it were damaged in any way, shape or form, he, Henry Segrave, would have to pay for it. Furthermore, he would receive not one penny piece from the Sunbeam coffers in the way of expenses.

'But,' said Coatalen, 'if you finish in this race, then we will talk again. If you complete the course, and only if you complete it, I might, just conceivably, find room for you in the team.'

Segrave tried the car out at the Easter Monday meeting at Brooklands and won easily. He now set about getting himself into training for the Grand Prix. He disliked alcohol, and so that was no problem. Giving up smoking was rather harder. However, he soldiered on—with the help of only a very occasional cigarette (requisitioned from somebody else: he manfully went around without them during this period)—until there he was, bright and clear-eyed, with reflexes as sharp as they can ever be, at Le Mans for the start of the race.

[1] They had been left behind by a German who made a hurried departure from Britain just before the outbreak of war.

If ever a driver earned a place in a works team, Segrave did. During the course of the event:
He had to change tyres fourteen times.
His mechanic was knocked out by a flying stone.
The oil tank was punctured by another stone.
The car overheated.
The ignition timing slipped.
He finished on six out of eight cylinders.
But he finished.

Major H. O'N. de H. Segrave was now a member of the Sunbeam team.

The 1922 French Grand Prix took place at Strasbourg, which had been returned to France by the Treaty of Versailles. It was won by Felice Nazzaro in a Fiat. The 1923 event was to be held over 500 miles on a 14-mile circuit near Tours. Three Fiats, three Sunbeams, three Voisins, four Bugattis, and a Delage, were among the starters. The Fiats were the favourites.

It was a beautiful summer's morning. From five o'clock onwards, spectators were making their ways along the fifteen-mile stretch of the road which linked the towns of Tours with the tribunes. Before very long it was jammed with traffic.

Down at the circuit, they were making last-minute preparations. The track was sandy, and looked as if it would throw up a good deal of dust. Presently, accompanied by the playing of the Marseillaise, the President of the Automobile Club de France arrived in a touring car. There were now about 50,000 spectators around the course. A system of loudspeakers was trying, in spite of a tiresome crackling which tended to blur the announcements, to keep them informed.

The racing cars were strung out in pairs over half a mile. At 8 a.m. the starter swept down his flag. Led by a motor-cyclist, the cars processed in line ahead for another half-mile, until they reached the starting line. At this point the motor-cyclist peeled off to the right; and, with a roar of fearful thunder, churning up the dust for all their rear wheels were worth, the pack suddenly took off.

The Fiat driven by Bordino was in the lead as they swept down to the first hairpin. De Vizcaya in a Bugatti took it much too fast. He was travelling at 100 m.p.h., which is no way to deal with a hairpin. He spun off, crashed through a fence which was supposed to be protecting spectators (or was it merely containing them?), and plunged through a mass of people. At last his car came to rest, bent and baleful, against a tree-trunk.

GRAND PRIX REVIVED
Cars stirring up the dust in the 1922 French Grand Prix at Strasbourg

RIGHT *Henry Segrave—after winning the 1923 French Grand Prix, there was only champagne to quench his thirst.* BELOW *A 2-litre Sunbeam getting into position for the start of the 1922 French Grand Prix*

THE SHORT AND THE LONG
ABOVE *The start of a three-lap cyclecar race at Brooklands.* BELOW
Count Louis Zborowski at the wheel of one of his monsters. Like his father, he adored big machinery.

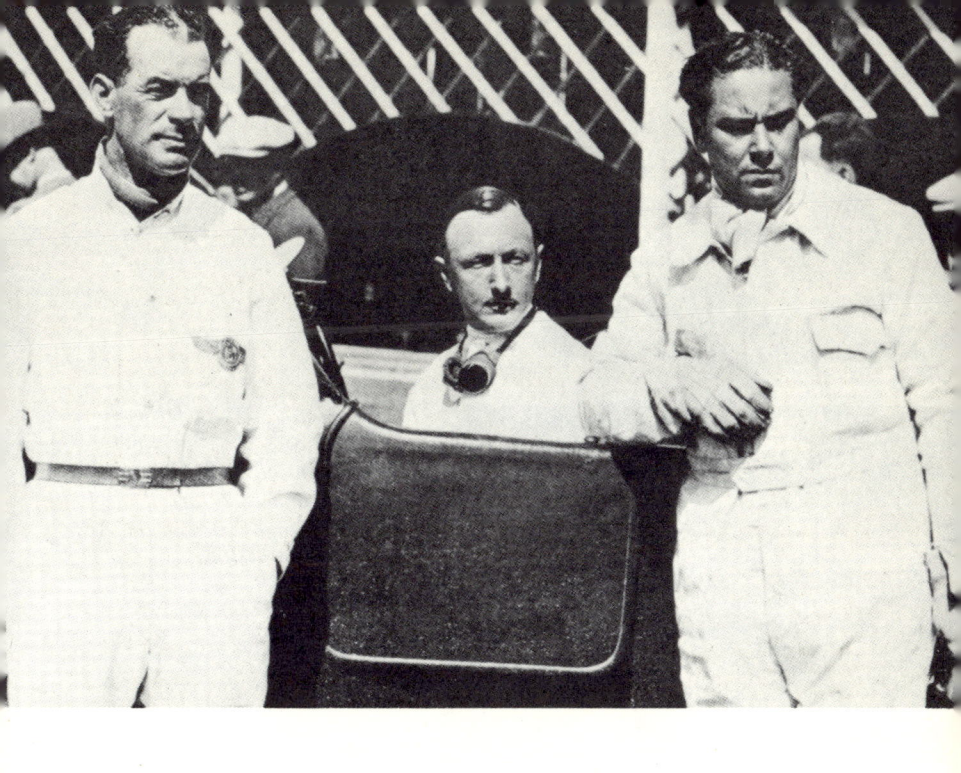

BENTLEY GLAMOUR
ABOVE *Birkin is in the driving seat, Barnato is on the right. For all their fame, 'the Bentley Boys' disliked being a catch phrase.* BELOW *Two of the 4½-litre conquerors, which were so successful at Le Mans*

TAKING TO THE ROADS
Count Masetti and his Mercedes in the 1922 Targa Florio

LEFT *An E.R.A. in Ulster for the TT.* BELOW *It is somewhat reminiscent of Le Mans, but this happens to be the start of the 1929 Tourist Trophy race on the Ards Circuit near Belfast*

FIRST TAKE A RECORD: THEN TRY TO BREAK IT
ABOVE *Building George Eyston's 'Thunderbolt'.* BELOW *Malcolm Campbell demonstrates one of his famous line of Bluebirds at Brooklands*

FOR ALFA ROMEO—AND ITALY
Tarzo Nuvolari—perhaps the greatest of them all

Campari—away from the circuits, he enjoyed opera and good cuisine

Nuvolari at the wheel of an 8-cylinder Alfa Romeo in the 1931 Monaco Grand Prix

TWILIGHT OF THE GODS
ABOVE *The Mercedes team of 1938. Left to right are: von Brauchitsch, team manager Neubauer, Richard Seaman, Hermann Lang and Rudolf Caracciola.* BELOW *Visitors to Mercedes. Only Hitler seemed to find the noise deafening*

CREATOR AND CREATED
ABOVE *Ferdinand Porsche with an apparently somewhat chilly Bernd Rosemeyer.* BELOW *The Auto-Union with Rosemeyer driving. This, or the Volkswagen* (it depended on your taste), *was Porsche's greatest creation*

One woman spectator had both her legs cut off: fifteen more were seriously injured.

On the track Bordino was well ahead in his Fiat, K. Lee Guinness (Sunbeam) was in second place, then came René Thomas in a Delage, followed by two more Fiats. After them there was quite a gap before the Sunbeams of Segrave and Divo came into view with the rest of the pack behind them. The leaders were surging past the grandstands at 100 m.p.h.

By the third lap, the Fiat strategy was becoming clearer. Bordino, who was lapping at well over 85 m.p.h., was setting a fearful pace. His obvious intention was to wear out the rest of the field, regardless of what happened to his own car. If it failed there were two more Fiats taking things rather more easily further back.

But K. Lee Guinness was also pushing it pretty hard. He was hanging on to Bordino's tail. They were now doing 110 m.p.h. on the straight—far, far ahead of the rest. Indeed, the other Fiats, which were now leading the remainder of the field, were a good mile behind them.

Thomas brought his twelve-cylinder Delage into the pits. It was overheating. Divo overtook de Cystria's Bugatti. Hemery's Rolland-Pilain came in belching smoke. De Cysteria skidded into a sandbank. Thomas got going again, until a stone pierced his petrol tank. Looking very disappointed indeed, he walked back to the pits—having taken a short cut through the woods from his stranded car.

And the cars were swaying and sliding and throwing up stones for all they were worth.[1]

You can hammer a car for just so long. Bordino's Fiat had been hammered for long enough. Suddenly, through the loudspeakers, came an announcement that it had stopped. It started again after a little coaxing; but its race was, to all intents and purposes, over. Presently there was another announcement. Bordino had retired with engine trouble. Guinness was now in the lead.

Further back, Segrave was driving a very steady race in spite of a slipping clutch, which meant that he couldn't exceed 4,600 r.p.m. On the fourteenth lap he was in fifth position.

But now the Guinness automobile was in trouble It, too, was suffering from a slipping clutch. As a further irritant, having chased Bordino, it was under fire from another Fiat driver, Giaccone, who was steadily creeping up.

[1] Tours was considered to be a very good circuit. Unfortunately, a race for touring cars had been held on the previous day. These machines had ploughed up the track somewhat, and covered it with loose pebbles.

On board the car, Guinness's mechanic, Perkins, was having one hell of a time. To increase the pressure on the ailing clutch he had tied a length of rope to the pedal. Now, in a horribly cramped position, he was having to cling to it for all he was worth. To make matters worse, the spare magneto, which should have been fixed to the floorboards, had broken adrift. It was racketing around, cutting chunks out of the driver's and mechanic's legs.

It was hot and bumpy and Guinness was having the very devil of a job holding the car straight when travelling at such high speeds.

The order had changed again. The various troubles on board his Sunbeam had demoted Guinness into sixth place. The Fiats of Giaccone and Salamano had come up into first and second places respectively. Divo had almost willed himself into third place.

Segrave was still lying fifth.

Divo's car had been using a lot of petrol, trying to catch the Fiats. Now Coatalen signalled him in to refuel. The car's filler cap was a quick-release type. One-eighth of a turn was all that should have been needed to get it off. Unfortunately, in the prevailing excitement, Divo lost his head. He turned the cap in the wrong direction, jamming it on harder than ever. It stuck fast. Nothing that Divo could do would shift it. He tried to chip it off with a chisel—without any effect at all. Outwardly, he contrived to seem calm and intent, but his actions were being slowed down by his overstretched nerves.

He struck the cap a blow with a hammer. It didn't budge. He threw the hammer down in disgust and tried a hacksaw. The blade snapped in two. After that there was nothing more he could do, except motor on, using the two gallons of petrol in the reserve tank. It meant that, every lap, he had to call in at the pits to refuel.

In the Sunbeam box overlooking the circuit they were eating cherries without apparent enjoyment. The only person who showed any signs of confidence in the outcome of the race was Mrs. Coatalen. But, then, Mrs. Coatalen was always very calm.

Guinness came in to change his mechanic. Poor Perkins was exhausted. At some stage he had banged his head on a protruding part of the car, and had been unconscious for over half a lap. Now, with his overalls covered with oil, dust and blood, he struggled over the pit counter. A mechanic named Smith replaced him.

But the Fiats were in trouble. Giaccone had come into the pits with a sick engine. Even after a number of adjustments it still wouldn't fire. They tried cranking it, and then attempted a push-start. There were a few half-hearted explosions, and that was all. They got the bonnet up again.

Salamano had skidded and gone through a wooden guard fence. He wasn't delayed for long, however, and neither he nor his car was damaged. Now, with 100 miles to go, a Fiat victory seemed to be in the bag. Salamano just had to keep on motoring.

And then, dramatically, he was overdue. The minutes passed without any news. Three minutes, four minutes, five minutes ... and presently an exhausted figure came stumbling into the pits. It was Feretti—Salamano's mechanic. The car had run out of petrol.

Feretti was just about dead on his feet. The Fiat manager passed a can with a big spout to another mechanic and told him to take over. The mechanic started off up the track. He hadn't gone very far when a pit marshal intercepted him with that indrawn, beyond-any-kind-of-human-appeal, look that officials often have.

There was, according to him, only one man who could take petrol back to the stranded car. Feretti. He had been the mechanic when the petrol ran out. It was his job, and nobody else's, to do something about it. If he hadn't the strength to get back, the car would have to stay where it was.

The crowd booed, but the official had the rule book in his pocket. They could throw rotten tomatoes at him, for all he cared.

Feretti then seized a bicycle. Steering uncertainly, with the can in one hand, he wobbled off towards the country. More officials, like a squadron of gunboats, bore down on him. Bicycling was not allowed. The journey had to be made on foot. Something in para so-and-so, sub-section something, it said so distinctly.

(More boos from the crowd.)

Loaded down with the heavy petrol can, Feretti hobbled off on a one-and-a-half-mile walk to the place at which his driver was impatiently passing the time of day.

Salamano still had 70 miles to go.

Divo brought his Sunbeam into the pits. It stopped. It wouldn't start again.

With all the opposition now out of the way, Segrave won the race comfortably at an average speed of 76·8 m.p.h. after a relatively trouble-free drive (the slipping clutch cured itself after 300 miles) lasting 6 hours 35 minutes 19·60 seconds. From start to finish, his tyres were never changed.

Up in the Sunbeam box, one imagines, the cherries were beginning to taste better.

Of course, as Segrave would no doubt have been the first to

admit, Guinness deserved a lot of credit for a Sunbeam victory. If he hadn't taken on Bordino and beaten him at his own game of wearing the opposition out, it might have been a very different story. Segrave's policy for the race had been to start slow and finish fast. It fitted in perfectly with what Guinness had been doing. Funnily enough, however, this doesn't seem to have been a deliberate strategy by Coatalen. When Segrave told 'The Patron' about his ideas some days before the race they were received rather cynically—almost, indeed, with disapproval.

But this was a typical Segrave victory. He was a controlled, beautifully disciplined, driver, who once said that 'you should never go faster than you have to to control the opposition'. When he went racing he usually wore a green outfit. Raymond Mays once described him to me as: 'A very nice, gentle, gentlemanly fellow. Very pleasant—with a nice smile. He'd always speak to you. This meant a lot when one was young. He encouraged young drivers.'

Even when receiving his trophy from the French Minister for War, Segrave was as urbane as ever—in spite of the fact that he had to take a long drink of champagne. Segrave hated champagne, but there wasn't any water available.

Divo, still driving a Sunbeam, won the Spanish Grand Prix of 1923, and Segrave won the Spanish event in the following year. After that, Sunbeam pulled out of Grand Prix motor racing and Britain, as a Grand Prix car-building country, went into the wilderness for thirty-three years.

8 Trial by distance

It was the first day of the Paris Motor Show in 1922. The Press and various motoring dignitaries were doing the rounds. Among the latter were Charles Durand, secretary of the Automobile Club de l'Ouest, and Charles Faroux, one of motor racing's elder statesmen.

Presently, the two men came to the Rudge-Whitworth stand. Emile Coquille, the company's agent in France, was there to greet them.

Before very long they were deep in conversation. The subject had been on their minds for some time: was motor racing making a sufficient contribution to the development of ordinary production cars?

Before the war it had, of course, got completely out of hand. The big racers which competed in Grand Prix events had little or nothing to do with the cars that ordinary people bought. After the war a limit of 3 litres had been woven into the Grand Prix formula. In 1922, the year in which Italy staged the first international Grand Prix to be organised outside France, the limit was cut down to 2 litres.

If the automobile's only development requirement was a high-speed travelling test bed this might have meant something. But, as motorists were beginning to discover, there was more to it than that. A car should not only be able to take one from A to B: it should also be able to do so with the greatest possible reliability and in reasonable comfort. This, in the combined opinion of Messieurs Durand, Faroux and Coquille, was where the sport fell short.

With almost any other group of people the talk would have been largely academic. In this case, however, the men concerned were able to translate their ideas into action. As secretary of the Automobile Club de l'Ouest, Durand had considerable influence over the uses to which the circuit at Le Mans was put. Faroux had a great deal of skill and experience in the organising of motor races; and Coquille had £4,000 of Rudge-Whitworth money with which to back any project that seemed to have merit.

The idea, as eventually worked out by them, was to hold a 24-hour test of endurance. It was to be open to all types of standard cars with four-seater bodies (an exception was made in the case of those with 1100 c.c. engines, which were permitted two-seater bodies). The cars would be required to travel at minimum average speeds, based upon the sizes of their engines. For example, the figure for a 3-litre engine was 35 m.p.h. At the end of each 6-hour period the situation would be reviewed. Any car that hadn't gone fast enough would be eliminated.

Those which completed the full 24 hours would be eligible to compete in the next year's event; and so on, into the third year, when the contest would culminate with a race. The winner of this triennial competition would be awarded the Rudge-Whitworth Cup.[1]

When the rules were published they stipulated that each car should have two drivers, but that only one of them might be on board at a time. Whoever was on duty had to carry out all his own repairs and refuelling. People in the pits were allowed to have spare parts in readiness, and even to hand them to him. But they must not touch the car.

All the cars had to be equipped with headlamps, though nobody seemed to be under any illusion about their probable effectiveness. Consequently, French Army searchlights were brought in. They were stationed by the roadside, with their beams directed down the track—in such a way that they provided the greatest possible illumination but didn't dazzle the drivers.

[1] The event was originally known as the 'Rudge-Whitworth 24-Hour Race'.

All told, thirty-five entries were received for the first event, which was held on May 26th and 27th, 1923. It was a good field and promised adequate excitement. Even so, the organisers felt that there were bound to be some dull moments for the spectators—especially at night. For this reason, they arranged a lavish bill of entertainment.

Among the attractions were a firework display, a cinema showing sporting films, radio programmes specially relayed from the Eiffel Tower in Paris, a dance hall with a jazz band, an orchestra, and an American bar run by a firm from the Champs Élysée. In addition to all this there was a large luncheon party at midday on the Sunday to which 500 fortunate members of the Automobile Club de l'Ouest were invited.

Wisely, perhaps, it was agreed to start the event at four o'clock on the Saturday afternoon, so that the night driving could be done when the competitors were still reasonably fresh. Up to a point, the course was similar to that followed by today's 24-Hour Race. The big difference came just after the cars had passed the grandstands. Instead of veering off to the right, under the Dunlop arch towards the esses, they sped on along a fast stretch of straight, which penetrated deep into the suburbs of Le Mans. Then, at a fiendish hairpin called Pontlieue, the road doubled back at an acute angle, rejoining the present circuit at Tertre Rouge. Since then, the course had been twice modified: in 1929 when the Pontlieue hairpin was snipped off, and in 1932 when the stretch of road which includes the esses was built. The original lap distance was 10·726 miles. Nowadays it is 8·36 miles.

If the organisers imagined that this would be simply an endurance test, they must have been somewhat naïve. Other people had attempted similar exercises in restraint (witness the eliminating rounds of the original Coupe des Voiturettes), only to be forced back to a basic truth about drivers. If two or more of them come under starter's orders, and then set off on a prescribed course, whatever happens is bound to turn into a contest of speed. It is inevitable: if it weren't for this urge to be fastest, there wouldn't be any more racing at all.

The course was, basically, a pretty fast one. Its shape was triangular, with adequately difficult corners linking the straights. Some while before the event began, motoring papers were reporting that a number of the drivers intended to average over 60 m.p.h. for the full period. In fact, the winner's average speed was 57·20 m.p.h., and so this estimate wasn't far out.

'As a general rule,' predicted *The Autocar*, 'fast sporting type cars will be used.' At the time, a number of French firms were building this kind of vehicle, and there was considerable competition among them. It didn't require a great deal of imagination to foresee what an effective advertising impact a victory at Le Mans would make. Among the cars which eventually turned up were a trio of 3-litre Chenard-Walckers, which were hotly tipped as the favourites, four Rolland-Pilains, a six-cylinder Delage, and a 3-litre Bentley. The latter, driven by John Duff and F. C. Clement, was the only car not equipped with front-wheel brakes. This, as it turned out, was to be a considerable disadvantage—particularly when it came to negotiating difficult hairpins like the one at Pontlieue.

In 1925 the traditional Le Mans start was introduced. Originally, it was somewhat harder than today's slightly modified version. Not only did the drivers have to sprint to their cars: they also had to erect their hoods and sidescreens before starting the engines. Thereafter they had to drive with them up for a prescribed period. This ruling lasted until 1928, when the regulation about hoods was dropped.

For the 1923 race, however, everything was much more simple. There was, indeed, a regulation which stated that the hoods might be left off altogether, and many of the drivers took advantage of it. The cars were lined up, for want of any better idea, in the order in which their entries had been received. They were started simultaneously, the little ones mixing it with the big ones, and all of them jockeying furiously for position in the rundown to the Pontlieue hairpin.

Two cars on the grid had saloon bodies built from wood and fabric leather. The twelve-cylinder Delage (not to be confused with its six-cylinder stable mate), the Excelsiors and a Berliet had the nearest approach to comfortable touring bodies. The rest of them looked a pretty tough, athletic, lot.

Throughout the afternoon of the 26th, the weather was ominous. One had the impression that, given half a chance, the deluge which Louis XV had predicted was about to begin. Possibly it was looking for some sort of signal; at any rate, as the starter swept his flag down, a brisk burst of hailstones ushered in the downpour which was to continue for the next twelve hours or so.

And so, churning up mud for all they were worth, the pack departed. Strangely enough, not one of the cars was equipped with a mechanical windscreen wiper. It was bad enough for the drivers of the big cars who, half-blinded, had to take off their goggles. For the men in the smaller machines, it was terrible, for they were more or less enveloped in a torrent of mud. Under these conditions windscreens were more of a nuisance than an advantage. The drivers of the little 1100 c.c. Saras did the only possible thing, and smashed theirs. And the driver of a Corre La Licorne, very prudently, put up his hood and kept it up for the rest of the event.

Had the entrants abided by the spirit of the contest, it might have been somewhat dull for the spectators. As it was, the whole thing developed into a race from the word go, and an enormously exciting one it was, too. There they were—going at it hammer and tongs under the worst possible conditions. The biggest cars were the two six-cylinder Excelsiors. Although they were designed as sports cars, they had large, comfortable bodies, and this was a disadvantage. Much better equipped for this kind of thing was Duff's Bentley. It wore the minimum-width mudguards, had a low windscreen, and every cubic centimeter of superfluous weight had been eliminated. It didn't even, which may sound somewhat imprudent, carry a spare wheel.

It soon became clear that the essence of the race was going to be a fight between the Bentley and the Chenard Walckers. Duff, who took the first four-hour spell at the wheel, was going very quickly indeed, and so were the two leading Chenard Walckers, driven respectively by Lagache and Bachmann (who were business partners, and had manufactured these cars).

The pits were a small line of wooden huts opposite the grandstand. If the cinema and the dance hall foresaw the shape of *Le Village*, which was eventually to spring up at the circuit, with its cafés, bars, fun-fairs, shops, and just about anything else the tourist wants, so, in the pit area, were there signs of trade hospitality to come. In this case, it was known as 'The Hartford Hotel'. It was arranged by the Hartford firm of shock-absorber manufacturers, and consisted of a pit fitted out as a restaurant. For the drivers there was onion soup, roast chicken, and, if they cared for it, champagne. In fact, the competitors cannot have been the only people who enjoyed the Hartford fare during the event. Over the 24 hours, fifty chickens, 150 gallons of soup, and 450 gallons of champagne were consumed. By 1926, two other firms (one of them Rudge-Whitworth) had cottoned on to the Hartford idea. Between them they supplied a bar, a cabaret, and such dishes as chicken, paté de foie gras, Prague hams and Bologna sausages. There were barmen in white jackets, and small tables with electric lamps on them. The overall effect, it was said, compared very favourably with the best restaurants in Paris—and if you had the right connections it was all free!

For the first three hours of the 1923 race nothing very dramatic happened and there were no pit stops. Then, just before nightfall, a stone broke one of the Bentley's headlamps. Very sportingly, the Chenard-Walcker team offered to provide a replacement. Unfortunately, it would have taken too long to carry out the change. The Bentley hurtled on with one lamp working and the other flickering on and off.

The army searchlights were doing their best, but the best wasn't quite enough. About one-third of the cars lost time during the night through the failure of their electric or acetylene lamps. On the two Saras the electrical circuits short-circuited. As the lights suddenly went out on one of them, the driver ran off the road. He was unhurt, but he was compelled to abandon his car.

Later, an Excelsior spun off and buried itself in a sandbank. The driver spent two hours digging it out. And, later still, the petrol tank on the Bugatti driven by R. Marie and L. Pichard was punctured. Marie (or was it Pichard? The record is uncertain) walked 1½ miles to the pits, collected two cans of fuel, and then returned to his car. Presently, taking it very gently, he brought the vehicle round, changed the tank all by himself, and drove off.

The Bentley was doubtless giving the French manufacturers a happy feeling about their four-wheel brakes. At one point it was closing up on Gros's Bignan. Suddenly, one of the latter's rear tyres burst. Gros jammed on his brakes, and Duff could see the blue smoke as the road scorched the rubber. In the Bentley's case, braking was not enough. Duff ran on to the grass. As his car came to a halt, he saw that its dumb-irons were practically touching the Bignan's tail.

By the Sunday morning, the rain had cleared away. The leading Chenard-Walcker was well ahead—partly because the Bentley had been handicapped by its broken lamp and partly because the Chenard-Walcker pitwork seems to have been better than its rivals'. Even if a mechanic couldn't work on the car, a good deal of time could be saved by having everything handy and making the driver's job as easy as possible.

At one time, the car driven by Lagache and Léonard was nearly 40 miles (four laps) ahead, but then Duff really went motoring. Steadily, he began to catch up. Lagache (or Léonard, whoever was driving at the time) received orders to shake him off. The pace quickened even more. The Chenard-Walcker began to lap at 64 m.p.h. Duff was going even faster. Shortly after 9 a.m., he took the lap record up to 64·7 m.p.h.

He was now sandwiched between the two leading Chenard-

Walckers. On his approach to the ninety-degree bend at Mulsanne he was drawing out to overtake the leader, when he suddenly saw that he was in danger of being bumped by the other car. Getting out of the way quickly, he went off down the escape road, letting the second Chenard-Walcker through. Then he shot off in pursuit, and overtook it in front of the grandstands. Thereafter, for lap after lap, he demolished his own record, relentlessly creeping up on the leader.

If it hadn't been for a flying stone the Bentley would probably have won. But at 11.45 a.m. the news came through. Duff was stranded. His petrol tank had been punctured. He was three miles away from the pits.

Presently, he came trudging in. The judges, who seem to have been more merciful than the pit marshals at the French Grand Prix of that year, made a quick decision. Since Duff had walked all the way back, Clement could take over. And, what is more, he could make his way to the Bentley by bicycle.

Luckily, there was a soldier nearby who had a bicycle with him. Clement promptly requisitioned it and set off. When, a few minutes later, he arrived back at the pits, the soldier's machine was in the back of the car.

The leak was in a highly dangerous place, just above the exhaust pipe. It was, indeed, little less than a miracle that the car hadn't caught fire. Clement now applied himself to the task of mending it.

His materials were somewhat rudimentary: a cork and some soap. However, he must have done a good job, for it lasted throughout the rest of the race, during which he broke the lap record on three successive occasions, taking it up to 67 m.p.h. When, at 4 p.m. on the Sunday afternoon, the cars were flagged to a standstill, the order was: Chenard-Walckers in first and second places, Bignans in third and fourth, and the Bentley in fifth.

The last car to arrive was a Chenard-Walcker, which was approaching the grandstand at 60 m.p.h.—just at the moment when Gros was walking across the track. In spite of violent avoiding action by both parties, Gros was hit and seriously injured. He was the only casualty of the event. Nor, indeed, had Le Mans yet begun its reputation as a car-killer. Out of the entire field, only three cars failed to finish.

In the following year Duff and Clement finished the job they had begun in 1923 by winning the Le Mans 24-Hour Race. Later, between 1927 and 1930, Bentleys won the event four years in succession—taking, in 1929, first, second, third and fourth places. Alfa Romeos pulled off a similar achievement when they won the race in 1931, 1932, 1933 and 1934, but the record in this respect goes to Ferraris, which won it continuously between 1960 and 1965 inclusive.

9 When in Rome (or Brescia, or Monza, or even Sicily)...

The Grand Prix business was growing. In 1922 Italy broke the French monopoly by holding an event for Formula cars at Brescia. In the following year the circuit at Monza was completed after an almost legendary job of building. Within six months of the initial slice of earth being turned, the track, its grandstands, and everything else, were ready for the first race. Three thousand five hundred labourers worked on the project, assisted by 200 lorries and thirty light trucks. They even constructed a special length of railway track, five kilometers long, over which a locomotive and eighty wagons transported supplies to the workers.[1]

Doubtless, this was intended as an example of the way in which the Fascisti got things done. Ernest Hemingway, who interviewed Mussolini soon after he had come to power, once described him as the 'biggest bluff in Europe'. Possibly he was, but he was also a very adept hand at publicity. He realised the value of king-size stunts, such as building a circuit in record time, and then causing cars to be constructed, which would win races

[1] Monza (lap distance: 7·6 miles) was the world's first artificial road circuit.

in no less record times. Indeed, he got the measure of motor racing tolerably early on. When, over a decade later, Hitler decided to get in on the act, he was merely following his Italian friend's example.

Spain held its first Grand Prix event in 1923, and Divo won it in a Sunbeam. The Spanish alacrity to support motor racing was hardly surprising, for the country's monarch, King Alfonso, was, of all crowned heads, the arch motoring enthusiast. Opening a new circuit at San Sebastian in 1924 (to which the Grand Prix was moved), Alfonso did a couple of laps at over 62 m.p.h. His speed compared very favourably with Segrave's when he won the Grand Prix of that year at an average of 64·46 m.p.h.

The first Belgian Grand Prix was held at Spa in 1925; and the first German Grand Prix took place on the Avus circuit, just outside Berlin, in the following year. But the Germans were busy on another project. The economy of the nation was in a parlous state, and there were large unemployment figures throughout the country. The areas of Koblenz and Cologne were particularly badly hit.

It was with the purpose of providing work for reluctantly idle hands in these two towns that the idea of building a huge racing circuit (the Nurburgring) in the Eifel district was conceived. One of the men behind it was Konrad Adenauer, then Mayor of Cologne and eventually to become, many years later, German Chancellor.

A secondary object in the minds of the planners was that of attracting tourism to the region, which, when all is said and done, is an extremely pleasant place.

Possibly with the notion of dragging the work out for as long as possible, they built a very monster of a circuit. The lap distance was over fourteen miles, there were 172 bends and a fantastic collection of switchbacks. The Nurburgring was completed in 1927 and in that year the German Grand Prix was held on it. It was won, appropriately enough, by a Mercedes.

In 1926 Britain, too, had conceived the brave idea of holding a Grand Prix. It had to take place at Brooklands, since there was nowhere else. By the introduction of artificial hazards, such as sand banks used to create bends, they put up a show of reproducing some of the conditions associated with road racing. The event was repeated in 1927; but after that, possibly because it seemed to be a somewhat thin imitation of the kind of thing they did on the Continent, it was dropped.

These years were witnessing the arrival of a new wave of big-time motor racing. There were the circuits, and the events, and the names. Some, like Antonio Ascari, seemed to emerge suddenly, burn with frenetic brightness and then, equally abruptly, to be snuffed out. Others, like Rudolf Caracciola—who leapt into the headlines when he won the first German Grand Prix—developed steadily until they appeared to overwhelm motor racing. To some extent it was a question of survival.

Take, if you like, the case of Antonio Ascari. He was born on September 15th, 1888, in a village not far from the place where, four years later, Tazio Nuvolari first saw the light of an Italian day. He moved with his family to Milan and became apprenticed to a bicycle maker. Later he trained as a car mechanic.

After taking part in a six-day endurance trial in 1911 he joined Alfa Romeo as a test driver. In that first event he gave a foretaste of his style. It was fearless, flamboyant, almost (as one writer has described it) acrobatic. If you went to watch Ascari you got your money's worth. You might also have been tempted to ask yourself: 'Is this too spectacular? Can a man continually drive like this and stay alive?'

Ascari believed in himself: not with conceit—that is far too petty—but with an extreme sense of his strength and ability, an intense awareness that he had been endowed with most of the qualities which make a great driver.

In 1919, after watching Campari win an event at Cremona, he is reputed to have gone up to the ace and said: 'I can drive like that,' and Campari is reported to have grunted 'Maybe'.

Eventually, he got into the Alfa Romeo team. He also became the Lombardy agent for their cars; and by all accounts, he was a very shrewd businessman.

Ascari did not reign for long. In 1924, driving a P2 Alfa Romeo, he won the Italian Grand Prix after a drive which was almost too breathtaking. On one of the bends he was skidding more and more every time he went round. Eventually a harassed marshal threatened to flag him in unless he restrained himself.

In the following year he won the Belgian Grand Prix, and then, on July 26th of that year, came the French Grand Prix at Montlhery. Ascari seemed to be on the top of his form. The success for which he had striven so long was his. He was a Name, a man at the Top. He had conquered motor racing, achieved the great prize which had hitherto eluded him with depressing agility. Life must surely have been pretty good.

At the start he shot away into the lead. Driving with all his customary panache, he stretched it out, second by second, minute by minute. After 150 miles he was four minutes ahead of the next car.

A light rain was falling. The track was becoming slippery. Taking a bend at 110 m.p.h., one of the wheels scraped against the fence. The car went out of control. Nobody knows what, exactly, happened. Like a mad thing, it hurled itself against the palings, tearing up posts, spinning wildly down the track, and then, as a kind of *coup de grâce*, ejecting its driver.

Antonio Ascari died on the way to hospital. Alfa Romeo promptly withdrew all their cars from the race as a mark of mourning.

Short, powerful, fair-haired Ascari had gone. He was a brave man, humble in a way, and extremely generous. If you went out with him he'd never let you pay.

When he died, his young son, Alberto, was just seven (his birthday had been thirteen days earlier). Many years later Alberto was to take up the story where his father left off.

Not all of them, of course, were big names. There was the Mercedes driver Otto Merz, who was killed while practising for one of the Avus races at Berlin. Merz was a man of immense strength. He could (or so it was said) lift a racing car up for the mechanic to change a wheel. His favourite party trick was to drive a nail through a two-inch wooden table-top with his bare fist. When talking about the dangers of racing he used to joke about feeling sorry for any milestone that might come into contact with his head.

A few eventually gave up driving. Like the young man who joined the Alfa Romeo team in 1920, and came second in that year's Targa Florio. His name was Enzo Ferrari.

Or the Mercedes driver, who came thirteenth in the Targa Florio of 1924. The race was won by his team mate Werner in 8 hours 17 minutes and 13 seconds. But this man, whose name was Alfred Neubauer, wasn't quite so fast. He finished over an hour behind Werner.

Neubauer, of course, was to become one of the greatest team managers of all time. He ruled his pits with the discipline of a Wehrmacht sergeant-major, the precision of a chronometer, and an intuition which his burly, rumbustious, appearance seemed to deny. It would have been interesting to have heard his comments on the Sicilian ordeal of endurance that year, when he put up what can only be described as a very moderate performance.

According to the reports, 50,000 Germans went to see this race: they took up 75 per cent of the space on the steamer from Naples to Palermo. Germany, Austria, Italy and France were all

When in Rome (or Brescia, or Monza, or even Sicily) ... 101

represented on the starting line, from which the thirty-seven cars set off at one-minute intervals. The Mercedes team consisted of Werner, the veteran ace Lautenschlager and young Neubauer. Of the starters, seventeen finished.

But the thing which would doubtless have interested Neubauer was the pitwork. The German method of changing wheels depended on a good deal on brute strength. Two men took the replacement wheels. Eight lifted the car up. Two more slipped jacks under the axles. It seems to have been swift and effective.

The Italian method was less tidy. There was always a crowd around the Alfa Romeo and Fiat pits. When a car came in they'd swarm in, doubtless with the best intentions, every one of them trying to help. Eventually, when things seemed to be approaching a state of total chaos, a carabinieri would notice that none of them carried the necessary passes. With a good deal of shouting he would sling them out. Often, because this was no mean task, he would have to call in other carabinieri and soldiers to help him.

But at some point in this great drama the tide would suddenly turn. Led by (of all people) the pit manager, the crowd would return, round on the militia, and throw *them* out. This particular phase of the ejection was usually accompanied by something not entirely unlike a bayonet charge.[1]

The 1924 Targa Florio must surely go down as one of Antonio Ascari's greatest races. He was leading on the last bend when, within sight of the finishing line, he skidded. His car swung round and blocked the track. Heedless of danger and the protesting soldiers, a crowd of onlookers (estimated at forty) rushed on to the road and tried to push Ascari and his car over the line. Unfortunately, everything appeared to have seized up. The machine just wouldn't budge. Eventually, they had to give up. The Alfa was hauled on to the verge to clear the track. A second or two later Werner passed by on his way to victory.

Afterwards a monument was erected by the roadside as a tribute to the giant effort which came to nothing.

But perhaps an even more vainglorious effort occurred in the Fiat pits. Bordino had just come in to refuel, when he passed out. They brought ice, water, and more potent restoratives, but he stubbornly remained unconscious.

---

[1] And then there was the case of the 1930 Targa, when Varzi's mechanic tried to refuel while the car was still moving. The rear end caught fire, Varzi drove on, and the luckless mechanic had to beat out the flames with a seat cushion. You may call it a miracle—but Varzi won the race.

Suddenly, at the back of the crowd, an impatient voice was heard to exclaim, 'The race is being lost!' And there, elbowing his way to the front, was no less a person than Felice Nazzaro. The supine Bordino was hauled out of the cockpit, and Nazzaro climbed in. 'Push!' he said. The mechanics obeyed, and off he went up the winding road.

Fifteen minutes later, Nazzaro returned. He was leaning on two helpers and they hurried him to an ambulance. Presently, the mechanic free-wheeled the car down from the mountain.

It afterwards transpired that towards the end of the fourth lap Bordino had found the road blocked by a line of stones (how they got there was never explained). He tried to pass between them, but the gap was too narrow. They tore a hole in his car's base plate. Presently, overcome by the Fiat's violent shaking and the intense heat of the sun on the back of his head, he flaked out.

Nazzaro, unaware of what had taken place and the fact that he was driving an ailing car, miscalculated a bend and overturned on a soft piece of ground. The car was not badly damaged, but Nazzaro sustained injuries to one of his shoulders and chest.

And that wasn't the end of the story. Bordino eventually revived. The car was got going again. And between them they finished the race.

In 1927 the Italian motor industry was in the throes of a huge economic crisis. It was virtually impossible to prepare special cars to compete in international events; and this, according to the prevailing Italian point of view, was a crisis within a crisis. Racing, they argued, was good for the motor trade and, which rated high up on the list at that time, good for national prestige.

While people were debating what to do about it, Count Franco Mazzotti, president of the Brescia Automobile Club, quietly produced an idea. 'How about a thousand-mile race for production cars over the roads of Italy?' he asked. The manufacturers liked it and, which was possibly more to the point, Mussolini approved of it. In that way, the Coppa delle Mille Miglia came about—though why it should have been *miles* in a country which uses the metric system has bever been explained.

The race was to be non-stop. The original course began at Brescia, went over the Apennines, through Florence, down to Rome, then northwards through Ancona and so, via Bologna, back to Brescia. The *podestàs* (autocratic mayors, who ruled local governments) were instructed to push through road-repair schemes as fast as possible, and 4,000 black-shirted Fascisti militia were attached to the police for lining the route. They did it conscientiously and sometimes with violence. Nevertheless, it should go to their credit that in the first Mille Miglia there was not a single accident. The crowd was kept completely under control; and the difficult task of opening and closing the roads to let the race through was accomplished without a hitch.

There were seventy-seven starters. Fifty-five finished. It was won by an O.M. driven by Minoia and Mirandi.

When all was over, the officials of the Automobile Club d'Italia seem to have been somewhat exhausted. Their collective comment was 'Never again!' That, however, was not the view of Mussolini. If he had any criticisms they were that the race had been a somewhat tame affair and hadn't generated quite so much publicity as he would have liked.

'But,' he said, 'it must certainly continue. It is definitely in the interests of industry—indeed, it is *necessary*.' Once again adequate supplies of armed militia were guaranteed for the policing of the route. And so, in 1928, it took place all over again. This time it was won by Campari in an Alfa Romeo at an average speed of just over 52 m.p.h. The big guns were beginning to move in.

Nevertheless, it was still an event in which the enthusiastic amateur could have a go. The drivers entered for the 1929 race included the Baroness Avanzo, with a 2-litre Alfa Romeo, and the actress Mimi Aylmer in a 3-litre Lancia saloon. Of the two, Miss Aylmer (who finished ninth in her class) was the more successful. The unfortunate Baroness overturned after completing 5 miles. Happily, neither she nor her companions were harmed.

Drivers who surely deserved special awards for endurance beyond the call of duty were Tamburi and Ricceri (Fiat) and Foresti and Coffani (O.M.). In both cases, though on different sections of the route, their cars collided with bridges. Again in both cases the fuel lines were damaged. And, finally, in both cases, they soldiered bravely on, hand feeding their thirsty engines with petrol.

Minoia, the Mille Miglia conqueror of 1927, had an unfortunate encounter with an Alsatian dog, which caused his wings and bonnet to be smashed out of all recognition. In this respect, he got off lightly compared with Bordino, who in 1928 had hit a dog when practising for a race at Alessandria (it's to the north of Genoa). His car swerved off the track, plunged into a river, and stood on its head. Bordino was drowned.

In Brescia, where the O.M. works were and a high spirit of O.M. partisanship prevailed, people sat up all night, listening to radio reports which were broadcast in the town's main square. They were to be disappointed. The race was won by Campari at a fraction faster than his race-winning speed of the previous year. But, then, his Alfa Romeo was the only supercharged car in the race, which may explain matters.

Grand Prix racing continued, though not very brilliantly. In 1929 the Monaco Grand Prix was inaugurated as what might, quite reasonably, be described as a protest. Ever since it had been founded the Automobile Club de Monaco had been denied international status. It had to accept the role of a kind of satellite to the Nice Auto Club. This rankled. After all, Monaco is an independent state, ruled by a prince, and there it was—being treated like a suburb of some French resort.

Presently, however, a man named Anthony Noghès had what can only be described as a stroke of brilliance. Nobody could object to Monaco having a Grand Prix of its own; and, if this happened, then it followed that the International Association of Recognised Automobile Clubs would *have* to recognise one more.

It was, when one comes to think of it, an extremely daring idea. Who, unless he were a genius or a madman, would consider it possible to hold a race for the world's biggest and fastest racing cars in the narrow, twisting, uphill-and-down-again, streets of Monte Carlo? But it *was* possible and it worked. Furthermore, it survived to the present day, which is more than can be said of a lot of events which were being held in the late 'twenties and early 'thirties.[1]

But perhaps things had got out of hand. Any town which had a tourist problem, an economic dilemma, or an inferiority complex, seemed to think that getting up a Grand Prix was the remedy. By 1933, matters had reached such a pitch that the new edition of the international rules for motor racing contained this paragraph:

'*Grand Prix* is only to be used for events of first importance and when the words are accompanied by the name of the country in which the race takes place. The race may only be organised by the appropriate national club.'

Previously, there had been a number of other changes and additions to the rules. In 1925, for example, riding mechanics were barred from Grand Prix races (they continued in other events for

---

[1] In 1933 it had the distinction of being the first race in which positions at the start were governed by practice times.

When in Rome (or Brescia, or Monza, or even Sicily) ... 105

some while afterwards), but it was still obligatory to have a mechanic's seat in the car. Driving mirrors were also obligatory.

As in all the previous races, repairs and refuelling were still the driver's responsibility, and he was only allowed one mechanic to help him.

In the following year a $1\frac{1}{2}$-litre limit was put on engine sizes. The mechanic's seat was still essential, though heaven knows why. It ceased to be essential in 1927.

Finally, as the 'twenties petered out, and the 'thirties came in, two mechanics were allowed to help the driver with repairs. Pressure refuelling (as opposed to cans) was permitted, and all restrictions were lifted so far as sizes of engines and cars were concerned. This was largely official recognition for a state of affairs which already existed. Ever since 1928, there had been an almost cynical disregard of the internationally agreed formula, and races were mostly run as *formula libre* events. But, by this time, Grand Prix racing had reached something of a nadir. There were so many events, that manufacturers couldn't possibly support them all; and, in any case, money was becoming tight. During the next year or so it was to become tighter still.

10 Into the 'thirties

Mussolini was obsessed by dreams of ancient Rome. The thing about the Romans was that they had an empire which looked like one. Theirs was a conquest not merely by soldiers but also by engineers and architects.

Il Duce shared his ancestors' enthusiasm for triumphal arches and kindred exercises in structural pomp. A motor-racing circuit was, perhaps, ideal. Not only could it be made to look suitably impressive: the very races had an heroic ring about them—particularly when they produced victories for Italy. If one wanted to live closer to the old Roman pattern they could be regarded as latter-day examples of chariot racing.

Tripoli, being in some ways a showpiece of Italian colonial power, was obviously a most suitable place for a circuit, and it was there that Mussolini caused a really swaggering example to be constructed in 1933. It was situated just outside the town, on the salt flats. The grandstands were hefty stone monoliths, and just beside the starting line there was a magnificently tall white tower.

The splendour of the place suited the Fascist image beautifully, and nobody can have been more pleased with it than Marshal

Balbo, the ambitious new governor of Libya, who was obviously taking his task of career building (as well as circuit building) very seriously.

A dapper figure, with a neatly trimmed beard and an elegant uniform, he looked rather like a Ruritanian prince when he went to the motor races. It was he who carried out the opening ceremony in May, 1933, and who, until 1940, started the big events and presented the prizes afterwards.

The first Tripoli Grand Prix, which took place in 1933, was not a very good advertisement for the integrity of motor sport. To add to the publicity for the new track, which was claimed to be the fastest in the world, a national lottery was organised. Tickets were on sale throughout Italy, and cost eleven lire each. Three days before the Grand Prix, thirty of them were drawn—one representing each of the drivers. Whoever had the winner was going to find himself richer to the tune of seven and a half million lire (about £80,000).

According to Alfred Neubauer, who wrote about it in his book *Speed was my Life*, a timber merchant from Pisa made an unexpected call on Achille Varzi at his hotel on the evening before the race. He had, he explained, drawn Varzi in the lottery, and he hoped to persuade him to win.

Varzi pointed out that his reward for a victory was likely to be somewhat less than £80,000. His visitor nodded, and said that he fully appreciated this. 'But,' he said, 'if you do as I say, you can have half the lottery money.' To show that he would be as good as his word, he produced a document, drawn up by his solicitor, which set the whole thing down in black and white.

The timber merchant departed. Varzi sat in a state of tortured meditation for a few moments, and then picked up the telephone. He wanted to speak to Nuvolari.

On the following day, Balbo sent the race on its way, with three Alfa Romeos (driven by Nuvolari, Borzacchini and Campari) in the lead. Varzi was somewhere in the middle of the pack, seeming quite content with his position.

By the end of the seventh lap Campari was out of the race with engine trouble. Shortly afterwards, he was seen in the canteen, peacefully sampling a bottle of Chianti. Nuvolari was still in the lead and Borzacchini was still chasing him. Chiron and Birkin were in third and fourth places.

Towards the end of the race it seemed inevitable that Nuvolari would win. Borzacchini didn't appear to be driving anything like flat out, and he kept on looking over his shoulder to see what

Varzi was doing. As it happened, Varzi was preoccupied with nursing along a car which quite obviously wasn't in the full bloom of health.

And then, just as it seemed as if nothing could rob Nuvolari of the race, his car began to slow down and presently came to a halt only a few hundred yards from the finish. He climbed out of the cockpit and, with a show of tragedy which would have done credit to an actor, exclaimed that he had run out of petrol.

A squad of mechanics hurried out from the pits carrying cans. But while they were filling up the tank, Varzi's and Chiron's cars came crawling round the corner. No—that isn't a misprint. They were *crawling*. Nuvolari started his machine up again, and joined in what appeared to be a funeral procession. He took second place; for Chiron was, in fact, a lap behind.

The Pisa timber merchant collected his winnings, but a kind of reckoning was at hand. On the next morning, the Tripoli motor-sport authorities assembled round a table. They accused Varzi, Nuvolari and Borzacchini of rigging the race, and threw the mantle of suspicion over Campari and Chiron. The suggested penalty was immediate disqualification and the loss of their competition licences.

But before the matter was put to the vote they had second thoughts. If the five finest drivers in Europe were debarred from the sport what on earth was going to happen to international motor racing? In the end they were let off with a warning, and the rules of the lottery were tightened up. Thereafter, the tickets were drawn five minutes before the race began, when the drivers were safely tucked up in their cars.

Commented Neubauer: 'Technicalities aside, any chance to increase the earnings from such a dangerous profession is worth taking. Good luck to them!'

Varzi and Nuvolari were tolerably wealthy men, but this was the first time that Borzacchini had come by such a large sum of money. In *A Racing Driver's World* Caracciola recalled an account by Chiron of this shy young driver's reaction to his sudden windfall:

'I went up to him' (Chiron observed) 'and said, "My God, that brief-case looks heavy! I suppose you're carrying your millions in it". Borzacchini winked and said, "Of course, I never let it out of my hands". I said, "But what are you doing with all that money?" "You know", Borzacchini whispered to me, "I lock myself into my room at home, close the shutters, make sure that no one else is around, and then I count the bills. When I'm sure they're all there, I turn on the fan and dance among the fluttering, floating thousand-lire bills." '

Alas—poor Borzacchini was not to enjoy his wealth for long. He was killed in the Monza Grand Prix of that year.

Death was always hanging around: unpredictably, working according to no very obvious rules. What, for instance, was one to make of two such cases as Geier, who survived a crash which seemed bound to be fatal, and Birkin, who was killed by a small burn?

Geier, as a new recruit to the Mercedes Benz team, was practising for the Prix de Berne in Switzerland. Taking a corner too wide at about 150 m.p.h., he skidded. The car shot across the road, crashed into a large tree, and fell apart in four distinct pieces. Geier was thrown out and hurled against a vehicle which was parked nearby. Almost every bone in his body was broken, and yet, after a year in hospital, he recovered.

Tim Birkin drove in the Tripoli Grand Prix of 1933. After an impeccable drive in his Maserati (he had no part in the lottery fiddle) he finished third.

It was Birkin's habit to go motor racing with a polka-dot silk scarf around his neck and in a short-sleeved shirt. During this race he caught one of his arms on the hot exhaust pipe and burned it. The injury turned septic. In a London hospital his old friend and Bentley racing companion, Dr. J. D. Benjafield, fought for his life. It was no good. Three weeks after the race, Tim Birkin was dead.

Birkin was one of the great drivers of all time. He was immensely rich and spoke with a fairly pronounced stammer. If this gave the effect of a nervous man, it couldn't have been more misleading. As S. C. H. Davis told me: 'He was an excellent driver when controlled. You might call him the archetype of the "Bentley Boy". He'd drive until he either broke the car or won. It was he, really, who supercharged the Bentley. If he'd had to work for a living, he'd have been quite somebody. And, as I say, when he was controlled, when he was driving as part of a team, he was excellent. But he needed iron control. He was rather like a fighter pilot.'

He was certainly a big attraction when he raced at Brooklands. On one occasion he is said to have flown to the circuit from Nice, won a race, and then celebrated his victory, that evening—back in Nice.

In spite of his reputation as a somewhat spectacular driver, he only had one serious crash. This was in the 1930 Tourist Trophy race at Ards in Northern Ireland. The course was very slippery at the time, and he was going into a particularly nasty bend. Suddenly his mechanic looked down at the floorboards of the car, as if something had broken. Birkin noticed the movement and asked, 'What's happened?' This momentary distraction caused him to make one of his rare mistakes. The first bit of the bend found him on the wrong side of the track.

He wrenched at the steering wheel, and the front wheels became unstuck. Travelling at 90 m.p.h., the left front hub-cap hit a telegraph pole.

The tail swung round, and the car went into an opposite skid on three wheels. Birkin's fear was that it would plunge into the crowd and hurt somebody. By a miracle, or so it seemed, he managed to avoid them. Now going at 60 m.p.h., the car struck a stone wall. A large chunk of wall came down, the car spun round and struck it again. More wall came down, and the car stopped.

Birkin and his mechanic climbed out unhurt, and walked away.

This 1930 T.T. was one of the more contentious of these events. There was a number of European stars on the list of drivers —including Nuvolari, Campari and Varzi with Alfa Romeos, and Caracciola with a Mercedes. The trouble started before the race had even begun. Much to everybody's amazement, Caracciola's car was disqualified.

It was the vehicle he had used, shortly before the T.T., at Le Mans. For the Northern Ireland event it was entered by Malcolm Campbell as part of a three-car Mercedes team. The other drivers were Campbell himself and Lord Howe.

The reason why Caracciola's car broke the rules was that it was equipped with an outsize supercharger. If Campbell's and Howe's cars had been fitted with the same type everything might have been in order. As it was, the scrutineers had to bar it from taking part. A thunderstruck Neubauer, who was representing Mercedes, promptly cabled the Automobile Club von Deutschland, asking them to verify that the decision was in order. A somewhat vague reply came back. It didn't advance Caracciola's case an inch. The German driver took the news philosophically, though his wife was very upset. As for the white Mercedes, it spent the race standing forlornly on a strip of tarmac in front of the grandstands.

Afterwards an editorial in *The Autocar* stressed 'the need for all entrants to read, understand, and abide very strictly by the regulations'.

Wherever the Alfa team went, the eye of Il Duce was upon them. He sent them innumerable telegrams, sometimes of congratulations,[1] and sometimes urging them to even greater efforts on behalf of Italy. Before this particular Tourist Trophy race he had despatched the following message to Nuvolari, Campari, and Varzi: 'I am sure that in a strange land each of you will battle only for a victory for the Italian flag, forgetting all jealousy and personal feuds.' It was somewhat longer than the simple 'start and win' bidding which he sent off to the Alfa team before the Italian Grand Prix of 1931, but it amounted to the same thing.

One is tempted to wonder how much the dictator knew of the inner conflicts and emotional upheavals that went on inside the Alfa Romeo ranks. That talk about 'jealousy and personal feuds' suggested that he was kept pretty closely informed. Varzi and Nuvolari were known to be frequently at loggerheads, though it has since been suggested that reports of their much vaunted rivalry were exaggerated. What is certain is that, more often than not, Alfa Romeo drivers were required to finish in a set order.

Rudolf Caracciola has recalled how, in his first race for Alfa Romeo (the Monaco Grand Prix of 1932), he deliberately held back towards the end to allow Nuvolari to finish first. His action was sufficiently obvious to draw boos from the crowd, but it met with the full approval of the team.

At Ards the Alfa drivers are said to have drawn matchsticks of uneven lengths to decide the finishing order. If this was so, it was clearly Nuvolari's day, for he came first. Campari was second and Varzi third. A mere 0·57 m.p.h. separated the speeds of first and third drivers.

During the event it was Campari who caused the trouble. At various points along the route there were stretches of road on which overtaking was prohibited. Campari was blatantly ignoring these restrictions. He was driving a brutally aggressive race, cutting in and almost pushing the smaller cars off the track. According to his own viewpoint, he was no doubt acting to instructions, for the Alfa strategy was clearly for Campari to force the pace and wear out the opposition, whilst Nuvolari took things fairly easily, nursing his car for the almost inevitable victory.

This was all very well, but the crowd didn't like it (boos galore) and nor did the officials. An angry message was conveyed to the Alfa pits. A signal was put up warning Campari to ease off a bit. It didn't have any effect.

[1] When Howe and Birkin won the 1931 Le Mans 24-Hour Race in an Alfa Romeo he sent them a telegram, congratulating them on a win for Italy.

Next time round, he was flagged in. Campari, who had aspirations to sing in grand opera, was in good voice that day. He wanted to know what the hell all the fuss was about. The pit staff made up with athletic gesturing what they lacked in decibels. The argument went on for a while, and then Campari drove off. It must have made some impression on him, for afterwards he drove rather more considerately.

The Autocar's comment was: 'Incidents of this kind are doubly unfortunate, because, to the thoughtless, they suggest overstrictness, or even partiality, on the part of officials, who, as a matter of fact, would be guilty of neglect of duty did they not take action to enforce rules laid down for the benefit of all concerned.'

To some extent it was the age-old problem of communication. The case of Caracciola's disqualification is another example. In Britain the officials carried out the regulations to the letter, whilst on the Continent they went by the spirit. The Germans, in a less vague mood than that in which they cabled their reply to Neubauer, described this episode as 'a hostile action'. It was certainly not intended to be.

Nevertheless, the race had its moments of comedy. The best turn was provided by Nuvolari. Early on, a car went out of control, and smashed the window of a butcher's shop on one of the corners. Afterwards, whenever Nuvolari went by, he stretched out his arm, as if he were trying to snatch a leg of mutton.

Nuvolari was short—so short that preparing a car for him was not easy. You had to build up the seat until it was just the right height. He was an abbreviated quickfire genius, who drove with a skill such as no other driver, before or after, has ever possessed. As a character, however, he is almost impossible to pin down. Indeed, talking to people, it seems as if everybody had his own Nuvolari.

S. C. H. Davis describes him as a humorist who 'was most amusing when things went against him'. Enzo Ferrari, who has never attempted to disguise his profound admiration for him, has pointed out that 'he was often caustic-tongued'. He looked friendly and yet he had few friends. He was difficult to come close to, and often very lonely. Sometimes his humour was of the 'sick' variety—as when he rebuked Ferrari for buying him a return ticket to Sicily for the Targa Florio. He might, he pointed out, be coming back in a wooden box.

Occasionally his skill seemed to be supernatural. In the 1930 Mille Miglia he was driving towards the finish at night. In front of him was Varzi, and he wanted Varzi to take things easy. That way, he'd be able to creep up behind and overtake him when the moment seemed most suitable.

The best way was to lull Varzi into a sense of false security; to make it seem that he had the road to himself, and that the nearest opposition was miles behind. Consequently, going very quickly indeed, Nuvolari drove with his lights off. Then, 30 miles from the finish, he switched them on, swept past, and won the race.

His contributions to driving techniques were seemingly endless. He invented the 'saw-tooth' method of cornering. He discovered how to tame the four-wheel drift and turn it from a calamity to an asset. And, of course, there was no car which he couldn't coax into a condition of obedience.

One of the most difficult cars in between-war racing was the Auto-Union. Stuck and Rosemeyer managed to handle it, and the latter did so brilliantly. But after his death nobody really got the hang of it until, in 1938, Nuvolari had a go. He didn't like the car, but he imposed his will upon it and usually made it behave itself.

Mussolini watched his comings and goings with interest and sometimes anxiety. When, for example, Nuvolari proposed to go independent in 1935 and race a Maserati of his own, a message came from Il Duce. It instructed him to give up the idea and join Ferrari's team of Alfa Romeos.

The motor-racing crowds loved him. Among the names they called him were 'Maestro' and, more flamboyantly, 'Son of the Devil'. But the description which fits him best was 'The Great Little Man.' He was outspoken, temperamental, passionate, a compressed bundle of unceasing energy, and, above all things, modest. In his grubby yellow shirt, or his Fair Isle pullover, he somehow managed to radiate greatness. If he had gone into a room where nobody knew him, people would have been bound to take notice of him and ask 'Who's that?'

Riding mechanic with him was a rare test of nerves. One of the most terrifying trips was before the Ulster T.T. of 1933. Nuvolari had been invited to drive the new M.G. K3 Magnette. He had never seen the car before the first morning's practice. He climbed into the seat, nodded to his mechanic (Alec Hounslow, now the foreman of M.G.'s Development Department), and drove off.

Now this particular car was fitted with a preselector gearbox. Nuvolari didn't realise that it wasn't entirely a 'no hands' job. There was a lever, and you were supposed to use it. Says Hounslow: 'He thought you just had to push down the accelerator without manipulating the lever. Consequently, we did a hair-raising first lap all in top gear. Afterwards, for the next lap or so, I worked the lever for him, until he got the hang of things.'

Although the riding mechanic had been done away with in Grand Prix races, he survived at Brooklands and the T.T. races until well into the 'thirties. It doesn't seem to have been a particularly enviable job, although there was never any lack of recruits. Pay was at the niggardly rate of 1s. 6d. an hour plus 2s. 6d. expenses, which had to cover all meals. The mechanic frequently went without sleep for at least one night, sometimes two, before the race, for he was busy getting the car ready. Sometimes, during the event itself, these men were so tired that they actually nodded off.

Their task on the circuit was to act as an extra rear mirror. All the time they were supposed to be looking backwards, in case somebody was trying to overtake. It was too noisy to speak to the driver, and so some sort of signalling was used. Usually, it took the form of banging him on the shoulder.

The races, particularly at Brooklands, were incredibly bumpy, and drivers and mechanics had to wear body belts, literally, to hold themselves together.[1] The driver had the steering wheel to hang on to. Lacking this means of keeping him in the car, the mechanic was usually held in by straps anchored to the floorboards.

It was, of course, a nightmare if you did not have confidence in your driver. S. C. H. Davis recalls an instance in which the director of a car-manufacturing firm, who wasn't a particularly good driver, was making a mess of cornering. His mechanic disapproved of his antics. Eventually he lost his temper and started beating the driver furiously on the back.

There was also a case in which a driver struck his mechanic.

Davis himself, when not driving, sometimes acted as mechanic for that most colourful or all racing figures, Count Louis Zborowski. Zborowski, whose father had been killed on the La Turbie

---

[1] Segrave and Davis were the first advocates of crash helmets. Les Leston tells me that they were built up from layer upon layer of linen coated with shellac. A cork lining was fitted to the inside. Raymond Mays recalls that they were cumbersome things. 'You had to get the straps right,' he told me. 'If you didn't make the right adjustment, they'd flop forward over your eyes.' The big improvement in helmets came in 1955, when fibre glass was first used for the manufacture of the shells. Two years earlier, in 1953, they had become compulsory for racing—replacing the cloth helmets which Grand Prix drivers wore.

hill-climb in 1903, lived in Kent. He drew his fortune in monthly instalments from property in New York. He was a very hairy driver indeed, and given to dramatic mood swings.

On the night before a French Grand Prix, Davis recalls, 'Zborowski and I were staying at a small farmhouse away from the bustle of Lyon. He was very much a Slav, you know, and he had this idea that he was going to be killed the next day. It was a wonderful night, with all the stars you could think of. We went outside and there we were, between 11 p.m. and 2 a.m., discussing infinity. Next day, I'm glad to say, all his forebodings had gone.'

Zborowski was famous for his Chitty-Chitty-Bang-Bang cars. The first of this celebrated breed was powered by a 23-litre 300 b.h.p. Maybach engine. It was said to have been taken from a Gotha aircraft used for the bombing of London in World War I.[1] Invariably dressed in a black shirt and a Palm Beach cap, he used to drive it, using trade-plates belonging to a firm of coach-builders, from his estate at Higham near Canterbury to Brooklands.

'He liked big, thunderous things,' Davis recalls. 'His father liked big engines, and the son secretly thought in terms of the father. He wanted the biggest engines he could get, and these came from aircraft.'

One of Zborowski's less welcome legacies from his father was a pair of gold cuff-links with the family crest on them. These had been worn by the latter during his disastrous run at La Turbie. His son had a morbid feeling about them and would never wear them—until, on the morning of the 1924 Italian Grand Prix, he suddenly put them into his shirt before setting off for the circuit.

He and Werner were driving Mercedes cars in the race. Werner was a Mercedes veteran; a tall, gaunt, rather sad-looking individual, with deep-set eyes and a large nose. On the forty-seventh lap Zborowski came in to refuel and change his tyres. Then he sped off, chasing Ascari, who was in the lead. Just round the first curve from the pits, one of his tyres burst and he crashed into a post. He was taken to hospital with a fractured skull and died soon afterwards.

Let Davis have the last word on this remarkable man:

'One moment he was in despair—the next in good spirits and humour. It would have suited his temperament to be a poet

[1] Another story was that it had been extracted from the wreckage of the Zeppelin Z19 which was shot down over London.

living in the Rue Pigalle. If he could have painted or sculpted it might have been better for him; but he couldn't. He expressed himself in his large cars.

'He was a good driver, provided he was rigidly controlled and not allowed to drive as fast as it was possible to drive. His cars were prone to engine troubles. He loved high speeds—he was like a Valkyrie or one of the horsemen of the Apocalypse.'

Did Zborowski experience a transcendental sense of foreboding when he broke his own rule, and put those gold cuff-links in his shirt that morning? Certainly Campari seems to have had no misgivings before the Monza Grand Prix of 1933.[1] He had just admired a stop-watch which the firm of Pirelli had given to one of his friends. He said that after the race he was going to get hold of a couple. He also told his mechanics to have a whole roast chicken ready for him when he finished. After so much hard work he would have a good appetite.

The race was to be run in three heats of fourteen laps apiece. The first four drivers in each would qualify for the final, which would take place over twenty-two laps.

During the first heat Trossi's $4\frac{1}{2}$-litre Duesenburg threw a con rod, which split the crankcase, spewing oil out on to the always treacherous South Curve. Moll, who finished second, hit the oil at a speed of over 125 m.p.h. He spun round three times, but managed to keep his car on the track. Afterwards, he notified the superintendent about the danger.

But the superintendent was busy. The second heat was due to start. Somebody went off in a car and made a pretence of sweeping away the oil with a broom. The intention may have been good but as a precaution it was totally inadequate.

The second heat started. Campari and Borzacchini took the lead, with Borzacchini just a little way ahead. As they reached the South Curve, Borzacchini landed on the oil slick. His car spun viciously, went out of control, turned over and trapped him underneath it. Campari, making a desperate effort to miss the wrecked car, shot off the track and hit a tree. He was killed instantly. Borzacchini died soon after reaching hospital.

That, one might have imagined, would have been enough for one day, but big motor races, like anything else in show business, must go on. They made further efforts to clear away the oil, and the third heat took place without any incident.

The drivers had been warned about the state of the course, and

---

[1] Not to be confused with the Italian Grand Prix, which took place on the same day—in the morning.

were clearly unhappy about it. Before the final they held a meeting to consider an invitation from the organisers to withdraw without any loss of honour. Lehoux who, with Czaykowski (they were both driving Bugattis), was co-favourite, suggested a compromise. His idea was that both he and Czaykowski should hold back a bit until the closing stages. Unfortunately, the latter would have none of it.

By now, the race was two hours late in starting. To make up lost time, the distance was reduced from twenty-two to fourteen laps. For seven laps nothing dramatic happened. Czaykowski led the field. He roared up to the South Curve on his eighth lap and suddenly went into a violent skid near the spot where Campari and Borzacchini had been killed. His car turned over, and the petrol tank exploded before help could reach him. Lehoux got by unscathed and eventually won the race. But by then there was no more interest left in it. Everybody wanted to go home and forget the whole thing.

It was hard to imagine that Campari was dead. He, of all the drivers, had the greatest relish for life. He was a portly, perspiring, individualist of enormous strength. Apart from motor racing, his two passions in life were singing and cooking. His girl friends had always been singers, he married a singer, and he once took part, with a professional company, in a performance of *La Traviata*. However, he had trouble with his low notes, and wasn't very successful.

Nor, according to Enzo Ferrari, was he a particularly talented cook. In *The Enzo Ferrari Memoirs* Ferrari gives an account of a meal which Campari prepared. The dish was *riccioline al sugo*, which is a Milanese speciality. 'At table,' Ferrari wrote, 'I excused myself on the grounds that I could not eat anything in the nature of spaghetti, but my friends declared that the riccioline was excellent, although a shade on the salty side.'

After the event at Monza, Campari had intended to retire from motor racing—to devote all of his time to cooking and singing.

Sometimes spectators got hurt. At 3 p.m. in the 1936 T.T. Race on the Ards circuit, J. Chambers in an old 1100 c.c. Riley was hustling through the town of Newtownards. Coming into a fast left-hander, he went into a front-wheel skid. There was nothing he could do about it, and nothing to protect the crowd of onlookers, who were separated from the track only by a length of rope. The Riley hit a lamp-post and then went broadside on to the pavement. Eight spectators were killed. Fifteen more were seriously injured. The fact that they should not have been there did little to dull the agony. Nor did it reprieve the Ards circuit. For the next two years the T.T. was held at Donington, which had been opened in 1933, and was the only road circuit in England.

11 Meanwhile—back at the factory...

The car is everything. If the designer cannot make the car go quickly, the driver can do nothing about it. If he cannot build a reliable car, nobody is going to win any races with it. If he designs a dangerous car, it is going to kill people. The driver is beholden to the designer for his victories and for his life.

Racing cars may be single-minded explorations into the art of going as swiftly as possible. Or they may be cars which were built for quite another purpose. They fall into the hands of enthusiasts, who modify them out of all recognition. A car which in its original state has been advertised as 'perfect for you and your family' may emerge into the kind of thing that only a motorist bent on suicide and mass murder would dream of using for a family outing.

Constructing a thoroughbred racing car costs a fortune. Adapting a standard production car is rather less expensive.

Raymond Mays has seen both worlds. In many ways, the problems which beset him during the between-war years of motor sport reflected those of British racing as a whole. If Mays had had his way, there would not have been that painfully long period when no British cars took part in Grand Prix events.

The story of Raymond Mays is essentially one of making do with the best he could get, of talking, arguing, sometimes pleading, with industrialists for their support. As a driver, he was undoubtedly brilliant. But if it hadn't been for his powers of persuasion he might never have made a name for himself on the tracks. Certainly (to go forward into the years after World War II) he would never have been able to mastermind the B.R.M.

Mays was brought up in the small town of Bourne in Lincolnshire. His father had been one of the pioneer motorists. He took part in local hill-climbs and, every now and again, mechanics would come up from Vauxhall or Napier to tune his cars. On one occasion, he took his son to a meeting at Brooklands.

'I was always hooked on cars,' Raymond Mays says. 'I lived them, dreamed them. They were really in my blood. I never thought of anything else. At school, I longed for the day when the motoring papers came out.'

With him at Oundle and, later, at Cambridge, was Amherst Villiers, who was to become the wizard of superchargers. Mays admits that he is 'not highly technical'. Luckily, there always seemed to be somebody around who was. At first it was Amherst Villiers—later, Peter Berthon, a young airman who had been injured in a crash, and who, years later, designed the E.R.A.

Mays's first racing car was a Speed Model Hillman in which, when still at Cambridge, he distinguished himself in hill climbs. Later, he raced a variety of models, which were modified and boosted—in the early days by Amherst Villiers and, later, by Peter Berthon. They included a pair of Bugattis, a supercharged A.C., an Invicta, the famous White Riley which was the forerunner of the E.R.A., a 3-litre supercharged Vauxhall Villiers, and a Mercedes.

This particular Mercedes, which had been brought over from Germany especially for him, was a terrifying monster. It had a wonderful engine, but the suspension was almost solid. At 125 m.p.h. on the bumpy surface of Brooklands, it was practically impossible to drive. He used it for one race—in which, after only just managing to keep it on the track, he came second. When it was over, Segrave, who had been watching, came up to him. 'Ray,' he said, 'you're damn lucky to be alive. If you take my advice, you'll never drive that car again.'

Mays Snr. was somewhat less than happy about his son's motor-racing activities. Once he told him: 'Motor racing is an unnecessarily dangerous sport, and one which you can ill afford. It is interfering with business, which is your bread and butter.'

The family business was concerned with the wool trade. As his father's health deteriorated, more and more responsibility fell on to Raymond Mays's shoulders. Furthermore, times were bad. It needed all the attention it could get; but, then, so did motor racing.

When the Rolls-Royce engine was being tested at the works for the Schneider Trophy air race of 1929, the Mayor of Derby had to step in and calm down the local citizens—who protested that the noise was keeping them awake at nights. The people of Bourne seem to have been more long-suffering. On countless nights, their sleep must have been disturbed, while Mays and his friends tried out the effects of this or that modification to an engine. For road tests, they used a series of long straight stretches across the neighbouring fens, which must have called for a good deal of restraint on the part of the local constabulary.

Clearly, Mays's ambition was to produce a Grand Prix car for Britain. Financed by that wealthy enthusiast and driver, Humphrey Cook, he did his best with the E.R.A. (the initials stand for English Racing Automobiles Ltd.). He was the E.R.A.'s number one driver, and did very well in road races and hill climbs in Britain, and also had a number of successes abroad. But its relatively small engine was never enough to compete with the big Mercedes and Auto-Unions in Grand Prix events. Compared with them, it was built on a shoestring.

This rankled, particularly after a trip to South Africa. He told me: 'I took with me masses of spares and one mechanic. We had to do all the work of preparing the car ourselves, though a party of naval officers volunteered to do the pitwork for us. This was just before the war, and the Auto-Union team had just been out there. They left behind a staggeringly frightening impression of the German might in engineering. German trade diplomats went along with them and, of course, the Germans swept the board.

'I visited a number of local businessmen to get their reactions. They thought that Germany was supreme: their engineering had gone over completely. It was terrifying. I was almost afraid. I thought it was time this country produced a winner, and this was the substance of the "white paper" I eventually sent out to raise support for the B.R.M. I was obsessed by the need for a British car.'

The B.R.M. came—but much later.

If there was any particular irony about the Sunbeam victory in the 1923 French Grand Prix, it was the similarity of the winning car to the Grand Prix Fiats of the previous year. The reason was that Coatalen had secured the services of Bertarione, one of the Fiat design team. Bertarione had virtually copied the 1922 Fiat; and so as things turned out, the current racing Fiat was beaten by a car that was, to all intents and purposes, an earlier model of the same breed.

This was a time when a number of people were making raids on the Fiat stock of talent. Among the raiders was Enzo Ferrari, an Alfa Romeo driver who was rapidly assuming responsibility for his employer's racing activities. Ferrari was hunting a man named Vittorio Jano—one of the greatest designers of them all.

When he called at the Janos' apartment in Turin, Vittorio was out. His wife said she thought it unlikely that her husband could be enticed away from Fiat's. It wasn't so much a question of loyalty to the firm; she doubted whether he would wish to move to Milan.

At this point, Jano came in. It must have required some pretty hard talking; but, by the following day, he had capitulated.

In *The Enzo Ferrari Memoirs*, Ferrari describes the impact on Jano on Alfa Romeo.[1] 'No description could do credit to this extraordinary man and his fertile brain . . . Once in Milan, Jano took command of the situation, introduced a military like discipline and in a few months succeeded in turning out the P2— the supercharged, 2-litre, eight-cylinder machine which made such a sensational debut in 1924. For example, it set up a record of about 125 m.p.h. along the 6-mile straight at Cremona. It was driven by Antonio Ascari on this occasion with Bazzi, who had worked on the car as his mechanic.'

But it did more than that. The first Grand Prix for which a P2 was entered was the 1924 French Grand Prix at Lyons. With Campari driving, it romped home at the head of the field. It went on to win the Italian Grand Prix of that year and in the following year the first Belgian Grand Prix. On both these occasions, Ascari was driving.

In 1929, Scuderia Ferrari was formed to take over Alfa Romeo's racing interests. The symbol, a prancing black horse, had been given to Ferrari after winning a victory at Ravenna in

[1] Founded in 1909. Started racing in 1911 (the same year as Bugatti). Alfa for Societa Anonima Lombarda Fabbrica Automobili, the company's original name. Romeo for Nicolo Romeo, who acquired it in 1915 to manufacture munitions.

1923. The success had been particularly spectacular and, afterwards, the crowd broke through the cordons and carried him off, shoulder high, in triumph. Among those who had watched the race was a couple named Baracca—the parents of a World War I fighter ace, who had been shot down in flames after destroying thirty-five enemy aircraft.

The Baraccas managed to get up to Ferrari and present him with a small shield on which was painted a prancing black horse on a yellow background. They explained that their son had always displayed it on his aircraft—to distinguish it from those of his fellow pilots. For the rest of his days as a driver (he retired in 1931, when his son, Dino, was born) Ferrari carried it on his car. It later became the emblem of the Scuderia Ferrari Alfas of the 'thirties—and, of course, the Ferrari cars when they were built.

At the end of 1932, during which they had won every major event but two (the Czech Grand Prix and the Avusrennen), Alfa Romeo decided to retire from motor racing. The reasons are somewhat vague, though they were probably financial. Certainly in the following year there was a big switch in the ownership of Alfa shares, and the firm's famous Monoposto cars were impounded. It was several months before even Ferrari, who had not the slightest intention of giving up motor sport, could get hold of them and race them.

Throughout the 'thirties, Scuderia Ferrari raced Alfa Romeos and employed the famous Alfa drivers. In 1937, he began to have ideas about building a car of his own, and in 1939 came the big break. After a dispute which, Ferrari says, 'was a crisis of conscience' and was largely over technical matters, Scuderia Ferrari and Alfa Romeo parted. When, after the Second World War, Alfas returned to racing for a few years, they found their old colleague on the side of the opposition. For, in 1947, he produced his first racing car.

According to Alice Caracciola (widow of Rudolf Caracciola), Ferrari was always in his shirt sleeves at races and he invariably wore a large pair of braces. He detested the idea of women in the pits, though he was gracious enough to make an exception in the case of Madame Caracciola. It was hardly surprising; for she was one of the most competent timekeepers who ever held a stop-watch. On one occasion, she spotted a mistake which the official timekeepers had made. She pointed it out to Ferrari, who made a protest which was accepted. Since it affected the finishing order, it made all the difference of 20,000 lire to his day's finances.

The big feature of the Le Mans 24-Hour Race in the 'twenties was the Bentley—or, as they used to say, the 'Bentley Boys'. This was not a name they particularly liked; but it was meant affectionately, and they had to put up with it. At one time, it was said, there were five millionaires driving for Bentley. This is probably an exaggeration. Wolfe Barnato (winner of the 24-Hour Race three times in succession), whose fortune came from diamonds, was certainly in this class, and Tim Birkin was never short of funds. Benjafield, who won at Le Mans in 1927 with S. C. H. Davis, was a doctor. Davis was a motoring journalist. But, to the general public, the 'Bentley Boys' spelt glamour. They drove cars which any well-heeled young blade-about-town could buy, and they drove them beautifully and at tremendous speeds. Furthermore, they brought success and glory to Britain at a time when the country could well use these commodities.

The master mind of the Bentley team was, of course, W. O. Bentley, who wasn't a particularly glamorous figure. By nature he was rather shy and he tended to shun publicity. Davis, who knew him well, describes him as 'not so much brilliant. "Methodical" would be a better word for him.'

He was one of a large family. In the early days, they nearly all raced motor cycles. At the Bentley dinner table there were always plenty of high spirits, but W.O. seldom joined in. He never had very much to say for himself, and often used to disappear from the scene for days on end. At the time he was wrapped up in thoughts of steam locomotives.

One of his brothers had the agency for Doriot, Flandrin and Parent cars. W.O. raced one of them in the T.T. event of 1914 and did tolerably well. Then war broke out.

He joined the Naval Air Service. At the time, the Admiralty wanted a more powerful engine for their fighter aircraft. He was sent up to the Humber works at Coventry where, working with a designer named Burgess, he was told to do something about it. Among his ideas was that of using light alloys, and the machine which this work produced (it was known as the Bentley Rotary Mk I) was the first to have aluminium pistons. It went very well.

Bentley had conceived the ambition to build a fast touring car. Burgess had similar notions and suggested that the answer might be a *real* Humber—the sort of car which, in his opinion, the Humber ought to have been, but wasn't.

This would probably have been a disaster. At any given time, any make of car has its own particular image, and, therefore, its own particular type of customer. The Humber clientele of those days was certainly not in the market for this sort of thing, and it is doubtful whether sufficient would ever have been sold. Presently the idea was dropped.

Neither Bentley nor Burgess had any thought of manufacturing cars for the sake of making money. They simply wanted to produce the finest that human skill and sweat and ingenuity could build. If they had a market in mind it was peopled by enthusiasts who were rich and who drove well. Above all things they were motorists who liked things that were very beautifully done.

This was not a proposition calculated to win support from any of the big car-makers—with the possible exception of Rolls-Royce, who might have protested that they were doing it already. Nevertheless, Horace Bentley (W.O.'s brother) succeeded in raising funds for it. One of the backers is said to have been Barnato, who was well rewarded—if not financially, then at least on the racing circuits.

When they went racing, the team was everything. Individualism was discouraged, and drivers were required to observe strict orders from the controller. Anyone who received too much publicity was liable to fall out of favour. Nor was this entirely unreasonable. When a well-known driver wins it is, so far as the public is concerned, *his* victory. If he fails, it is the *car*'s fault.

W. O. Bentley was unlikely to swell any driver's ego beyond reasonable proportions. Says Davis: 'He'd praise you only when that praise had really been *earned*.' Similarly, if anybody made a mistake, he was treated to some pretty harsh remarks.

Of course, the drivers did get publicity—with so many victories and with such colourful personalities it was inevitable. But this certainly didn't turn anyone's head; and when something did go wrong, everyone felt very badly about it.

Mind you, Bentley was always just. Much to most people's surprise, one of the T.T. races found him riding mechanic. Afterwards, he explained: 'I took on the job because I thought our mechanics were beginning to consider themselves heroes. After the race I realised they were right.'

He and Burgess may not have produced the perfect touring car, but they came very close to it. Bentley pulled out of motor racing after 1930, just when the depression was really biting and money was becoming seriously short. Tim Birkin, who (somewhat to W.O.'s disapproval) had commissioned Amherst Villiers to supercharge his car, continued to keep the marque alive. But the reign of the Bentley Boys, which had lasted for just short of six years, was over.

The late nineteen-twenties were the heyday of the Bugattis. With drivers such as Chiron, and Williams and Benoist, they were winning races with almost monotonous regularity. As early as 1923, although they were not particularly successful, they were pioneering new shapes. At the French Grand Prix of that year, the so-called Bugatti 'Tank cars' created a mild sensation by their advanced style of streamlining.

Bugatti was Ettore Bugatti—autocrat, artist, engineer, genius. Born in Milan, his father was one of those amazingly versatile people who crop up from time to time and cause their friends to compare them with Leonardo da Vinci. It is tough on anybody to be saddled with such a comparison, for he is bound to come off worst. Nevertheless Bugatti Snr. was a painter, sculptor, wood-carver, architect and furniture designer. He also invented and manufactured string-instruments; and, on one occasion, designed a suit of clothes for himself. He did all these things very well.

At an extraordinarily precocious age, his son, Ettore, was having shrewd ideas about internal combustion engines and their applications. He never had any formal training as an engineer, nor could he possibly have found the time for it. At the age of nineteen, when many youngsters are still wondering what to do with their lives, he was on his way to a town near Strasbourg to design cars for the De Dietrich company. He was to be paid on a royalty basis and, since he was still under twenty-one, his father had to sign the contract on his behalf.

Inevitably, he would one day have his own firm, and it wasn't very long in coming. By January, 1910 (he was then twenty-eight), he had taken over premises at Molsheim in Alsace, and the first machine tools were arriving. During the course of that year five cars were produced and, with Ernest Friederich at the wheel, Bugattis had taken part in their first races.

Ettore Bugatti once wrote that: 'My father attached great importance to his two sons being able to work with their hands, and a cabinet-maker's work is the best of groundings for mechanics.' This belief seems to have had a marked effect. His brother, Rembrandt Bugatti, became a famous sculptor; and he, himself, took an almost unbelievable delight in good craftsmanship.

At the works, everything *shone*. Many of the tools were made in the factory—for the simple reason that there was nothing quite like them on the market. The Guv'nor certainly wasn't going to entrust their manufacture to establishments where the standards were less exacting.

A correspondent from *The Autocar*, who visited the works in

1930, had this to say: 'Everything is done perfectly and in its order. Time is not wasted, naturally, because a good workman does not waste anything, but there is no undue haste. The great thing is not to do the job so that it will merely satisfy the *patron*, but so perfectly that it will draw a word of commendation from him.'

Bugatti's labour relations policy reflected some of the paternal aspects of feudalism. Nobody was likely to remain on the payroll for long if he wasn't an above-average workman, and so it was difficult to award wage increases for sheer merit. Instead, Bugatti devised his own system. It was based on the principle that people should be encouraged to be thrifty. Since he considered them to be reasonably well paid, he believed that they should either be saving up for their old age, or else improving their living conditions. Those who could satisfy him that they were doing one or the other of these things received increases. It was rather like the parable of the talents.

Molsheim seems to have been a happy place to work, and the employees obviously thought the world of the Guv'nor. However, there was one force against which even this secure citadel of loyalty was not proof: trade unionism. When a wave of strikes knocked much of the wind out of France in 1936 (they caused the Le Mans race of that year to be cancelled), Bugatti imagined that his own men would keep on working.

To his bitter dismay, the agitators had been busy at Molsheim. One day, the red flag was waved at the works. The men put down their tools, and even went on protest marches. It may have been a striking exhibition of the Solidarity of Labour: to Ettore Bugatti, however, it was as much a personal affront as a blow in the face.

With his mind inflamed by thoughts of man's ingratitude, he departed for Paris, and left the management of Molsheim to his son, Jean.

Two of the great men in motor racing during the last five decades have been Ettore Bugatti and Enzo Ferrari. Ironically, they both suffered the same sort of personal tragedy: the death of a son, who, had he survived, would (in each case) inevitably have taken over the business.

Dino Ferrari died as the result of a nephritis virus. Jean Bugatti was killed when testing a car one evening near Molsheim. A stretch of road had been cleared for the run. Jean Bugatti was reaching full revs when, suddenly, a cyclist appeared and began to cross the road. Jean braked hard. The car swerved and hit a tree. He was crushed against the steering wheel and killed outright.

The cyclist escaped with cuts and bruises. Three years later, however, he committed suicide.

Ettore Bugatti was stubborn. He paid no heed to what his competitors were up to, and practically none to public taste. Fortunately the latter had considerable respect for his ideas, and loyally went on buying his cars—even though he would never, under any circumstances, equip them with left-hand drive.

As a designer, he never used a slide rule and seldom a drawing board. Once, when working in his room in Paris, he roughed out his ideas on the mantelpiece.

According to one of his calculations, his cars won over 10,000 [*sic*] races and established thirty-seven international records which were still standing in 1939. They, certainly, are the source of his fame. Nevertheless, they shouldn't be allowed to obscure his other achievements. During the First World War, he designed aircraft engines, which were the only ones to be produced in America under a European licence. They were also the first in France to undergo a successful test run of 10 hours. He designed railcars (the type of engine produced for the fabulous Bugatti 'Royale' car was used in some of them),[1] a yacht, speedboats, gadgets galore, and even the chandeliers for his home.

His interests and enthusiasms seemed to encompass everything that anyone could think of. Apart from bad workmanship, the thing which he seems to have disliked most of all was the word 'genius', when people applied it to him. Significantly, in her excellent book *The Bugatti Story*, his daughter, L'Ebé Bugatti, contrives to avoid its use. It was done, she writes, 'out of respect for his wishes'.

When the Auto-Union came on to the scene in the mid-'thirties, it was an entirely revolutionary racing car. By putting the engine at the rear, it anticipated this trend by well over twenty years. Auto-Union was a joint enterprise by four firms: D.K.W., Wanderer, Audi and Horsch. But, above all things, it was the creation of its chief engineer, Dr. Ferdinand Porsche.

Porsche's was also a somewhat precocious talent. His father was a tinsmith in the Austrian village of Maffersdorf. At the age of fifteen, young Ferdinand installed electric lighting in the house. This amounted to very much more than, simply, wiring the place

---

[1] At one time, Bugatti railcars held the World Record of 122 m.p.h. timed over 6 miles, and the World Record for a long distance run—90 m.p.h. on the 313-mile run from Strasbourg to Paris.

up: he had to build a generator, which he installed in the cellar.
By 1900 (he was then twenty-five), he had produced his first car. One of its interesting features was the fact that it was powered by two electric motors, one on each of the front wheel hubs.
Having established this, his next idea was to do away with batteries. He replaced them with a generator and called the new system 'mixed drive'. This, of course, was much more than a passing novelty. The 'mixed drive' principle has since been applied to railway trains. Porsche himself used it on one built specially to haul the enormous 26-ton Skoda mortar, 'Big Bertha', in World War I. In the Second World War, the system was used in the deadly Tiger tank (which was another Porsche invention).
In 1905, Porsche joined the Austrian Daimler company. One of his earliest designs for them was also his only failure. It was a 30 h.p. touring car—named the 'Maja' in honour of one of Emile Jellinek's two daughters. Jellinek was a wealthy financier who had money in both the Austrian and German Daimler companies.
The car never did well. In this respect, Maja Jellinek was less fortunate than her sister, after whom another car (made by the German company) was christened. Her name was Mercedes.
In 1907, the Austro-Daimler company began to build motors for airships. Five years later, an air-cooled flat-four aero engine came off Porsche's drawing board. It was probably the most significant design he ever produced; for, out of this thinking, eventually sprang the Volkswagen, the Porsche, and the Auto-Union.
After the First World War, Porsche joined the German Daimler company, largely because he attached a lot of importance to motor racing, and his colleagues at Austro-Daimler didn't. He remained there for six years—long enough to establish a line of supercharged Mercedes-Benz sports-racing cars, and to create some trucks and tractors as well. Then, after a brief sojourn back in Austria, he moved to Stuttgart and set up his own design office.
In 1932, he received an invitation to visit Russia. When he arrived there, he was treated like a visiting potentate, and was offered the job of taking charge of the country's motor vehicle production. On the face of it, it seemed a tremendous opportunity. He was to be allowed unlimited research facilities, and would be able to experiment to his heart's content. But there was one snag: on no account would he be able to leave Russia. He turned the offer down.
It was probably just as well. In technical matters Porsche liked to have his own way. Whenever he found himself in a state of disagreement with his colleagues, he quit.

When he was entrusted with the design of the Auto-Union (it was originally called the P-Wagen, 'P' being for Porsche), he threw away all existing ideas and produced what was probably the hairiest racing car there has ever been.

The Auto-Union had scarcely been tested, when Porsche received an order to design a people's car. As the former was furious and unforgiving, so had the latter to be meek and mild. By 1937, a batch of thirty had been produced. A random sample of Nazi SS men tested them for two million miles, and could find no fault.

Hitler wanted to call the new car 'K.D.F.' after the initials of his Strength Through Joy organisation, but more sober councils prevailed. It was christened the Volkswagen.

Alice Caracciola described Porsche to me as 'a man who looked rather like Einstein, with a furry little moustache. He was always sympathetic, wise and kind.' But, above everything else, he was a dedicated man. He read practically nothing that wasn't technical. He disliked going to the theatre; was practically tone-deaf so far as music was concerned; and, in spite of belonging to two yacht clubs, he didn't care for sailing. Indeed, his only relaxations seem to have been motion pictures and hunting. If he found a film he enjoyed, he'd go and see it over and over again. As for hunting, he had one reservation which seems to be a sharp negation of the whole idea. He refused to kill anything.

12 Interlude on sand and salt

Ever since the duel between Chasseloup-Laubat and Jenatzy, a number of racing drivers had been struggling for the distinction of being the fastest man on earth. Among the less obvious contenders was Henry Ford, who, on January 13th, 1903, took his famous '999' special on to the frozen waters of Lake St. Clare, a few miles away from Detroit, and quietly hoisted the record from 84·73 m.p.h. (by Duray in his Gobron-Brillie) to 91·37 m.p.h. It remained there until January 28th of the following year, when W. K. Vanderbilt set off in a Mercedes on Daytona Beach, Florida, and raised it to 92.30 m.p.h. Later, in 1904, Louis Rigolly went motoring on the Ostend road and became the first man to crack the magic number of 100 m.p.h.

The last run before World War I was at Brooklands. On June 24th, 1914, L. G. Hornsted with a Benz did 124·10 m.p.h.

After nearly every war there is a sale of government surplus materials. If you shop around carefully, you can usually find some bargains. Among the better value in the way of leftovers from the First World War were aero-engines. The Aircraft Disposal Co. Ltd. had 30,000 for sale, and it was possible to pick one up for under £100.

One of these machines—a hefty 18·25-litre V12 affair producing 350 b.h.p. at 2,000 r.p.m.—eventually found its way into a single-seater Sunbeam designed by Louis Coatalen. The result was a car which travelled so fast that hardly anyone dared use it. Among the few who did was K. Lee Guinness. On a blustery day in May, 1922, he took the monster out on to the track at Brooklands. When he had finished, the land speed record stood at 133·75 m.p.h. This, incidentally, was the last occasion on which the run was made on an artificial circuit. Two years later, Ernest Eldridge, driving a Fiat, clocked 146·01 m.p.h. on a stretch of road near Paris, and this was the last time that a public highway was used. Afterwards, it was done on a sandy beach and then, later, on salt flats.

The chassis of Eldridge's car had originally been a part of that fast old Fiat, 'Mephistopheles', on which Felice Nazzaro beat Edge's Napier, 'Samson', back at Brooklands in 1908.

Malcolm Campbell had been anxious to buy the giant Sunbeam as soon as he heard about it, but Coatalen refused to sell. Eventually, after a good deal of argument, Coatalen loaned it to him for a record attempt on the sands at Saltburn. Campbell did 138·08 m.p.h., which should have been a record. However, the Commission Sportif Internationale (who were responsible for supervising these exercises) disallowed it. Apparently, the timing hadn't been carried out by synchronised stop-watches.

Campbell approached Coatalen again. This time, after further horse-trading, the latter agreed to sell the car. Campbell painted the word 'Bluebird' (after Maeterlink's opera of that name, which he rather liked) on to the bonnet and set off for Pendine sands. This time, more attention must have been paid to the stop-watches, for his average speed of 146·01 m.p.h. was accepted. In the following year, also at Pendine, he raised his own record to 150·87 m.p.h.

Record bids were now coming fast and furious. Every year produced its harvest of new ones and swept away the litter of old ones. In 1926, on April 28th and 29th, Parry Thomas made two attempts.

Thomas was a quiet Welshman who lived with a pack of Alsatian dogs in a house called 'The Hermitage' on the edge of the aerodrome at Brooklands. For a number of years, he had worked for Leyland's, for whom he developed the famous 7-litre straight-eight Leyland-Thomas luxury car. Naturally, since, to his mind, it was the only logical thing to do, he converted one of them for racing. In spite of the very severe handicapping which was imposed on a car of this size, he won a number of races in it.

RED AND GREEN
ABOVE *Farina winning the 1950 British Grand Prix at Silverstone in a 1½-litre Type 159 Alfa Romeo. In that year, the Italian ace also won the first World Championship of Drivers.* BELOW *At last—a Grand Prix victory for Britain. Stirling Moss winning the 1957 European Grand Prix at Aintree in a Vanwall*

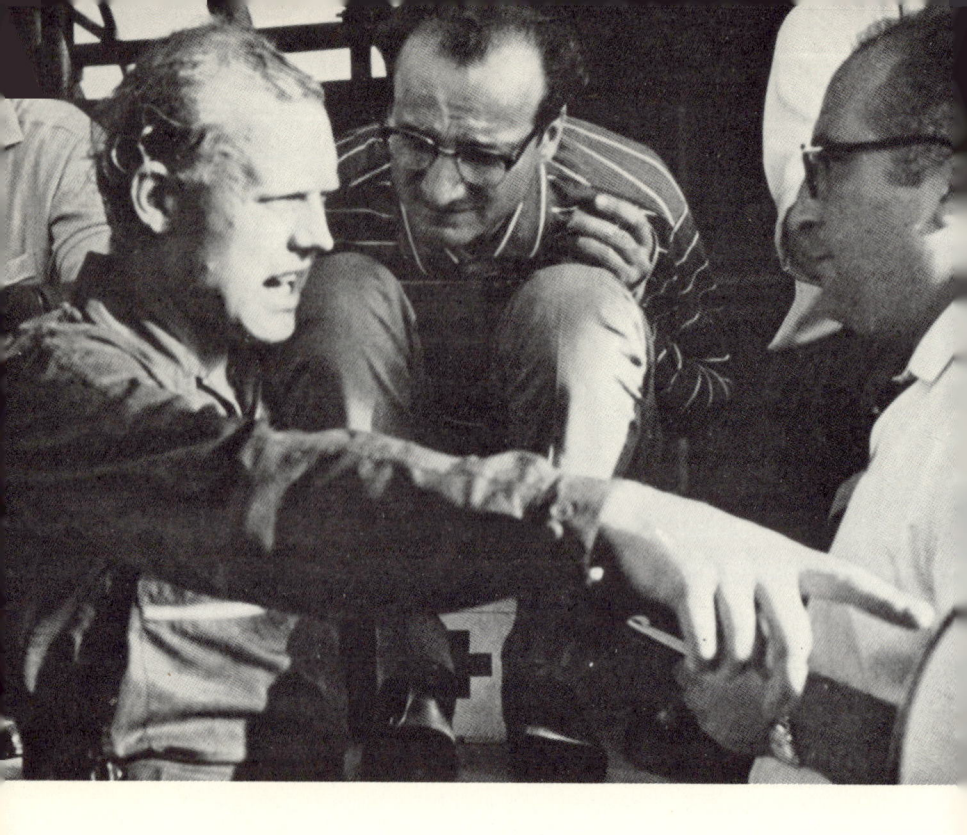

ON TOP
ABOVE *Mike Hawthorn in command of the situation at the pits.*
BELOW *Fangio in command of the track*

WHAT'S WRONG WITH PUTTING IT AT THE BACK?
The Coopers, father and son, created the 500 c.c. racing car. What better place to put the engine, they decided, than at the back. Which they did. Of course one thing led to another: the cars became bigger and so did the engines—like (below) this Cooper-B.R.M., which Stirling Moss drove at Aintree

DEATH IN THE AFTERNOON—AT LE MANS
ABOVE *Levegh in his Mercedes shortly before crashing at Le Mans in 1955.* BELOW *A battered Austin-Healey blocks part of the track; a pillar of brown smoke gropes towards the sky; and more than eighty people, including Levegh, are dead*

THE GREAT ONES
Stirling Moss

Juan Manuel Fangio

Alberto Ascari

Jim Clark

STYLES OF STARTING
ABOVE *The sprint at the start of the Le Mans 24-hour race.* BELOW *Gurney, Surtees and Ginther on the grid at Brands Hatch*

AUTOMOTIVE ROCKETRY
Craig Breedlove's 'Spirit of America'. When the 'chutes failed, Breedlove got his feet wet

BIG WINGS, LITTLE WINGS
ABOVE *Jim Hall's Chaparral before the start of the 1967 Le Mans 24-Hour race.* BELOW *Graham Hill in his Lotus-Ford at the 1968 British Grand Prix. It was in this car that Hill won the 1968 World Championship of Drivers*

Apart from the occasional game of tennis at the Queen's Club, he had no interests in life apart from his beloved racing cars. He seemed to avoid people, though he was surprisingly soft-hearted about children. Shortly before his death, he endowered the 'Babs' cot at the Great Ormond Street Hospital for Sick Children.

'Babs' was the name of his record car, which was otherwise known as the 'Higham Special'.[1] It had originally been one of Count Louis Zborowski's chain-driven Chitty-Chitty-Bang-Bangs. After purchasing it from the Count, Parry Thomas took it back to Brooklands to give it the treatment. One evening, a mechanic who was working late, chalked the name 'Babs' on the massive V12 aero-engine. Parry Thomas liked it, and the name stuck.

And so 'Babs' and Thomas went to Pendine. The result of the first day's runs was to take the record up to 169·30 m.p.h. On the following day, he raised it to 171·02 m.p.h.

In March of the following year, he tried again. On the second trip, however, one of the chains snapped at over 2,000 r.p.m. It sliced through the steel guard and killed Thomas instantly. The wreckage of the car was afterwards buried in the sands—where, so far as I know, it remains to this day.

Segrave, with thirty-one 'firsts' to his credit out of a total of forty-nine events, gave up circuit racing in 1927 to become a director of the Portland Cement Company. He also wrote a book entitled *The Lure of Speed*, designed a car body for the Hillman Segrave Coupé, and set about demolishing the World Land Speed Record. In that year, with assistance from another aero-engined Sunbeam, he took it up to over 200 m.p.h. (203·79 to be precise) at Daytona Beach. Then, with financial help from two of the Portland Cement directors, he started work on designing the most famous of all his cars, 'Golden Arrow'.

'Golden Arrow's' big moment came on March 11th, 1929, at Daytona, when Segrave took her twice over the mile and left the record at 231·44 m.p.h. (23·89 m.p.h. faster than the speed of Keech's White Triple[2] in the previous year).

On that same visit to Florida, he also broke the World Water Speed Record in his boat *Miss England*. As he heard over R.M.S. *Olympic*'s radio on his voyage back to Britain, this brace of broken records earned him a knighthood.

But Segrave was approaching the end of his days. Back in

---

[1] After Zborowski's estate in Kent.
[2] An extraordinary car, this: it had one engine at the front and two at the back.

K

England, he applied himself to designing a new *Miss England*. When she was completed, he took the £25,000 boat up to Lake Windermere for a further attempt on the water record. This time, he had to beat 92·86 m.p.h. He made two runs at an average speed of 98·76 m.p.h. Then he set off on a third, on which he proposed to go flat out with the object of exceeding 120 m.p.h. At some point, *Miss England* struck an obstacle, turned over at full speed, and sank. One riding engineer was killed instantly. The other survived. Segrave was brought ashore with both arms broken, a crushed thigh, broken ribs and head injuries. Two-and-a-half hours later, he was dead.

The ace's ashes were taken up by his father in an aircraft, and scattered over the playing fields of Eton.

John Cobb was killed on Loch Ness, when attacking the World Water Speed Record in 1947. He had held the World Land Speed Record three times. Donald Campbell, who briefly held the land record after a remarkable performance by his car 'Bluebird II' in Australia, was also killed on water.

The last run at Daytona was made by Malcolm Campbell in 1933, and the record went up to 272·46 m.p.h. For his next attempt (in 1935), Campbell took over the Bonneville Salt Flats in Utah.[1] He made two runs that year. On the first, he did 276·82 m.p.h. and on the second, 301.13 m.p.h.

Captain G. E. T. Eyston is the only surviving record-breaker of those days. When working on this chapter, I went to see him at his house in Winchester.

Eyston was a consulting engineer. He specialised in superchargers. They were used, among other applications, in the highly successful M.G. sports racing cars and in a Bentley which, driven by Birkin, took the lap record at Brooklands. He had plans to build them for aero- and diesel engines.

Before making his assaults on the World Land Speed Record, Eyston had served a very thorough apprenticeship in the art of speed. He did a great deal of motor racing. In his remarkable little car the 'Magic Midget', he broke a number of class records for M.G.; and he also captured the world 1-hour, 12-hours, 24-hours, and 48-hours endurance records in other cars. Two of the 1-hour records were made at Montlhery in a Panhard with a plywood body, which had originally been designed for speed trials on the beach at Ostend. The others were done at Bonneville in a car of his own design called the 'Speed of the Wind'.

[1] The problem, as the cars went faster and then faster still, was to find an expanse of land long enough for the attempt.

For his attack on the World Land Speed Record, Eyston designed and built an eight-wheeler which he named 'Thunderbolt'. It was powered by a pair of Rolls-Royce 'R' aero-engines. One of them had had amazing history; for, before becoming the fastest engine on land, it had been used in Supermarine seaplanes competing in the Schneider Trophy air races. On two occasions, it had set up a new air speed record.

When Donald Campbell attacked the land speed record in 1964, huge sums of money were involved. Campbell himself was paid substantial retainers by his sponsors. In Eyston's case, the sums were much more moderate. He told me: 'We received reasonable money from Castrol and some from BP before we did the runs, and a little more if we succeeded. It covered our expenses with a little surplus. We also had splendid help from many people in the motor industry.'

He made his first run in 1937, and took the record up to 312 m.p.h. In the following year, having shed 2,000 lb from the weight of his car, he tried again. This time, his speed was 345·50 m.p.h. Then John Cobb took over the Salt Flats with his Napier-Railton, and did 350·20 m.p.h. Eyston replied with 357·50 m.p.h. In the following year, Cobb did 369·70 Finally, in 1947, still with the Napier-Railton, Cobb brought things very close to the elusive 400 m.p.h. mark by travelling at 394·20 m.p.h.

Eyston's car had an enclosed cockpit with a windscreen and canopy that were both taken from a Spitfire aircraft. The entire fuselage was crammed with machinery and, as Eyston told me, 'the hardest job was to find space for the man. The superchargers were alongside one, and they were revolving at 36,000 r.p.m. It would have been bad news, if anything had happened to them.'

Heat and exhaust fumes were another problem. The exhaust manifolds, which were very thin, were unpleasantly close to the driver. The slightest leak would have filled the cockpit with carbon monoxide. To overcome this unpleasant possibility, Eyston devised an ingenious fresh-air device in which a mask, rather like those which the dentists used for administering gas, was strapped over the driver's face and connected by a length of tube to the outside world.

The heat was intense—particularly on his final run, when he decided to do away with the radiator. He replaced it with a 60-gallon tank, filled half with water and half with anti-freeze (to put up the boiling temperature from 100°C to 105°C). Rolls-Royce engineers said that it would come to the boil at the end of the run, and it happened just as they had predicted. Steam valves were fitted into the system: they blew just before the end.

On this attempt, the cockpit became so hot that Eyston stuck to the seat. He raised the record to 357·50. The trouble came afterwards, when they tried to get him out of the car.

Bonneville Salt Flats extend over an area about 90 miles long by 40 miles wide. Much of it is covered with scrub. Only a section, about 10 miles in circumference, is suitable for running cars on. But, before anything could be done on it, a great deal of preparation had to be carried out.

Eyston used to arrive at the flats anything up to five weeks before making his attempt. He then had to survey the course, which was in a somewhat rough condition. To smooth it down sufficiently, it had to be scraped with iron rails.

On the day of the run, he used to get up at 2.30 a.m., wake up the rest of his crew, and be ready on the starting line just after dawn. 'I liked to do it then,' he said, 'for the flats were at their coolest and the air temperature was cool. At midday, it was so hot that you could hardly touch anything. July was the best month, for the salt was hard. By mid-November, when I once did the record, it was getting softer. I remember that there was a snowstorm on the horizon and, by midday, it was snowing hard.'

He used to wear overalls and a cloth helmet. He never wore a belt.

There was a run of 5½ miles up to the measured mile which was marked by red banners at either end. The timekeepers were out of sight of the starting line. They telephoned through when they were ready (on one occasion, Eyston was kept waiting for two hours, while they sorted out some trouble with their apparatus). Initially, a compressed-air motor was used to start the engines, but this wasn't very satisfactory. One engine got going, and the other didn't. In the end, it turned out to be better to receive a push-start from a Ford truck.

The route was marked by a black line, which had to be followed slavishly, and there were no objects against which to measure speed and distance. Indeed, Eyston recalls, there was very little sensation of speed. After 300 m.p.h. a light sideways wobble set in, owing to the tyres becoming distorted by centrifugal force. It was as if the car were running on knife edges. 'But', Eyston told me, 'after 300 m.p.h. one really couldn't guess how fast one was going.'[1] There was nothing except the din of the engines and the intense heat.

---

[1] Ordinary car instruments were installed in the cockpit. Cobb and Campbell both used cameras, which photographed the dials and provided evidence for any review of the runs which might take place afterwards. 'Thunderbolt' was not fitted with a camera.

Interlude on sand and salt   137

'The heat,' he said, 'surged up into the cockpit as if one were sitting on a stove.'

First gear took the car up to 60 m.p.h., second gear brought it up to 240 m.p.h.—'after which,' he said, 'one engaged third gear. You then had four miles in which to grind out the record.'

By no means the least of the problems was that of stopping the car. It was no use applying the brakes until the speed was way down below the 180 m.p.h. mark, otherwise they'd have burnt out. As an experiment, he tried using air brakes. He applied them at full speed, which was considerably faster than they were normally used on aircraft. 'I didn't feel a thing when they came on,' he told me, 'but the air disturbance, caused by their application, crumpled all the panels. I had to renew them after each attempt.'

It took $5\frac{1}{2}$ miles, after which he described a series of large circles, before the car came to a halt. After this, the return trip had, according to the F.I.A. regulations, to be made within an hour. If it wasn't, the whole thing was nullified.

In his 1938 attempts, Eyston shared the salt flats with John Cobb. Before making his first run, he had prepared two courses, one of which his rival used. 'But,' he told me, 'Cobb and I were in opposite camps. We didn't see a great deal of each other. He had a family business in the City—they were fur brokers. I didn't get to know him well until he made his attempt on the water record at Loch Ness. I acted as manager for that, and we became friendly. I was very distressed when he was killed.'

'Thunderbolt' was exhibited at the New York World Fair in 1939 and, some years later, at centenary celebrations in New Zealand. Whilst on show at Wellington, there was a fire and the car was destroyed. Eyston appears to have received the news without any undue emotion. 'My cars,' he told me, 'were very useful tools for a special purpose. They all worked quite well, and had fully come up to expectations'.

A World Land Speed Record attempt is something which captures the public's imagination. Indeed, while working at Bonneville, one of the problems was crowd control. Once, Eyston recalls, there was a queue of cars, forty miles long, on one of the approach roads.

But did these spectacular drives contribute anything to the stock pile of technical knowledge? Or, was it sufficient to attack a record, simply because it was there? Everybody has his own answer to this. Eyston being, before anything else, an engineer, can point to a number of advances which his work with 'Thunderbolt' helped to make possible. There was, for example, the testing of tyres with reference to the very fast landing speeds of fighter and bomber aircraft in World War II.

There was also something to be learned about transmission systems, which was used to good advantage in wartime tanks. Finally, there was a contribution to the development of self-ventilating disc brakes. In spite of the fact that a similar principle had been used in German tramcars about eighty years previously, these were still something of a novelty. For the short speed records, however, they were essential, for how else could brakes best be ventilated? Furthermore, they provided a bigger surface than drum brakes.

Perhaps, when all is said and done, the World Land Speed Record has helped to improve the breed.

13 Children of the Gods

By the end of 1931, the European motor industry had become limp from the depression. The worst-hit nation was Germany, where nearly half the young men between the ages of sixteen and thirty-two were out of work, and the country was on the verge of bankruptcy. Not surprisingly, as the year tottered towards its painful conclusion, Mercedes Benz announced that they intended to pull out of motor racing.

In twelve months' time Alfa Romeo were to make a similar decision, though their withdrawal was more of a paper transaction. Waiting in the wings, eager to take the cars over as soon as the factory would release them, was the indefatigable Enzo Ferrari.

Within Germany, the forces which create history were brewing up their own dark remedy in the form of National Socialism. On January 30th, 1933, President Hindenburg conferred the chancellorship upon Adolf Hitler. By March of that year, Hitler had become a dictator.

One can't help wondering what might have happened had the German leader devoted himself to the theatre, rather than to politics. He may have been the most evil statesman the twentieth century has so far produced, but he was a brilliant showman. He liked his Wagner and his massive displays of pomp, heroic architecture, and huge noises such as those of brass bands, canon fire, and racing cars.

Possibly he had taken notice of his friend Mussolini's attitude to motor sport: at all events, he had not been long in power before he offered a prize of £40,000 to the constructor of the most successful German racing car to travel the circuits in 1934.

At Mercedes Benz they began to smile again and went back to the drawing boards. At Chemnitz, four smaller firms—D.K.W., Wanderer, Audi and Horsch—formed a consortium. The chief designer of the new firm, which called itself Auto-Union A.G., was Dr. Ferdinand Porsche.

Eight years previously, Porsche had produced a rear-engined single-seater racing car. It had only competed in a few events, and it hadn't been very successful. Nevertheless, the principle must have seemed to be sound, for, when it came to this new car, Porsche had no hesitation in putting its whopping great 4·36-litre V16 engine at the back.

The Auto-Union (or 'P-Wagen', as it was originally called) was one of motor racing's most closely guarded secrets. Even the German racing drivers were denied any details of it at first. It had originally been intended to test a prototype at Nurburgring at the end of 1933. However, the circuit was frost-bound and much too slippery. The trials were postponed for a month. Then, with Hans Stuck at the wheel, they were carried out on the Avus circuit near Berlin.

It travelled at 150 m.p.h. In March, 1934, with Stuck again driving, the Auto-Union made its second appearance at the Avus. This time, it covered 134·9 miles in 60 minutes and broke the world 1-hour speed record. Stuck was unable to take the corners at more than 80 m.p.h. Consequently, on the long, very fast straights, he must have been doing about 170 m.p.h.

Clearly, then, the Auto-Union was a very fast car. It was also an exceptionally difficult one to drive. Of all the racing cars ever built, this was almost certainly the most unforgiving. Not the least of the problems was that occasioned by putting the driver up front. When the rear wheels broke away, it sometimes took a fraction of a second too many for the news to reach the cockpit. Unless the driver reacted quickly, he was in very dire trouble.

Nobody ever quelled the Auto-Union. Three men, Bernd Rosemeyer, Varzi and Nuvolari, came to terms with it.

Alice Caracciola described Rosemeyer to me in these terms:

'He was *alive*. When he won, he really won. He was the happiness of three years of motor racing: without him, it would have been dull. He was a passionate young man, one of those bright stars that illuminate everything. He drove like a motor-cyclist—as if he had two wheels instead of four. He was without any fear: gay, young, blue-eyed. Perhaps, when you think of it, he was *too* fearless and *too* passionate. But you couldn't wish him otherwise: he was so full of enthusiasm and so passionately gay.'

Rosemeyer's career with Auto-Union lasted only three seasons. Like Nuvolari, he had originally competed in motor-cycle races. With almost unbelievable tenacity, he had pestered Willy Walb, the Auto-Union manager, for a trial. Presently, his persistence was rewarded. He was instructed to report at Nurburgring one day in November, 1934.

Writing about him in *Great Racing Drivers*, Cyril Posthumus recalls: 'On the great day, he turned up at the Nurburgring wearing a lounge suit. "Where are your overalls?" asked Walb. "Well, this is a great occasion for me—my première in a racing car—so I thought I'd dress up for it," quipped Bernd.'

Walb told him to put on some overalls and get into the car. As the result of this outing, he was signed on as reserve driver. Eventually, after bombarding the long-suffering Walb still more, he was given his first opportunity to take part in a race. From that moment, his fame was assured.

Hitler clearly meant the revived German motor racing set-up to take all the records that were going. For these attempts, he had caused two special stretches of autobahn to be built for this purpose. One was between Frankfurt and Darmstadt. It was an ingenious piece of construction; for, instead of the customary central reservation between the two carriageways, there was a row of removable concrete posts.

Before an attempt, soldiers were stationed by the roadside. Presently, by means of a field telephone, an order was passed down the line. Each soldier took a few paces smartly forward, removed the concrete post, and then retreated to his previous position.

The other was near Dessau.

Early one January morning in 1938, the Mercedes team was out in strength on the latter. They had with them a new car, built for record-breaking, and Rudolf Caracciola. The object was to beat Rosemeyer's Auto-Union record of 250 m.p.h. At 8 a.m., Caracciola made his first run. Soon afterwards (from Caracciola's account, he just had long enough to smoke a cigarette), the car was turned round, and he made the return trip. The average speed for the two was 265 m.p.h.

He went off a second time, and took the record up to 271 m.p.h. By now, the wind was getting up, and they all went away to enjoy a late breakfast.

In his book, *A Racing Car Driver's World*, Caracciola has left us some vivid accounts of what it was like to drive at these fantastic speeds along this stretch of road. 'The road before me seemed to shrink,' he wrote, 'becoming narrower and narrower, till it was a slender white ribbon. The trees on either side merged into a solid black wall.'

And: 'A wind had sprung up, just a faint morning breeze, but I could feel it trying to push the car to the right while I bucked it with the wheel.

'Again the road constricted to a narrow, white band with overpasses that seemed like small black holes, and at the speed I was going I had to steer accurately to pass through them. But even before the brain had grasped what was to be done, the car had already streaked on.

'I couldn't understand that my brain should be slower than the speed of my car. Again and again I had that strange impression that I had to aim in order to get through.'

While the Mercedes boys were still at breakfast, news reached the hotel that the Auto-Union team, complete with a very fast projectile and Bernd Rosemeyer, had arrived at the autobahn.

By this time, the 'faint morning breeze' had increased considerably. The tree tops were waving, the sky had become overcast with torn-off shreds of clouds scuttling across it. This was no weather for record-breaking. Furthermore, the Auto-Union attempt was totally unnecessary. Germany had all the prestige she could possibly need. This apparently impulsive action was taking inter-team rivalry to absurd lengths. Indeed, it was turning the whole thing into a race.

If Rosemeyer had been less fearless, he might have paid heed to the signs. As it was, he probably regarded them as adding spice to the challenge. He set off on his first run, and failed to break the Mercedes record. A few moments later, he went off again. This time, he didn't come back. A gust of wind hit the car as it came out from beneath one of the underpasses and sent it spinning off the road. Bernd Rosemeyer was killed outright.

Years later, Alice Caracciola told me: 'If he'd lived, it would probably only have been a reprieve. As a Luftwaffe pilot, he'd almost certainly have been shot down early in the war.'

Inevitably, the German appetite for records could never be fully appeased until it had the ultimate—the World Land Speed Record. To this end, Porsche designed a car 29 feet long, which weighed three tons and was powered by a V12 Daimler-Benz engine rated at 2,500 b.h.p. It was thought to be capable of 405 m.p.h. and had short wings to keep the wheels on the ground. The original idea had been to make the bid on the salt flats at Bonneville. But then the authorities had the notion that if Germany was going to break the record, it was best done on patriotic German concrete and not upon alien salt. This created a delay, and then the outbreak of war caused the whole thing to be cancelled—which may have been just as well.

By the middle of 1934, Mercedes Benz and Auto-Union had become virtually unbeatable. Even the Alfa Romeos couldn't compete with them. There were one or two attempts to slow down the thunderous silver cars—such as when, in a French Grand Prix, they introduced a chicane—but they were of no avail. The Italians may have imagined that they were on to a sure thing in the 1939 Tripoli Grand Prix. The Grand Prix formula of those days was a free-for-all. However, for this race, the Tripoli authorities imposed a $1\frac{1}{2}$-litre limit on engines. This, they imagined, would put the big Mercedes cars out of the running.

They clearly had an inaccurate impression of Mercedes Benz determination. When the ship left Naples for Tripoli, the familiar trilby-hatted figure of Alfred Neubauer was seen to be on board. There were also the Mercedes drivers and some mysterious shapes swathed in tarpaulin.

Unbeknown to anyone outside the factory, Mercedes had been quietly designing and constructing $1\frac{1}{2}$-litre cars to comply with the rules. With Lang and Caracciola driving, they took first and second places in the race.

With France torn apart by strikes and economic upheavals, not even the great Bugatti was in a position to challenge the German might. In 1936 and 1937, the French Grand Prix was relegated to the status of a sports car race. There was no Le Mans 24-Hour Race in 1936. In the following year, the French may have found some crumb of comfort in the fact that it was won by Wimille and Benoist in a Bugatti, with Delahayes finishing second and third and a Delage in fourth place. But, in Grand Prix races, their day was over.

Between 1934 and 1939, Mercedes won thirty-two victories, and Auto-Union twenty-two, making a total of fifty-four for Germany. Alfa Romeo won eight. As in so many other aspects of the Axis relationship, and in spite of the fact that both his son and chauffeur were now racing drivers, Mussolini had to content himself with the role of junior partner.

On the Grand Prix front, nobody else won anything at all.

German motor racing had become an obsession. The cars were the pride of the country. The drivers represented an élite who might be forgiven almost anything. Caracciola, whose first wife had committed the cardinal Nazi sin of having Jewish blood in her veins, had elected to live in Switzerland after 1928. But this didn't detract from his position as one of the heroes of the Third Reich.

Indeed, such was Hitler's regard for the prestige created by successful motor racing, that he gave the sport its own Korpsführer. This was a rough-mannered Bavarian with a deep voice named Hüehnlein, who was given to making enormously long-winded speeches after races. The drivers had to stand there patiently listening to him, when all that they really wanted was to get back to the hotel and have a hot bath. Caracciola had described him as 'a bumbling, good-natured fellow, who had honestly believed in his national-socialistic ideals'. Certainly, unlike most members of the Nazi Party's hierarchy, he made no attempt to cash in on his position. He lived, very modestly, in a three-roomed flat in Munich. He died in 1942.

According to Alice Caracciola, 'Motor racing was at its gayest before the politics began. After nationalism, it had the Fatherland on its shoulders.' The prize for winning the German Grand Prix was 20,000 marks. The winner could do whatever he pleased with it, so long as the money remained in Germany.

In his *Split Seconds*, Raymond Mays recalls winning a German hill-climb in those days. It was made perfectly clear to him that he might as well spend the prize money on the spot, for he would not be allowed to take it back to England. Mays at the time needed every available item of currency for development work—no matter whether it happened to be a pound or a reichsmark. Eventually, he decided to smuggle the money out by pushing the notes up the exhaust pipes of his car and into the manifold. At the frontier, the German Customs authorities insisted that each of the sparking plugs be taken out. Luckily they never thought to look elsewhere, and Mays got the cash home.

The keystone of the Mercedes team was Alfred Neubauer. He was an enormous man, half-Czech, half-Austrian, who had entered the motor industry by way of Austro-Daimler and, after a not particularly successful phase as a Mercedes driver, had gone in for management.

Alice Caracciola told me: 'Neubauer was life in every finger. He had very small feet and hands. He moved surprisingly quickly and, in view of his weight, he was remarkably agile.'

He ruled the pits with the ferocity of a Prussian sergeant-major. Away from the motor-racing scene, however, he was a most genial person. Over dinner, with a bottle of champagne inside him, he could keep the company amused for hours with good stories, which he told extremely well. He was also an art lover, and would often slip away to admire some masterpiece in a church or a museum.

His trade mark at the circuit was his black and red flag. He used it to wave drivers in for refuelling or else to wave them on. On one occasion, when he considered that the Press was making a nuisance of itself, he hit a journalist over the head with it.

It was Neubauer who devised the Mercedes system of rewards. Ten per cent of all prize money was deducted for the mechanics. What remained was divided by three and shared equally by the top drivers. The idea, of course, was to reduce the importance of winning—and, therefore, make it easier for Neubauer to weave his tactical plots.

When an occasion called for it, Neubauer was capable of considerable courage. During the German Grand Prix of 1938, Von Brauchitsch's car, with 80 gallons of fuel on board, caught fire at the pits. Neubauer rushed up to it, helped the driver to get the steering wheel off, dragged him out of the cockpit, threw him on to the ground, and beat the flames out with his own coat.

With true Mercedes efficiency, the burning car was saved and Von Brauchitsch was able to go back into the race. However, he didn't get very far. After 3 miles, he spun off on one of the bends and was later seen walking back to the pits with the steering wheel in his hand.

Four men made up the Mercedes team: Rudolf Caracciola, Hermann Lang, Manfred von Brauchitsch, and a young Englishman named Richard Beattie-Seaman.

Lang was a mechanic who had worked his way up, via test driving, to the top. He was a quiet, shy person, always a little bit apart from the others, who was saving up to build a house for his wife and two sons. He was an excellent driver, taking a very precise approach to the art, and yet he never excited the crowd in the way that Rosemeyer or Caracciola did. At the time of writing, he is still employed at the Mercedes plant.

Von Brauchitsch was considered to be the wild one of the team. He had steel-blue, rather hard eyes, which appeared to burn exceptionally brightly. On the circuit, he sometimes seemed to be undisciplined. However, he survived, and nowadays is living somewhere in East Germany.

Seaman was an Old Rugbeian from an immensely wealthy family. He was tall and dark and quiet. Somebody once described him to me as 'the kind of Englishman who'd look good in a silk dressing gown, smoking a cigarette in a long holder'. When he went motor racing, he wore suède shoes with special fireproof soles.

His parents had hoped that he'd make a career for himself in either law, politics, or else the diplomatic corps—something which would go with the large Edwardian Daimler his father used. It was, indeed, his father's chauffeur who taught Dick Seaman to drive and, thereby, started off the chain of events which was to defeat his parents' plans.

With his friend, that enormously wealthy amateur driver, Whitney Straight, Seaman decided that motor racing could be run on a business basis. It wasn't long before he had become one of the favourites of Brooklands, where, according to William Boddy, the atmosphere was still one 'of sartorial elegance and garden party surroundings'.

When still at Cambridge, he learned to fly and, like many of today's drivers, used to pilot his own light aircraft to meetings. He owned several cars of his own. Among them was an ancient 1½-litre Delage, which had been designed eleven years previously, and in which he won four races.

It was his determination and ability with the Delage that brought him to the attention of Neubauer. He was summoned to the Daimler Benz factory, invited to do a test run, and presently offered the position of reserve driver.

He moved to Germany, where, to his mother's disapproval, he eventually married a German girl.

His big opportunity occurred in the German Grand Prix of 1938. After sixteen laps, he arrived in the pits to refuel 10 seconds behind Von Brauchitsch. When the latter's car caught fire Neubauer gave Seaman a push in the direction of the chequered flag. Caracciola was suffering from a stomach upset at the time, and Lang's car had been misfiring; now, with Von Brauchitsch in trouble, the twenty-five-year-old Englishman was the Mercedes Benz team's only hope.

Seaman did as he was told and won the race in front of a crowd estimated at 350,000. Afterwards, *The Autocar* happily headlined its editorial 'An Englishman is the Toast of Germany'. When Korpsführer Hüehnlein presented him with the trophy, he was seen to give a somewhat unconvincing Nazi salute. Afterwards, he remarked to a journalist that 'I only wish it had been a British car'.

The political situation was becoming increasingly grave. In 1939, Mussolini instructed his drivers not to compete in the French Grand Prix. For Seaman in Germany, things must have been extremely difficult. At least once, he thought about packing up and coming home. However, his friend, Lord Howe, reassured him that he was serving the country's interests by staying out there.

Then came the Belgian Grand Prix of 1939. The race began in heavy rain and the circuit was so slippery, that even Caracciola (who was nicknamed 'The Rainmaster') skidded. On the twenty-second lap, while chasing an Auto-Union, Seaman spun off at the very tight hairpin which goes by the name of La Source. His car hit a tree and, before help could reach him, it had caught fire. When they did get close enough, there was some difficulty in removing the steering wheel. Eventually, they got him out. He was severely burned but still alive.

The energetic Dr. Glaeser, who acted as medical officer to the Mercedes Benz and Auto-Union teams, accompanied him to hospital in the ambulance. As well as burns, Seaman was suffering from a severe kidney injury and his right arm was broken.

He revived sufficiently to talk to his wife. But, shortly after midnight, Richard Beattie-Seaman died. Among the wreaths at his funeral was one from Adolf Hitler.

That excellent American writer Ken Purdy once gave it out as his opinion that 'Of those in the Mercedes team, Rudolf Caracciola was the best'. Certainly, whenever people compile lists of the five greatest drivers his name always appears on them. His parents owned an hotel at Remagen on one of the banks of the Rhine. Young Rudolf, however, wanted no part of an hotelier's career. He became apprenticed at a garage, later became a Mercedes dealer in Berlin, and took up motor racing. He won the first German Grand Prix at the Avus circuit in 1926.

When Mercedes withdrew from motor sport at the end of 1931, he joined the Alfa Romeo team for a year. Afterwards, he joined forces with Chiron to form their own *équipe*, which was called the Scuderia C.C. They bought a couple of cars from Alfa Romeo, and Daimler Benz put a diesel truck at their disposal.

While practising for the Monaco Grand Prix of 1933, Caracciola had one of the two serious crashes which marred his career.[1]

---

[1] The other occurred while practising for the Indianapolis '500' in 1946. Some unknown object struck him on the head, and he lay unconscious in hospital for eleven days.

Due to brake failure, he hit a stone wall and sustained a bad leg injury, which kept him in hospital for over a year. By the time he was released, Mercedes were back in the game.

After 1928, he and his first wife, Charlotte, lived mostly at Arosa in Switzerland. One day, Charlotte was out ski-ing with friends, when she was killed by an avalanche. For Caracciola, this tragedy, added to all the agony he had endured from his damaged leg, made it seem like the end of the road. Eventually, it was his friend Chiron who went up to Arosa and talked him into taking an interest in life, which meant motor racing, once more.

In 1936, he married Alice Hoffman. As early as 1929, he had bought a plot of land at Lugano with the idea of building a house on it. Now, securely wedded to Alice and at the peak of his fame as a driver, he at last got around to it.

Like so many other drivers, he was a quiet man. He disliked night clubs and parties. He believed that drivers preferred the company of other drivers since only they truly understood the hazards of their profession. Even on these occasions, however, he tended to drift away. At a party on board ship, he'd silently wander off on his own, to commune with the stars from the boat deck. On land, he'd slip away in his car and go for a drive.

He was a man who needed to be married, but didn't particularly want girl friends. He had no hobbies. His wife once tried to interest him in the idea of stamp collecting, but it didn't catch on. He read little, but wasn't averse to doing jobs around the house. By nature he was very neat, and his long, sensitive, fingers (which were in marked contrast with his powerful, stocky figure) handled things delicately, precisely. He wore white shirts, which he always kept on hangers, smoked fairly heavily, and used a lemon preparation to remove the brown stains from his fingers. He took an occasional glass of champagne or whisky, but disliked brandy. Above all things, he enjoyed lying in the sun.

Unlike Chiron, who talked voluably and often became excited, he was a very calm person. Once, just before a race when all the other drivers were in their cars, his wife asked: 'Hadn't you better get in yours?' He smiled and replied: 'They can't very well start without me. I'm in the front row.'

Said Alice Caracciola: 'He loved his engine. He'd only go extremely fast if it was necessary to go extremely fast. "Why tire the engine unnecessarily?" he used to say. He asked of the motor as much as it could give without killing itself. That is why he had so many victories.

'He was always very disciplined. He believed in the pit singals and obeyed them blindly. He once said: "The pits know everything —they are cool-headed." '

Rudolf Caracciola, who survived all the hazards of the circuits, died of a liver complaint in 1959. He was only fifty-eight years old. 'But,' says his widow, 'perhaps he died at the right time. There was no anticlimax, no bathos. Perhaps he died at a moment when life would begin not to mean so much. Maybe it was better.'

In 1939, motor racing was about to die for a second time. When Great Britain declared war on Germany on September 3rd, 1939, Nuvolari, Lang and Von Brauchitsch were busy racing an Auto-Union and a pair of Mercedes at Belgrade. When, in the following year (Italy, remember, was still neutral), the Tripoli Grand Prix took place, the Alfa Romeos had the field to themselves once more. The inimitable reek of the Mercedes Benz exhaust fumes—which, according to Raymond Mays, 'smelt like boot polish and acted like tear gas'—was missing.

Characteristically, the first action of Caracciola when war broke out was to telephone his friend Chiron in Italy. Chiron, being Monagasque, was in danger of being interned. Thanks to Caracciola's call, he reached Switzerland just in time. Later, Chiron ran an escape route for crashed R.A.F. aircrews, and survived to take part in post-war events. Nowadays he is general manager of the races at Monaco and of the Monte Carlo Rally.

Robert Benoist, who was also engaged in underground activities during the war, was less fortunate. He was murdered by slow strangulation in Buchenwald.

' "Now! Now!" cried the Queen. "Faster! Faster!" And they went so fast that at last they seemed to skim through the air, hardly touching the ground.'
                    LEWIS CARROLL *Through the Looking Glass*

Part Three
Towards the present

14 Where do we go from here?

In the improbable event of a car ferry being wrecked on a desert island, one might expect the various nationals on board to react in equally various ways. The Americans would attempt to buy up all the vehicles and resell them. The British would line the cars up, bumper to bumper, from one end of the island to the other, and then grumble about the traffic chaos. The French would organise a motor race.

The ink was scarcely dry on the surrender documents before they were busy arranging the first post-war event. It took place in the Bois de Bologne, Paris, on September 9th, 1945. The race itself was known as the Grand Prix de la Liberation: the first prize was called the Coupe des Prisoniers. Huge crowds turned out to watch it. Amid great enthusiasm, Jean-Pierre Wimille was the first to cross the finishing line. He was driving a 4·7 Bugatti.

It was a most appropriate victory, for Wimille had a very good war record. He had served in the French Air Force until France capitulated. Then, with a number of other drivers, he worked for the Resistance. Later, he became a liaison officer in North Africa.

Peace was a great blessing, but it certainly didn't produce

plenty. So far as ordinary motorists were concerned, there were no new cars to be had—only time-scarred second-hand jobs at prices which reflected those of the black market. Petrol was equally scarce and pretty inferior stuff it was, too. In Britain another six years were to go by before branded motor spirit returned to the garages. In the meanwhile, people had to content themselves with a loathsome concoction known as 'Pool Petrol', which was guaranteed to cause any engine to pink.

However, this did nothing to daunt the enthusiasm of the motor-racing men. Raymond Mays was composing the appeal which, if things went as he hoped, would produce a grand prix car for Britain. Alfa Romeo were lovingly unwrapping a batch of Type 158s, which had been carefully stored away during the war. Enzo Ferrari was putting finishing touches to drawings, which, by 1947, would produce the first of his own noble breed.

The revival of grand prix racing was tolerably quick. In 1946, the Belgian and Spanish events were held once more; and by the following year everything was almost back to normal—though it was not until 1950 that the Allied forces quit the large military establishment which had been set up at Nurburgring, and the German Grand Prix could take place again.

In Britain, of course, there were problems. Brooklands had always been the place for motor racing. Admittedly, in the 'thirties, there had been Donington, but this had never achieved the mystique of the older circuit. Perhaps, in a way, Brooklands was a symbol. If you took it away, you removed motor racing from Britain.

The trouble about Brooklands was the aircraft industry. The needs of the First World War had caused little sheds to become big ones. During the Second, things had got completely out of hand. The circuit had been requisitioned by the government for the building and repairing of Vickers aircraft. Supports for camouflage netting had badly damaged the surface of the track, and the fact that some sections had been used for the manufacturing process hadn't helped matters. The buildings, of course, had proliferated.

It required a considerable exercise of the imagination to recall the days of Bentleys belting along the top of the banking, and the garden party airs and graces of the members' enclosure.

Financially, there was less to complain about. Brooklands was a public company. During the war years its affairs had been in the hands of three businessmen, one of whom was Sir Malcolm Campbell. They had produced what Mr. C. W. Haywood,

Chairman of Brooklands (Weybridge) Ltd., described in a statement issued to shareholders on December 31st, 1945, as 'a thoroughly sound balance sheet'.

People were now looking forward to the day when the planemakers would take their stuff elsewhere, and the circuit could revert to its original role.

The first hint that things weren't going to be quite so simple occurred when the Bentley Drivers' Club filed an application to use the track. It was treated with an air of evasive secrecy, which suggested that something nasty was going on beneath the surface. Before very long there was talk of a plot by Vickers Armstrong and the Ministry of Aircraft Production to buy the circuit outright.

By the end of January, 1946, the fate of Brooklands as the nation's motor-racing Mecca was sealed for ever. Accompanied by such statements as 'The government considers it desirable that the present occupancy be continued', it was revealed that the Brooklands directors had accepted an offer of £330,000 from Vickers Armstrong.

Commented *Motor*: 'One of the earliest results of a Socialist Government is to deprive the motorist of one of the only two places in this country where long-distance, high-speed motoring events could be held and witnessed. Deplorable as such an action may be considered from a purely sporting viewpoint, it is even more remarkable as proof that unco-ordinated planning leads to far worse results than unregulated private action.'

The Brooklands directors were accused of having sold the circuit 'down the river at precisely the moment when a testing track is most needed for the development of cars for the export market', and it was pointed out that 'a car which can't sustain a steady 60 or 70 m.p.h. without a breakdown or excessive fuel consumption will be rated a faliure'. Producing such a model of high-performance reliability was going to be difficult, since Britain was now one of the few countries in the world where manufacturers were without any high-speed testing facilities.

In their own defence, the directors of Brooklands pointed out that it would have been some considerable time before the track could have been reopened for motor racing. With the prevailing shortage of labour and materials, it would have been a monstrous task, simply moving such a large chunk of the aircraft industry to another site. And, even if that were done, there was a big job of reconstruction to be carried out before any racing could take place. During this period, it was quite possible that the ministry might slap a compulsory purchase order on the circuit. Wasn't it, surely, better to settle for ready cash—rather than for a long period of inactivity and uncertainty?

The argument continued. While it was still blazing, a luncheon was given at Claridges on March 2nd, 1946, by the newly formed British Motor Racing Research Trust to publish details of a new grand prix car to be called the B.R.M. (for British Racing Motors). The chairman of the Trust was Donald McCullough of B.B.C. fame. The master mind was, of course, Raymond Mays. Among the guests was Henderson Tate, Regional Controller, Ministry of Supply, who said that the project was of great personal interest to him. 'The government,' Mr. Tate explained, 'feel that there is no doubt that the participation of a British racing car team could have none other than the greatest advantages and far-reaching effect. It must raise prestige abroad, and it is an opportunity of "waving the flag", which is so important today.'

Nobody seemed to find any undue irony in the fact that, at that particular moment, there was nowhere in which to 'wave the flag' in Britain, and nowhere to test the potential flag-waver.

As it happened, by a nice stroke of justice, the very aeroplanes which had destroyed Brooklands were to be the salvation of English motor racing. The Ministry of Defence had built a war-time aerodrome near a village in Northamptonshire. It was used for the training of bomber pilots. Afterwards, it fell into disuse until the R.A.C. decided that it could be transformed into a motor-racing circuit. The club's officials approached the ministry, which presently agreed to lease it for motor sport. The name of the village was Silverstone. Nowadays the lease of the circuit is held by the British Racing Drivers' Club.

Later on, another track was built at Aintree. The British Grand Prix was held there on four occasions between 1955 and 1962. Then, after Aintree had capitulated to a property development deal, the Grand Prix circuit at Brands Hatch in Kent was opened. Since 1964, the British G.P. has been held at Brands Hatch on even years and at Silverstone on odd ones.

The first British Grand Prix to be run at Silverstone was on September 28th, 1948, before a crowd of over 100,000 spectators. The Alfa Romeo team was having a spot of financial trouble at the time (later solved by a £50,000 grant from the Italian government) and was unable to be present. Enzo Ferrari was having other, less clearly defined, worries and his cars weren't there either.

However battered she may have been by the misfortunes of war, Italy's status as a motor-racing power had in no way diminished. It was just like the good old days of the three-cornered fights between Alfa Romeo, Auto-Union and Mercedes-Benz—except that there were no longer any Auto-Union or Mercedes cars. Consequently, the Alfas won everything in sight with quite monotonous regularity.

When it was announced that they wouldn't be present at Silverstone, there must have been an almost audible sigh of relief. Now, with a bit of luck, some other country would get a look in.

In fact, it didn't work out quite like that. Armed with a pair of 4CLT/48 Maseratis, Luigi Villoresi and Alberto Ascari drove night and day across the Continent, and arrived at Silverstone just in time to put in four laps of unofficial practice.

Ascari had shown himself to be faster than anyone else; but, since it hadn't been official, he and his fellow countryman were stationed on the last row of the grid. The circuit turned out to be rather slower than people had expected it to be, and it was also somewhat slippery. However, the two Italian maestros cut through the field like a pair of knives through soft butter. Villoresi finished first, in spite of the fact that his rev counter was shaken adrift at one point in the race, and spent the rest of the time lodged underneath the clutch pedal (thereby depriving him of the clutch). Ascari finished second, and Bob Gerard came third in an E.R.A., which pleased the crowd no end. It was the first time a British car had been placed in a Grand Prix for many a long day, and the first time that a British driver had finished anywhere near the top since the death of Dick Seaman.

There are generations of drivers—just as there are generations of cars. During the last war, a number of the former had retired from the sport. Some had been killed. But, for the first two or three years of peace, the old names kept on cropping up, and they were usually out in front. When the Italian Grand Prix was resumed in 1947, it was won by Trossi in an Alfa; and, in that same year, the first post-war French G.P. was won by Chiron in a Talbot-Daracq. Wimille, who was signed on by Alfa Romeo, was adding to his collection of trophies. Varzi had staged a come-back in 1946 after nine years in retirement (some of them in a nursing home undergoing a narcotics cure), and was showing that the old hand had lost none of its cunning; and Raymond Sommer was driving extremely well—though with less success than his considerable panache deserved.

There is, behind motor racing, a strange and terrifying brutality. The process of natural selection is carried out with no mercy and without regard to past performances. Whatever evil god governs the sport wields the chopper and, *bang*, a driver is gone. More often than not, there is neither rhyme nor reason about it.

The years of 1948 and 1949 were wretched in this respect. Achille Varzi, however temperamental and uncertain he may have been in his private life, was one of the most careful drivers of them all. Nobody was more particular about the way in which his car was prepared: few people took greater pains to ensure that, in the heat of a race, the heart never overruled the head.

Consequently, he had only suffered one serious crash. That was at Tunis in 1936, when the rear suspension of his Auto-Union collapsed. He left the road at 125 m.p.h., but emerged from the wreckage unhurt.

Enzo Ferrari has gone on record as saying that he surpassed even Nuvolari for 'the cold perfection of his style'. Certainly, as many writers have remarked, Varzi was the ice and Nuvolari was the fire. But all his cold, calculating brilliance wasn't enough to protect him on June 30th, 1948, when he was practising for the Grand Prix at Berne.

It was raining. The road was wet and greasy. He drove into a left-hander at 110 m.p.h.—and then, suddenly, his experimental Alfa Romeo broke away at the back. It went into a broadside skid, hit a pole and turned over. Varzi, who was wearing a cloth helmet, had his head crushed. He was killed in the driving seat.

In January of the following year, Jean-Pierre Wimille was practising for a round-the-houses race in Palermo Park, Buenos Aires. His car was a little Gordini-Simca. There had been some talk about its steering, which seemed to be worrying him. At all events, he came round a corner very quickly, found that spectators had drifted over on to the track, and braked hard. The car skidded and crashed. Wimille died ten minutes after being admitted to hospital.

Crowd control was always one of the less satisfactory features of events in South America. In 1953, an enormous number of people turned out to watch the Argentine G.P. On the 32nd lap a spectator walked across the track just as Farina was coming up in his Ferrari. Farina swerved violently, went into a skid and shot into a thick cluster of onlookers. He escaped with a broken ankle, but fifteen spectators were killed and another thirty had to be rushed to hospital.

Then it was Raymond Sommer's turn. In 1950, this extremely colourful character, who was variously known as the 'Wild Boar of the Ardennes' and 'Cœur de Lion', was driving a little 1100 c.c.

Cooper in a minor French event. The steering broke: he crashed and was killed. Later on, Peter Collins, Stuart Lewis-Evans and Wolfgang von Trips were killed in grands prix events. On the whole, however, far more major drivers have perished in minor races or else in practice. Furthermore, the majority of fatalities have been caused by the car hitting a tree or a post. That is one of the reasons why more top drivers have lost their lives on Continental circuits than in Britain, where there are fewer trees lining the tracks.

But there is always somebody, waiting as it were in the wings, ready to take over. The driver who finished fourth in the race which cost Wimille his life was an Argentinian mechanic whose name, according to one motoring magazine, was 'Sangio'. Later in the year, when this obviously very promising performer finished second in the Argentine Grand Prix (in those days, they called it the Eva Peron Grand Prix), they got it right, and people in Europe began to talk about Juan Manuel Fangio.

After the last war, and heaven knows how they'd managed to live with it for so long, the Association Internationale des Automobile Clubs Reconnus changed its unwieldy name to the somewhat more simple Fédération Internationale de l'Automobile. This august institution, which has its headquarters in Paris, is concerned with all aspects of motoring. To make things easier, the general assembly (it meets once a year, usually in October) is divided into two sections: the Section Internationale de Tourisme de Technique et de Circulation, which is a rather long-winded way of saying 'touring', and the Section Sportive Internationale. The latter deals with motor sport matters and is subdivided into two further sections: the Commission Sportive Internationale (founded in 1922) and the Comission Internationale de Karting.

If one goes on with this game of opening up boxes, only to find smaller ones inside, the C.S.I. can be made to yield others, such as a technical committee, a circuit owners committee, and so on.

When one considers how many people (and, indeed, vested interests) are involved, it sometimes seems a miracle that the C.S.I. manages to achieve anything at all. As the body responsible for international motor sport, it has to produce a policy which will ensure that racing is fast enough to be exciting; that it is no more dangerous than is absoutely necessary; and that it contributes something to the breed of cars in general.

During the two years following the war, Formula 1 was run on a *formula libre* basis, while the C.S.I. fished around for a suitable set of regulations. The deliberations produced, in 1947, a 4½-litre limit for un-supercharged engines, 1½ litres for supercharged.

This formula survived for the next seven years. In 1954, it was changed and Formula 1 engines were confined to 2½ litres un-supercharged. In 1961, the limit was reduced still further to 1½ litres un-supercharged. Finally, in 1966, it was raised to 3 litres un-supercharged, or 1500 c.c. for blown engines.

The C.S.I. never wants for critics. The decision which caused the greatest uproar was that 1½-litre limit of 1961, which was enforced entirely in the interests of safety. People said that it made racing dull; that it inhibited development work; and, though the logic of this is hard to see, that it made motor racing less likely to contribute to the evolution of the ordinary production car. Even the drivers were against it, for they asserted that it gave them less opportunity to show off their skills. Nevertheless, one has to remember that the 1955 crash at Le Mans, in which eighty-one spectators and one driver were killed, had alarmed the world. During a comparatively short period, such fine drivers as Peter Whitehead, Ken Wharton, Raymond Sommer, Archie Scott-Brown, Luigi Musso, Stuart Lewis-Evans, Peter Collins, Ivor Bueb, and Jean Behra had all been killed in motor races. Something, clearly, had to be done to halt this appalling toll of casualties.

Possibly the C.S.I. went too far in the opposite direction. Major Harold Parker, the R.A.C.'s delegate to the F.I.A., told me: 'Cutting down the size of the cars wasn't necessarily making them go any slower. They could be made to go just as fast, and it made everything more expensive and less manageable. The manufacturers in the U.K. were very cross.

'And so we decided to get the Formula back to 3 litres. This would mean that they wouldn't have to spare the metal. But, again, the manufacturers cursed—even though we thought it might encourage more development of engines and chassis.'

Meanwhile, during the post-war years, the Italian cars were turning out to be virtually unbeatable. At the 1949 General Assembly of the F.I.A., the Italian delegate, Count Antonio Brivio, suggested that there should be a World Championship of Drivers. The Assembly agreed, which must have pleased the Automobile Club d'Italia enormously. There was little doubt that, in 1950 and into the foreseeable future, the championship would be won by an Italian driver at the wheel of an Italian car.

Things worked out as Brivio must have hoped they would. In the first year (1950) the winner was Giuseppe Farina in an Alfa Romeo. In 1951, an Alfa Romeo was again the champion's mount, though the title holder was Juan Manuel Fangio from South America. At the end of the year, Alfas retired from single-seater racing, but this did nothing to diminish Italian supremacy. For the next two years. Alberto Ascari, driving Ferraris, won the championship.

It was not, indeed, until 1954 that the first signs became apparent of Italian overlordship coming to an end. It was all strangely reminiscent of a period twenty years earlier. The threat, then, had come from a team of silver cars, each with a three-pointed star on its front, and led by a portly racing manager named Alfred Neubauer. Now, for the second time in history, Neubauer was on the march.

15 Le Mans super spectacular

It took the Circuit Permanent de la Sarthe, which is where the Le Mans 24-Hour Race is held each year, four years to recover from the battering it had received during the war. For a brief period in 1940, the aerodrome at Le Mans was used by the R.A.F. in the face of bombing from the Luftwaffe. Presently, the British airmen moved out and the German airmen moved in. They expanded the airfield and used the long stretch of straight, which passes the pits, as a runway. All this was accompanied by opposition from the R.A.F.

The final damage was done by the German airmen, as they, in turn, moved out. There was no question of leaving the place as they had hoped to find it. They blew up just about everything in sight.

What with one thing and another, it was not until the beginning of 1949 that the Automobile Club de l'Ouest was able to start repairing the damage. The project was government aided, and work to the tune of £130,000 was carried out.

It was, as everyone agreed when they turned up for the race on June 25th and 26th, 1949, a very fine job. A line of concrete pits,

¼-mile long, had been built. There were large concrete grandstands, a pavilion for the timekeepers, a restaurant which could seat 1,000 people, a press box complete with telephones and a bar, a tunnel under the track, a bridge over it—oh yes, and tourist offices, an art exhibition, small bars, tobacconist stalls and umpteen magazine stalls.

The Le Mans 24-Hour Race has always been much more than a motor sport event. It is France off duty, a place of inconsequential happenings, a series of spectacles, some of them big and some of them small, and the biggest of all being a number of cars which race round the track for hours on end, surrounding the island in the middle by a band of steel and uproar.

Nineteen forty-nine's Le Mans 24-Hour Race was just as it should have been. The Minister of Transport and Tourism arrived in state, and everybody booed him, which was rather unfair. Wasn't it his government which had done so much to finance the reborn circuit? Still, everybody boos somebody at Le Mans. If there isn't a cabinet minister handy, they catcall the policemen (affectionately called 'poulets' in that part of the world). It's all in the general mood of being, as the French so neatly put it, *en fête*.

Fifty-two cars took part in the race, which was won by a Ferrari driven by Chinetti and Lord Selsdon. Nowadays, they have rules about how long a driver can and can't drive at Le Mans. In those days, they let them use their own discretion. Chinetti used his to the extent of motoring for over twenty-two hours out of the twenty-four. Towards the end, his clutch was slipping badly, and the cockpit was swimming in oil. Nevertheless he came home 9·92 miles ahead of the second car (a Delage).

Possibly because of the trouble during the later laps, his average speed was 4·28 m.p.h. slower than that of Wimille and Veyron, when they romped home to victory at Le Mans in a 3·3 Bugatti back in 1939.

Throughout the history of the 24-Hour Race, there have been phases in which the event has been won for several years on end by a particular make of car. During the 'twenties, it was the Bentley; in the 'fifties, it was the Jaguar; and in the 'sixties, it was the Ferrari. The pay-off for Jaguar is the easiest to see, for the cars in question represent a missing link in the production sequence. In the beginning, there was the XK120, which sired a motor racing offshoot known as the C-type. This, still on the circuit, begot the D-type which, in turn and returning to production cars once more, produced the E-type. People talk about motor racing improving the breed, but it is seldom that one has an opportunity to see it happening quite so vividly as in the Jaguar history of five victories in seven years at Le Mans. No doubt, one could even pinpoint a moment in the evolution of the E-type, when Le Mans and other racing experience had taught the designers all they needed to know. If it can be traced, it would certainly coincide with the moment at which Sir William Lyons, the presiding genius of Jaguar's, decided to pull out of motor racing.

Now and again, throughout the course of history, there is a disaster which is so overwhelming, so apparently final, that it takes on a significance which transcends the actual happening. The loss of the *Titanic* was such a case. It was much more than the sinking of a ship. It grew in popular imagination, until it seemed to be the end of an epoch.

In motor racing, the Paris–Madrid race was possibly on the scale of the *Titanic*. The Le Mans disaster of 1955 certainly was. Afterwards, many people predicted that it would be the end of motor racing for ever (they said the same thing after Paris–Madrid); and even those who imagined that it would survive the catastrophe, agreed that the sport would never be the same again.

Back in 1952, a fabulous Mercedes-Benz sports car named the 300SL (3-litre, six cylinders) had produced a sensation in motor-racing circles. It arrived out of the blue, took second place in that year's Mille Miglia, first and second at Le Mans, and first and second in the Panamericana race. Then, as suddenly as it had arrived, it departed.

Nobody fooled themselves that this was just a flash-in-the-pan effort on the part of Mercedes. There *had* to be some sort of follow-up. It was almost as if the 300SL was a scout car, executing a brisk cavalry-style manœuvre ahead of the main body.

Sure enough, the next round came in the middle of 1954, when Mercedes-Benz returned to Formula 1 racing. In the following year, there was a team of three cars and the indomitable Neubauer on parade at Le Mans. Among the drivers were Fangio, Moss, Kling and a Le Mans resident who raced under the name of Pierre Levegh (his real name was Bouillon—Levegh being an anagram of his uncle's name 'Veghle').

Levegh was just short of fifty. He was a wealthy industrialist, who owned an interest in a Paris garage and raced for pleasure. His racing career began in 1938, when he drove a Darracq. During the 1947 French Grand Prix at Lyons, his car skidded on a patch of oil and plunged into the crowd. Four people were killed and eleven more seriously injured. Levegh himself spent several weeks in hospital after the crash.

His place in the Le Mans Mercedes-Benz team was partly due to the firm's wish to employ a French driver for a French race. There was also a nice touch of chivalry about it. In the 1952 24-Hours Race, it had been Levegh's misfortune which made it possible for the Mercedes cars to pull off their 1–2. He had been driving for nearly twenty-three hours on the trot and was almost numb with fatigue. With only an hour and a quarter to go, while he was in the lead, a con rod on his Talbot broke and he had to retire. This left the way clear for the two German cars to streak ahead to victory.

Practice for the 1955 Le Mans 24-Hour Race was marred by two unfortunate incidents. The first occurred when Moss was pulling out of the pits rather too hurriedly, and hit a D.B. which was being driven by a Frenchman named Storez. This car hit Jean Behra, who was waiting for Musso to return with the Maserati they were supposed to be sharing. Behra was hurt and had to be taken to hospital.

Late on the Friday evening, with only a few more minutes of practice time to go, Bayol in his 3-litre Gordini somersaulted, overturned in a field, and was carried away with a fractured skull. It seems probable that he took off while going over a hump at between 135 and 150 m.p.h., and tried to correct while he was still airborne.[1]

The race itself was obviously going to be a hard-fought contest of strength and speed between Jaguar and Mercedes—with Mike Hawthorn and Ivor Bueb leading the one team, and Fangio and Stirling Moss the other.

Punctually at 4 p.m., in the Le Mans custom, the starter swept down his flag and the drivers sprinted across the track to their cars. They started their engines and, amid the greatest noise in the world, the race began. From the very beginning, the sports car prototypes were travelling at grand prix car speeds. The 1954 lap record (117·44 m.p.h.) was promptly disposed of by Castellotti in a Ferrari on the second lap (117·49 m.p.h.). Fangio and Hawthorn were passing and then re-passing each other. The vast crowd settled down happily to watch what was obviously going to be the most exciting Le Mans of them all.

The cars had to travel a minimum of 32 laps before refuelling. The Jaguars and Mercedes were going very very sweetly indeed.

[1] The first essential in such cases is to keep the front wheels straight, so that you land squarely on the track.

During the first two hours, none of them came into the pits. By 6 p.m., the leaders were circulating at speeds well ahead of the old lap record. Hawthorn, for example, polished off his first 28 laps at an average speed of 118·9 m.p.h.

It was five minutes past six. Hawthorn, who was approaching the end of his forty-second lap, was due in to refuel. His co-driver Ivor Bueb was waiting for him at the pit counter. Hawthorn's Jaguar was going like a fighter aircraft, but Fangio wasn't far behind him. When he looked in his mirror, Hawthorn could see Fangio and his vivid silver Mercedes.

He wasn't going to surrender an inch of track. He was going to keep on at full bore until the last possible moment. It was reasonable. His Jaguar was equipped for just such a tactic. Its very powerful disc brakes were more than adequate for the occasion.

Thus the procession approached the pits: 1. Hawthorn—going like the clappers, and having just broken the lap record again. 2. Lance Macklin in an Austin-Healey, which wasn't going anything like so fast. 3. Levegh in a Mercedes, which was travelling about 40 m.p.h. faster than Macklin's car. And, behind Levegh, Fangio. Levegh was poised to overtake Macklin. Fangio, in his own sweet time, was ready to overtake Levegh.

Hawthorn jammed on his anchors and swung over to the right *en route* for the pits. Macklin, caught somewhat unawares, jammed on his brakes—and lost it. The wheels of his car locked, and the rear end slid round to the left just as Levegh was coming through.

Levegh's Mercedes hit Macklin's Austin-Healey. The Mercedes spun round several times in the middle of the track, charged into the bank opposite the pits, turned over, shot up into the air, and presently dived into the ground, where it snapped in half just behind the engine bulkhead.

Then it exploded.

The engine and front assembly erupted over the bank and into the midst of the crowd. The tail and the rest of the frame settled on the edge of the track, blazing furiously.

All this happened in less than four seconds. At one point, Macklin's car must have been travelling backwards at 60 m.p.h. By some curious twist of fate, the British driver was unhurt. Fangio managed to avoid the litter of bent and burning metal, and went on through.

Levegh was killed outright.

He was the third driver to die within three weeks. Ascari had just been killed while testing at Monza—whilst, over in America, Bill Vukovich had been killed in a multiple shunt with three other cars in the Indianapolis '500' race. Vukovich had won the '500' in 1953 and 1954.

Hawthorn handed over to Bueb, who went on his way. Suddenly, there was a great silence. And then the loud-speakers got busy transmitting orders to doctors and ambulances. When, finally, the cost was counted, it became clear that over eighty spectators had been killed and over 100 injured. The authorities wondered whether to stop the race.

Wisely, they decided against it. The one really important thing was for the medical services to be able to move about as freely as possible. If that huge crowd had been dismissed, the roads would have been jammed, and it would have been impossible to evacuate the injured. Goodness knows how many more would have died.

Neubauer's first reaction was to withdraw his cars. But it was a big responsibility, and he needed the approval of top brass back at the factory. He tried to get on the phone to Stuttgart. Every line was jammed with outgoing calls. For the next five hours, the two remaining Mercedes cars kept on racing. Shortly after 11 p.m., Neubauer got through. Yes—withdraw all cars. Fangio and Kling returned to the pits. Quietly their cars were taken to the paddock and covered in tarpaulins.

Hawthorn and Bueb won the race, but it was an empty victory. There was no longer anyone to race against. And, in any case, no victory was worth that kind of price.

And then there was the aftermath. Switzerland, Spain and Mexico reacted promptly—by banning motor racing completely. The French government put an embargo on the sport until the rules were revised—which meant that the French Grand Prix of that year had to be cancelled. The German Grand Prix was also cancelled. As for the future of the 24-Hour Race, it hung in the balance for some while.

Of course, there was no lack of opinion about what should be done. One popular thought was that the habit of mixing big cars with small ones was all wrong. How was it possible, these people asked, to run a race in safety, when some of the competitors were capable of between 180 and 200 m.p.h., whilst others could manage no more than 110 m.p.h.? Surely, it would be better to run two races?

Another popular notion was that the number of entries was much too big. Under the rules, sixty cars were allowed to take part. This required 120 drivers, and where could you possibly find 120 men gifted enough to cope with the kind of driving Le Mans required?

Lawrence Pomeroy published his own, highly individual prognosis. Before the 24-Hour Race disaster, he pointed out, the probability of a spectator meeting violent death could be measured at 500,000 : 1. Now the odds had diminished to 170,000 : 1. Equated in terms of life insurance, this meant that a £20,000 life policy for attending a major European race meeting, which might once have cost 5d., would now cost 1s. 2d.

Presently, everything was sorted out. The Le Mans 24-Hour Race *was* to continue, but on a vastly improved circuit. Indeed, £400,000 was to be spent on improving it. The track past the grandstands was to be lowered by $6\frac{1}{2}$ in., and the road widened at this point. The earth removed was to be used to build terraces in front of the stands. So-called 'fortifications' were also to be built to protect the grandstands.

The pits were to be razed to the ground and rebuilt further down the road, enabling the corner by the Dunlop arch to be eased off a shade. The old pit road was to be used as an escape road, and the new pit area would be considerably wider.

A new system of signalling, working by remote control, was to be introduced. Signallers were to be stationed at a point near Mulsanne. They'd receive their instructions by telephone from the main pit area.

With the reconstruction programme came new regulations, Thus:

1. The entry list had hitherto been confined to sixty cars. Now only fifty-two would be allowed to compete.

2. To satisfy the alarm about the ever increasing speeds of prototypes, they would henceforth be limited to $2\frac{1}{2}$-litre engines.

3. The car bodies had to be bigger: in other words, they had to be less like two-seater racing cars and more like everyday sports cars. Racing windscreens were forbidden. Every car had to have a full-width screen.

4. The tanks of cars were limited to about 22 gallons capacity (or, about 295 miles of motoring). The minimum distance between refuelling stops was cut to 28 laps.

5. A 92-octane fuel—either straight petrol, or else a mixture of benzole, alcohol, and petrol—had to be used.

6. Apart from the prototypes, all the cars had to be catalogued models as sold to the general public (which meant that at least 100 had to be manufactured every year).[1]

The Automobile Club de l'Ouest wished to change the date of

[1] As a kind of saving clause, the regulations also contained the words 'or provided for'.

the 1956 24-Hour Race out of deference to the families of those who had been killed. This turned out to be more difficult than they bargained for. Whatever date they picked seemed to clash with some other event. At the Easter Monday meeting at Goodwood that year, there were again rumours that the 24-Hour Race was to be cancelled.

In fact, they did manage to find a date—July 28th and 29th. Apart from an exciting moment, when Paul Frère spun into the bank on the second lap, the race was undramatic. It was won by a privately entered 3·4 Jaguar.

Lance Macklin raced again: in the 1955 Tourist Trophy race, which took place on the Dundrod circuit in Northern Ireland.

Jim Mayers, the son of a wealthy glass manufacturer, was driving a Cooper in the race. For some while, he had been trying to overtake a somewhat slower Mercedes saloon belonging to the Vicomte de Barry, which was keeping to the centre of the road. Presently, on a downhill stretch, Mayers decided to gave a go.

The Mercedes kept on steaming ahead—bang in the middle. Mayers wove to the left and to the right, looking for a gap big enough to let him through, when he suddenly lost control. His car went up the bank and hit a concrete gate post, bounced off it and crashed down on to the middle of the track, and then burst into flames.

A cauldron of blazing wreckage blocked the road. Mayers was killed instantly.

Ken Wharton, who was close on Mayers's heels in a Frazer-Nash, tried to get through on the right. It was too narrow. His car hit the bank, ricocheted off and crashed into the far side, where it caught fire.

Next Bill Smith tried to get through on the left. His Connaught hit the bank with an almighty slap and seemed to dig itself in. Smith was thrown out and killed. Wharton survived.

Among other drivers involved in this fearful shunt was Lance Macklin. He, too, crashed into the bank. He climbed out of his car, took off his crash helmet, and walked away back up the hill.

At that moment, Lance Macklin walked out of motor racing. The whole thing was too fearfully reminiscent of the recent disaster at Le Mans.

The Le Mans 24-Hour Race survived its catastrophe. The

Mille Miglia did not—though, numerically, it was much less serious. The year was 1957.

The Marquis de Portago and his passenger, an American friend of his named Gunnar Nelson, had just cleared Mantua. The Marquis was driving a 3·8 Ferrari, and was lying fifth. Before them was a long stretch of straight road.

Portago got a move on. He must have been travelling at about 150 m.p.h. when it happened. At first, it looked as if a tyre had burst. Later, it became pretty well certain that it was due to mechanical failure. His rear axle had been in a poor state when he clocked in at Mantua, and another driver afterwards reported having seen a wheel and half-shaft by the roadside near the accident.

But the cause is unimportant. Suddenly the Ferrari began a frantic, frightening, zigzagging from one side of the road to the other. Then it left the road and went right into the crowd. Portago and Nelson were killed, and so were five adults and six children among the spectators.

In his book *The Fast Ones*, Peter Miller describes how to cope with spectators. 'The only way to shift the crowd from the corners [he wrote] was to blip the accelerator and slide the tail over wide, which normally did the trick. It made an additional hazard if spectators clustered at a bend as you couldn't tell until the last possible moment whether it was a left-hander or a right-hander. But in some ways they helped, because if you approached a corner at speed and it was deserted it was a sure sign that it was safe to take it flat out. The crowds only congregated, like vultures, where there was a chance of bloodshed.'

In fact, the place at which Portago crashed had seemed to be a comparatively safe place for onlookers. Furthermore, Williams's remedy depends upon a healthy car. If, as was obviously the case with Portago's Ferrari, it had developed a fault, there was nothing which could be done.

Afterwards, there were appeals to save the Mille Miglia. *Motor* headed its editorial 'Reform not Abolition', and advocated that controls through towns, on the lines of the pre-Paris–Madrid races, might be the answer. It also suggested that cars with maximum speeds of over 150 m.p.h. should be confined to closed circuits.

However, the Italian authorities were not to be deflected from their decision. The Mille Miglia was abolished—which left the Targa Florio as the only true road race on the calendar. And the Targa survives to this day.

16 Green over red

Every generation of drivers produces its heroes: the stars which burn more brightly than all the others, the men of genius who are acclaimed as the greatest of all time—but who, since the conditions of motor racing differ so considerably from one age to another, are probably more truly described as the greatest of *their* time.

The nineteen-fifties witnessed the ascent of two men of genius. One of them was a large, heavily built Italian, with an engaging smile and a modest attitude, named Alberto Ascari. The other was a quiet, gentlemanly, Argentinian named Juan Manuel Fangio.

Alberto Ascari was seven years old when his father, Antonio, was killed at Montlhery. From the age of eleven, he developed a passion for motor-cycle racing, which naturally filled his widowed mother with anxiety. This was of great concern to him. As he developed his skill as a racer, he tried to underrate the glamour of the sport by referring to it, simply, as 'my trade'. After he married, he endeavoured to make his home as unlike that of a racing driver as possible. There were no monumental displays of trophies: they were tucked discreetly away in a corner cupboard.

Nuvolari and Varzi had both learned their art on motor cycles, and so did Ascari. Presently Luigi Villoresi began to tutor him in car racing. He took part in his first Grand Prix in 1948 when, in a 1½-litre Maserati, he won the San Remo event. In the following year, he was signed on as a works driver by Ferrari and the long string of victories began. In 1952 and 1953, still driving Ferraris, he won the World Championship of Drivers.

Ascari was always a spectacular driver. He could go so fast that it bordered on recklessness—or, he could handle a car so gently, so smoothly, that it was like an artist executing a delicate design. He always seemed to know which approach was needed; and, even though his instinct was continuously urging him to be out in front, he could hold back when his shrewd sense of tactics suggested it.

Strangely enough for a man who was so successful, he had a strong sense of financial security. At the end of the 1953 season, when he was right on top of the world, Lancia made him an offer. The gist of it was that he would receive a regular income irrespective of the rewards for winning races. Ferrari couldn't match it, and so Ascari moved over to Lancia—in spite of the fact that the firm's grand prix car wasn't yet ready and he'd have to miss a number of events.

By 1955, the new Lancia was ready, and Ascari set off with it to Monaco. The Mercedes team were out in force. Stirling Moss, who was driving one of the German cars, set a scorching pace, Ascari was in second place, trying desperately to make good the 1½ minutes which separated him from the leader.

Twenty laps from the finish, Moss's engine blew up. He just made it to the pits with himself, his engine and the rest of the car drenched in oil. Split seconds later, unaware that he was now in the lead, Ascari came roaring out of the tunnel towards the harbour wall.

At this point, there's a left-hand bend. As he went into it, the wheels on his Lancia locked: he slid sideways across the road, bounced off a bollard, shot up into the air, flew over a cabin cruiser and finally, with a splash and a cloud of steam, dived into the harbour.

Presently he could be seen, still wearing his blue helmet, swimming with a strong overarm stroke towards the shore. He was hauled into a boat with only bruises on his back, a cut nose, and a certain amount of shock to show for his misadventure.

Villoresi, who was driving a Ferrari in the race, saw what had happened. He hurried into the pits to ask whether his friend was all right. When he had been reassured, he went back into the race again.

Ascari went home to recuperate. Four days later, he became restless. Although he hadn't fully recovered, he drove over to Monza, where the Ferrari team was testing a 3-litre machine for the Supercortemaggiore 1,000 km sports car race. He was to have taken part in this event; but, owing to his ducking at Monaco, he'd withdrawn.

He fell into conversation with the Ferrari people. He ate a couple of sandwiches, and then came the inevitable question, 'Mind if I have a go?' Of course they didn't mind. Although he'd left the team, it had been under perfectly friendly circumstances. In any case, whatever Ferrari had done for Ascari had been more than adequately repaid.

One lap, 2 laps . . . just after coming round the curve which is now known as Curva Ascari, he braked suddenly. The car spun and shot off the track, throwing its driver about 25 yards, Alberto Ascari died on the way to hospital.

What went wrong? You can take your choice from the following theories, none of which has been substantiated: 1. He had a blackout resulting from his Monaco injuries. 2. A workman walked across the track (subscribers to this idea even go so far as to suggest that his identity is known, and that he later became a patient in a lunatic asylum near Milan).[1] 3. A deer ambled across the track and Ascari tried to avoid it. 4. The back axle seized up.

The air of mystery which surrounds his death is accentuated by the number of coincidences which link it with his father's. For instance, the P2 Alfa Romeo in which Antonio was killed, and the Lancia which Alberto was contracted to drive, were both designed by Vittorio Jano. Both men were thirty-six years old when they died. Both died on the 26th of the month. Neither accident has ever been fully explained. And so on.

Enzo Ferrari once asked Alberto Ascari why he was so strict with his children. The latter replied: 'I don't want them to become too fond of me. One of these days, I may not come back, and they will suffer less if I keep them a bit at arm's length.'

Juan Manuel Fangio was one of those who survived. Everybody liked Fangio. Raymond Mays once told me: 'He stood out through greatness and simplicity. He was very humble, but a great man.

[1] Or, as another theory has it, he made a full confession to a priest.

Everybody looked up to him and respected him. He was so likeable.'

And, from Tony Brooks: 'He was charming. A real gentleman. Even though, at the wheel, he was totally committed, he had time to respect the social graces, to fulfil his position at the top. Drivers are paid performers, and they owe this to the public and their sponsors. In the 'fifties people like Fangio often did things for nothing. They were prepared to write off many hours putting in appearances at motoring functions or whatever.'

This remarkable man was the son of a house painter in Balcarce, Argentina. He trained as a mechanic, and presently was entering cars tuned by himself in South American events. By the time he invaded Europe, he was already thirty-eight years old and beginning to put on weight.

His first European season was in 1948. It was unspectacular. He only started in one race and never finished it. The car blew up.

1949 was a very different matter. He took part in ten events, won four of them and was placed in two more. By the end of the year, he had been signed on by Alfa Romeo. Thereafter, his rise was astronomic. He just missed being World Champion Driver in 1950; won the championship in 1951; lost it to Ascari the next two years—and then, between 1954 and 1957, he won it four years in succession.

You can no more analyse the style of Fangio than you can explain how Leonardo da Vinci painted a great picture. People talk about his huge powers of concentration—how, on a circuit, his mind worked with the accuracy of a computer. But what do these things mean? They talk about his instinctive genius, but they've said this about other drivers. Fangio had some sort of magic touch, which put him at the top and kept him there. That, imperfect as it may be, is the nearest one can come to any definition.

He retired from motor racing after the Argentine Grand Prix of 1958. In that event, he was beaten by Stirling Moss, which was, perhaps, appropriate. He had often said that Moss was his logical successor as champion. Actually Moss never won the World Championship; but that is another, large and highly complicated story.

In 1951, when Alfa Romeo withdrew from Formula 1 motor racing, Fangio was the hottest property on the market. It may sound like an enviable situation, but it had its snags. The trouble was that nobody could afford him.

For the next couple of years, the Argentinian ace went into the wilderness. He took part in one or two races for Maserati, such as winning the Argentine G.P. (1952) and the Italian G.P. (1953), and had a serious accident in the Monza G.P. of 1952, which kept him away from racing for a while. In any case, the Maseratis of those years were no match for the Ferraris. Not that it really mattered to Fangio. The greatest was yet to come.

The shape of the future had been signalled by the sensational performance of that 300SL Mercedes in 1952. Mercedes-Benz had made a singularly quick recovery from the war. By the early 'fifties, the factory was back in full production: the order book was fat, and exports were expanding. To speed them up, the 300SL, with such revolutionary features as doors which were hinged on the roof, was launched as part of a publicity campaign. In a smaller way, it was comparable with the Ford effort at Le Mans in the mid-'sixties.

When the 300SL was withdrawn at the end of the year, it was by no means the end of things. In the factory at Stuttgart-Unterturkheim, the research department engineers were secretly working on a single-seater racing car. There were many revolutionary features involved. By no means the least of them was that the engine was to be fitted with direct fuel injection.

It needed Mercedes-Benz to do things on this scale. According to one estimate, the new racing shop was staffed by no fewer than 1,200 technicians. When the car was completed, it was valued by one observer at £3 an ounce. And, when the racing programme eventually got going in 1953 and 1954, it was said to cost the firm £60,000 a month. Still, the Mercedes-Benz turnover for 1953 was £75 million, so no doubt they could afford it.

Presently a prototype was ready. It was known as the W196. Karl Kling, the company's chief tester, took it out on one of the tracks at Unterturkheim and reported well of it. Later, it was tried out on a stretch of road 30 miles to the north-east of Stuttgart, where it reached 160 m.p.h. on the flying kilometer. Finally, on the circuit at Hockenheim (near Mannheim: it was more commonly associated with motor-cycle racing in those days), four cars driven by Kling, Lang, Hans Herrmann (a young up-and-comer), and Uhlenhaut (the designer/tester) were turned loose. They all lapped at a steady 125 m.p.h.

The 'Silver Arrows' were ready. Naturally they needed drivers who could bring out the best in them, and so Neubauer got in touch with Fangio.[1] Presently, when the talking stopped, the latter signed a 15-month contract. He was to be paid at the rate of £1,500 a month.

[1] He also signed on Stirling Moss.

All told, seven versions of the 'Silver Arrow' were produced. Once they had got over their early troubles, they began to win race after race after race. Or, to be rather more precise, they won thirty out of the forty-six events in which they took part. They helped Fangio to win his World Championships of 1953 and 1954. And, then, their mission accomplished, they were withdrawn.

One school of thought suggests that Mercedes-Benz retired from motor racing as a result of the 1955 Le Mans disaster (for much the same reason as Lancia withdrew from racing after Ascari had been killed). In fact, the whole racing operation was keyed in with the firm's marketing policy. The Mercedes executives felt that successes on the circuit over a period of from one to two years might be good for sales. And, if any further proof is needed, there's Fangio's contract for *fifteen months*.

After his Mercedes stint, Fangio took the championship in 1956 in a Ferrari, and in 1957 in a Maserati. But the reign of Continental cars in motor racing, which had lasted for so many years, was nearly over. In Britain, interesting things were happening. The country was at last about to become competitive in Grand Prix racing.

It would be nice to write about the British Renaissance. Unfortunately—apart from Edge's Gordon Bennett victory and the Bentley days at Le Mans—the country's international motor-racing reputation was hardly worth talking about, let alone reviving.

The fact that, in the nineteen-sixties, British cars were to dominate the world was largely due to two projects. Strangely enough, initially, they were completely contradictory. Raymond Mays appealed to industry for money to build the B.R.M., because he wanted the country to have a competitive Grand Prix car—the most powerful and highly expensive type of vehicle in the world.

On the other hand, Charles and John Cooper built their famous little '500's' as a reaction against the high cost of racing, which was putting it right outside the average driver's scope.

Mays knew that the object of his operation was to win international trophies: the Coopers never even thought about it. And yet, by one of those weird strokes of irony, they got there first.

The trouble with the B.R.M. was committees. Initially, the enterprise was controlled by a trust of which Tony Vandervell (chairman of Vandervell Products Ltd.), Alfred Owen (head of Rubery Owen), and Bernard Scott (personal assistant to Oliver

Lucas) were members, and Donald McCullough was the chairman. There was also a financial and planning sub-committee, a production sub-committee, and an information sub-committee. The design of the original car was by Peter Berthon with assistance (on its V16 engine) from Rolls-Royce. The number of firms supplying components was enormous. At one time, no fewer than 350 of them were in on the act.

Within the ranks, there was strife. Vandervell and Mays never hit it off and there was general dissatisfaction about the car's inability to win races. Eventually things reached such a state that, at a meeting in Stratford-on-Avon on September 4th, 1952, the trust was wound up. After a number of offers for the cars and equipment had been considered and rejected, Alfred Owen stepped in and bought the project up. Thus the Owen Racing Organisation was formed, but another ten years had to pass before the B.R.M. became the mount of a World Champion.[1]

Tony Vandervell was a man who didn't believe that committees were an effective way of achieving anything. He became more and more impatient with B.R.M. methods, and eventually pulled out. This did not, however, mean that he had lost his enthusiasm for motor racing—nor that he was no longer eager for Britain to have a Grand Prix car that would win races. Indeed, as time went by, the latter became something of an obsession with him. He was continually talking about 'the bloody red cars' and how anxious he was to wipe Italy off the face of the motor-racing map.

His company was an extremely prosperous firm of bearing manufacturers. Since Vandervell was an autocrat, he ruled the factory—as he ruled most things—with uncompromising firmness. When Vandervell said 'We're going to go in for motor racing', there was no one to argue with him.

He began by buying a $1\frac{1}{2}$-litre supercharged Ferrari (he seems to have found no undue irony in the fact that he began his career as a motor-racing *entrepreneur* by using the very cars he had pledged himself to conquer), for the stated purpose of testing his Thinwall bearings. Mays drove it in a British Grand Prix, and afterwards described it as 'the very devil'.

In 1950, Vandervell bought another Ferrari—this time a $4\frac{1}{2}$-litre V12 version. He caused it to be highly modified, and raced it under the name of the 'Thinwall Special'. It never won any major events.

Inevitably, he had to produce a car of his own. The first of the Vanwalls appeared in 1954—without any great success. By 1957,

[1] Graham Hill.

and five versions later, however, things had become very much better. Stirling Moss, Tony Brooks and Stuart Lewis-Evans were driving for him. Moss and Brooks between them won the British Grand Prix at Aintree: Moss on his own won the Pescara and Italian Grands Prix.

The following year was a strange one, and must surely prove how unsatisfactory the points system, used for determining the World Championship, was at that time. During the course of the year, Stirling Moss won four Grands Prix (one in a Cooper, the rest in Vanwalls) and Tony Brooks won three (all in Vanwalls). Nevertheless, when the season came to an end, Mike Hawthorn, who had only won the French Grand Prix, was champion.

If these had been production-car races, in which reliability is obviously an important factor, it might have meant something. Since Formula 1 is a test of speed, and the driver's one task is to make his car go as quickly as possible, it was a negation of the whole idea.

Nevertheless, Vanwall won the constructors' award—and, as Vandervell had hoped, the red cars had been virtually routed.

He was a strange man: tough, impatient, technically very sound (his cars followed the Mercedes example by using direct fuel injection), tremendously ambitious and yet remarkably reserved in some respects. Tony Brooks described him to me as follows: 'Vandervell knew what he wanted, said what he thought. He wasn't a popular figure, though everyone respected him.'

One might have imagined that he would see his racing cars as an excellent way of building up publicity for his firm. Surprisingly, publicity was something he seemed to avoid. He was reticent with the Press, and often observed that the only thing which mattered was results. Perhaps this was the businessman speaking: success is something best shown by a satisfactory audit and least served by talking.

However tough Vandervell may have seemed to be on the outside, he was by no means insensitive. In his monograph on the *Vanwall Grand Prix Car* for Profile Publications, Denis Jenkinson described Vandervell's reaction to the death of Stuart Lewis-Evans nine days after his crash in the Casablanca G.P. of 1958. Vandervell said: 'If it wasn't for my bloody silly passion for racing cars, and my obsession to beat the red cars, this wouldn't have happened.'

'Obsession' was right. He was only really interested in taking part in Grand Prix events—and, once the future of the World Championship seemed to be secure in the hands of other British constructors, he was content to pull out. In any case, his obsession had come pretty close to ruining his health. In January, 1959, he announced his retirement from motor racing 'on doctor's orders'. He was sixty at the time, and heading for a nervous breakdown. In fact, he did produce two more cars—both of them with engines in the rear—but they never amounted to anything. A 1958 version of a Vanwall was presented to the Montagu Motor Museum at Beaulieu, and the Vanwall story came to an end.

The people who put the engine at the back were the Coopers. Indeed, this amazing father and son team, whose only asset was a garage in Surbiton, not only revolutionised the shape of the racing car—they also discovered the next generation of drivers.

After the last war, a handful of enthusiasts had played around with the idea of building small racing cars powered by 500 c.c. motor-cycle engines. The idea had been relatively successful, though there was one enormous drawback. There were hardly any organised races for them.

Nevertheless, these lively midgets appealed to the Coopers, who decided to build a pair of them. Their original designs were based upon a highly modified Fiat '500' chassis powered by a Speedway J.A.P. engine. They were raced for the first time in 1948. Later, they were produced in several different versions. Basically, however, there was a 500 c.c. edition, powered by a Norton engine, for track events, and a 1,000 c.c. with a J.A.P. engine for hill-climbs.

Five-hundred c.c. racing caught on. It became the starting point from which Formula 3 developed, and, wherever they went, the little Coopers were invincible. When the first British Grand Prix was held at Silverstone in 1948, there was a supporting event for these cars. Among those taking part was a cream-coloured Cooper with a youngster aged eighteen behind the wheel. This young man, who had already won a '500' race at Goodwood that year, was described by *Motor*'s reporter as 'up and coming' and received praise for the fact that 'he is very fast, and corners on the limit to gain seconds from possibly faster cars'. His name was Stirling Moss.

Peter Collins was another young driver who began his racing in Cooper '500's'; and, when the Coopers produced a Formula 2 car, with a 2,000 c.c. Bristol engine based on the prewar B.M.W., one of their first drivers was Mike Hawthorn. Until then, Hawthorn had been doing his racing in uncompetitive old Rileys. Now all that was to change, and it was his performance in a Cooper-Bristol which eventually brought him to the notice of Enzo Ferrari.

When building their '500's', the Coopers had decided that the only sensible place to put the engine was at the back. Later, when they began to build bigger cars, they decided that the principle still held good. Among other things, it did away with such inherently unsatisfactory components as a long prop shaft.

In many ways, it was a brave decision. When, in the early 'twenties, a Dr. Rumpler produced a rear-engined racing car at the Daimler-Benz works in Germany, it was regarded with a great deal of scepticism and was never fully developed. Later, of course, Dr. Ferdinand Porsche took up the idea for his Auto-Unions, and was very successful. But that, before the Coopers got busy, was the only experience anyone had ever had of such a system.

One day, a quiet spoken Australian, who'd been reasonably successful with a Cooper-Bristol in Australia and New Zealand, turned up at the Cooper plant. His name was Jack Brabham. Presently Brabham suggested that if they could build a similar car around the 2,000 c.c. Bristol unit, it might do well in Formula 1 events. John Cooper was extremely enthusiastic about the idea. He invited Brabham to assist with the building of the car and, when it was completed, to become a works driver.

But the Bristol was not to be the race-winning engine which put Coopers right at the top, and gave Brabham his World Championships of 1959 and 1960. That distinction belongs to a unit built by Coventry Climax during the war for fire brigade trailer pumps.

One of Brabham's first outings in a Cooper-Climax was in the Monaco Grand Prix of 1957. Much to everybody's amazement, he was lying third when, on the last lap, the fuel pump bracket snapped off. Undaunted, he jumped out of the car and pushed it over the remaining distance. Two other cars overtook him on the way, but he managed to finish fifth. For those who looked for omens about the future, this was something which merited fairly serious consideration.

There was even more to think about after the Argentine Grand Prix in the following January. This event had been preceded by one of those rows which sometimes crop up in motor racing. The official name of the race was the Argentine Temporada (or, as *Motor* quipped, 'Bad Temporada'). The date of it was fixed for January 19th. By mid-December, the British teams hadn't been invited to compete, and there was some doubts about whether the event was going to take place at all. Even by January 8th, the R.A.C. still hadn't seen a copy of the regulations: the distance of the race was unknown and there was uncertainty about what kind of fuel was to be used.

At its 1957 General Assembly, the F.I.A. had decreed that, henceforth, only commercially available petrol should be used in racing cars. This put paid directly to exotic mixtures which were commonly known as 'liquid dynamite' and, indirectly, to superchargers (which produce all sorts of problems unless alcohol is used). One of the questions was whether the Argentine authorities intented the race to conform with the new F.I.A. fuel regulations, or not.

While Vanwall and B.R.M. were still wondering whether the race was on or off, Ferrari and Maserati were quietly crating up their cars and shipping them out to Buenos Aires. This suggested that the Italian factories knew that the race was *on* at a time when the U.K. constructors thought it was probably *off*.

The R.A.C. protested. A spokesman for the Argentine Automobile Club replied that a cable had been despatched on December 17th saying that the race was definitely on—and that, furthermore, he had received a cable back, stating that the British teams wouldn't have their cars ready for racing until April.

This was going *too* far. The R.A.C. applied to the F.I.A., asking for the race to be removed from the list of events which qualified for the World Championship of Drivers. As soon as they heard about this, the Argentinian authorities chipped in with the suggestion that this was a lot of nonsense, since the championship only concerned drivers and had nothing to do with cars. This was not entirely true, for 1958 was the first year of the Formula 1 Constructors' Championship.[1]

By the time the wrangling was resolved, and it was known in Britain that there would be a race and that it would be run on pump petrol, it was too late for Vanwall and B.R.M. to do very much about it. There was, however, one British car which did succeed in crossing the Atlantic in time. It was a Cooper-Climax, built by Rob Walker, that doyen of private entrants, in a small garage at Dorking. The driver was Stirling Moss.

Moss had been intrigued by the rear-engined Coopers and, after trying one out at Casablanca, had said that he'd always be happy to drive one whenever his other commitments allowed. In 1958, he was under contract to Vanwall; but—with that marque, as you might say, grounded—he was available for this race.

The Cooper looked tiny compared with all the other cars on the

[1] The R.A.C. didn't press its protest after the race was over, and the whole matter was quietly dropped.

grid. Once it took off, however, there was no mistaking its power. It was quicker on corners than the Maseratis, but its getaway was quite phenomenal. Rob Walker had been worried about the effect of pump fuel on its performance, for there'd been no time for any detailed experiments. However, Alf Francis, his chief engineer (previously Francis had been Moss's mechanic), was unperturbed. After the Boxing Day meeting at Brands Hatch (in which, with Brabham at the wheel, the Cooper had run away with the *Formula Libre* event), he had bench tested the engine, and found that it went perfectly well. With a 12:1 compression ratio, it produced 180 b.h.p. on pump petrol against 182 b.h.p. on alcohol.

It took 35 laps for Moss to get into the lead, and after that nobody could get near him. When the race was over, his tyres were almost down to the canvas; but this was a mere detail. It was very rare in a *grande épreuve* for a private entrant to secure a place in the face of titanic opposition from the works teams. Rob Walker had done that and more.

The beauty about the little Cooper was its lightness and simplicity. During the 1959 and 1960 seasons, it won the constructors' and drivers' championships in spite of the fact that it was giving away half a litre to the opposition. But what it lacked in power it more than made up for in lack of weight. Furthermore, it was a beautiful car to drive.

Tony Brooks told me: 'With engines at the back, the cars were much easier to drive than are front-engined cars. They required less effort to drive precisely and to reach the limit of adhesion. Now the designers were doing some of our work for us; but the problem of sensing and consistently driving just inside the limit remained.

Colin Chapman of Lotus was the next to adopt the rear-engine principle: B.R.M. followed and so did Ferrari, until the day came when all Grand Prix cars had their power plants at the back. Perhaps that Argentine Grand Prix of 1958 was one of the most significant races in the past two decades.

17 Faster, faster, fastest

If one of those continually talked-about visitors from Another Planet turned up on earth, he'd no doubt find many perplexing things. Motor racing, assuming he came from a competitive community, might be within his understanding; but I'm not at all sure whether he'd manage to make any sense out of the World Land Speed Record.

Racing is a struggle by man against man, car against car. Record breaking is a much more introverted occupation, in which one man and one vehicle are pitted against a stop-watch. Huge sums of money are spent on the act of trying to chip seconds off somebody else's time. The result of it all is a set of figures. If they record less time and more speed than the previous statistics, they win—and everybody becomes very excited. If they don't, the car is taken away, modified, and then the driver has to risk his neck all over again.

In 1947, John Cobb dug out the Napier-Railton which had served him so well before the war, took it to Bonneville Salt Flats, and hoisted the magic number up to 394·20 m.p.h. Later he made an attempt on the water speed record, and was killed. For the next sixteen years, his land record was unbeaten, and virtually, unchallenged.

Cobb's 1947 record was the last time that an internal combustion engine made the running. Keeping in step with the aircraft world, the jet engine took over. At enormous expense, Donald Campbell, son of Sir Malcolm, built his own 'Bluebird'. It was powered by a Bristol Proteus turbo-jet engine, weighed four tons, and had a potentially vivid performance. The list of sponsors was as long as your arm, which was just as well, for the car cost over £1 million.

In 1960, Campbell and 'Bluebird' arrived at Bonneville. After only eleven days of trials, Campbell got up one morning, pointed his car in the right direction, and blasted off in pursuit of the record. Having accelerated to 350 m.p.h. in 24 seconds, 'Bluebird' was suddenly hit by a strong gust of wind. Seconds and 1,000 feet later, she came to a stop. Campbell was hauled out of the cockpit. He wasn't too badly hurt, but the car was wrecked almost beyond repair.

Three years later, in a rebuilt 'Bluebird', he made another bid—this time on the dry bed of Lake Eyre in Southern Australia. Again, ill fortune attended him. Having worked up to a speed of about 250 m.p.h., the project was suddenly halted by heavy rains, which flooded the lake. It was not until the following year (1964), that he achieved what he had set out to do, and clocked up 405·451 m.p.h.

This was a record—but only of a kind. While Campbell was making his much vaunted preparations, a number of Americans from California had been busy with their own record breaking, and doing it on very unorthodox lines. The leaders of this land speed record splinter group were a young man named Craig Breedlove and a slightly older one named Art Arfons. Breedlove's vehicle was called the 'Spirit of America'; Arfons's, 'Green Monster'.

Breedlove had first go. On August 5th, 1963, he went to Bonneville, put in some hard driving, and covered the required distance at an average speed of 407·45 m.p.h.

In the following year, there was a spate of bids at Bonneville. The first was made by a driver named Tom Green, who travelled at 413 m.p.h. in his jet car. Then came Arfons, who raised the record to 434·2 m.p.h.—followed by Breedlove, who crossed into 500 m.p.h.-plus country with 526·28 m.p.h. Arfons had the last word with 536·75 m.p.h.

It may strike you as odd that, since Breedlove had achieved 407·45 m.p.h. in 1963, Campbell's 405·451 m.p.h. in 1964 counted as anything more than a brave attempt. The answer lies in the vehicle which the former used during his first two years. It consisted of only two elements: a B-38 wartime bomber engine bolted on to a three-wheeler body. Apart from the fact that it hadn't any wings, it looked very much like a fighter aircraft.

Since attempts on the World Land Speed Record had always been made in cars, the authority for them was the F.I.A., which ruled that they must be made in a vehicle with four or more wheels, employing direct drive to at least two of them. Breedlove's 'Spirit of America' only had three wheels and no direct drive at all.

Consequently, his record fell outside the F.I.A.'s sphere of recognition. As a three-wheeler, however, 'Spirit of America' was accepted by the Fédération Internationale Motorcycliste, which recognised that a new record had been set up for motor bikes. Breedlove could claim to be the fastest man on wheels, which means very little for there is no such title officially; he could claim to be the fastest man on a motor cycle; but he couldn't claim the World Land Speed Record.

Campbell's car, in spite of its gas turbine engine, paid some respect to orthodoxy, by having four wheels, with direct drive to all four of them. Consequently, although he was never the fastest man on wheels, he did, albeit for a short period, hold the World Land Speed Record. It may sound silly, but there it is. The F.I.A. rules in this respect have since been modified.

Once, during an interview I had with him at London Airport, I asked Breedlove why he decided to build a three-wheeler. 'The fastest thing known used to be an arrow,' he told me. 'An arrow is aerodynamically perfect. Its thrust is such that it will only go forward in a straight line. And it isn't only a question of streamlining—there's also a question of stability. If you try to throw a dart backwards, you find it won't work. As soon as it leaves your hand, it swings round in the air and travels point forward.

'Such factors as wind can slew it off course, so obviously corrections have to be possible. But fundamentally, an arrow is the right shape. As a matter of fact, I had originally intended to make "Spirit" a four-wheeler. But then it occurred to me that a vehicle comes nearest to an arrow when it's a three-wheeler. That's why I made it that way.'

Breedlove, who did all the design and development work on 'Spirit of America'—and much of the construction—had no formal training as an engineer. He was a passionate drag-racing enthusiast, who began modifying his first Ford at the age of fourteen, raced it when he was sixteen, and well before his twenty-first birthday had exceeded 200 m.p.h. in a strange device known as a belly tank car.

The fundamental of this type of vehicle is the belly tank from a B-38 bomber. You put an engine into it, fit wheels, and build a cockpit up in the front of the tank. To drive it, you have to sit in a humped-up position, with your head between your knees. It is extremely uncomfortable; but, with any luck, you travel very fast.

Compared with Campbell's £1 million 'Bluebird', the cost of building 'Spirit of America' was only about £17,000. Nevertheless, there was nothing shoddy about it. Breedlove has very strong views about what he calls the 'piles of junk' in which some drivers have attempted records. 'You only get one thing from a pile of junk', he told me, 'and that's a one-way ticket to the mortuary.'

Nevertheless, during his session at the salt flats in 1964, he very nearly lost his life. There is only one way of slowing these machines down, and that is by means of a parachute. After his last run, he dispatched the first chute. As it fluttered out into the slipstream, it was torn to shreds. A second parachute suffered a similar fate, and the vehicle careered on its way. It smashed through a line of telegraph poles, snapping one of them in half, bounded across a shallow lake and then over an embankment, and finally plunged into a canal twenty feet deep.

To the surprise and relief of onlookers, Breedlove climbed out of the cockpit unharmed and swam to the bank.

In the following year there was another gathering at the salt flats. Breedlove was there with a new car, which he called 'Spirit of America Sonic 1'. It had four wheels, but its shape still managed to suggest an arrow's inspiration. Arfons was also present with one of his 'Green Monsters', and the annual battle got going.

Breedlove scored first, on the morning of November 2nd, with an average speed of 555 m.p.h. A few days later, Arfons pushed the figure up to 576 m.p.h. And then, early in the morning of November 15th, Breedlove crossed the 600 m.p.h. frontier with 600·601 m.p.h.

And there (at the time of writing) things have remained. One suspects that Breedlove will be content to wait until somebody breaks his record before having another go. Arfons has turned his attention to the water record, with a curious craft which is virtually a jet-propelled hydrofoil on wheels. The idea of the wheels is to reduce the drag.

Sooner or later, of course, somebody will break through the sound barrier on wheels, but that will be an extremely hazardous and difficult undertaking.[1] The addition of the words 'Sonic 1' to the name of his 1965 car may suggest that Breedlove has ambitions in this direction. For the moment, though, he is well content.

[1] According to an expert at the National Physical Laboratory, with the thermometer at 92°F and humidity registering ·59, the speed of sound at Bonneville Flats would be about 780 m.p.h.

18 For the time being

The Le Mans 24-Hour Race is so big, so flamboyant, that it eclipses all similar events. There are, of course, several other long-distance races, which are measured either in time or distance. For the latter, 1,000 km is a favourite figure, though some are shorter (the Austrian Grand Prix, for example, which is over a distance of 500 km). There's a 1,000 km race at Nurburgring, at Monza, at Spa and at Montlhery. In Britain, the B.O.A.C. '500' Race was originally run over 500 miles, but now it lasts for 6 hours. Also in Britain, the Tourist Trophy race is still held annually. After that business on the Dundrod circuit in 1955, the R.A.C. finally gave up its attempts to hold it on public highways, and transferred it to a closed circuit. It took place at Goodwood until that track was shut for racing (it's still used for testing) at the end of 1964. Since then, it has been run at Oulton Park.

The toughest, most rugged circuit in this realm of motor sport is undoubtedly that of the Targa Florio in Sicily, where this event is still held each year (it's now the oldest motor race in the calendar). The road circuit at Mugello, in Italy, runs it a close second, and the annual sports car race which takes place there has been described as 'the nearest thing to the Mille Miglia'.

Over in America, they began to hold long distance races in 1952, when the 12 Hours of Sebring was inaugurated. Ten years later, they dreamed up something similar at Daytona. For the first two years, the Daytona was run over a distance of 500 km. Then it was stretched to 2,000 km. In 1965, they switched to a time basis, and ran it for twelve hours. Since 1966, it has been a twenty-four-hour race.

All these events are for sports cars and sports prototypes.

Ever since 1955, the regulations for the Le Mans 24-Hour Race have changed with an almost capricious abandon. In 1960, Ferrari began his period of Le Mans dominance, when his cars won the race of that year and of the five following years. This was a record. Neither Bentley nor Jaguar had quite so many victories in a row.

The supremacy of one particular breed does not necessarily make motor racing more interesting. Indeed, it probably has the opposite effect. However, the latter years of the Ferrari reign became very exciting indeed. With virtually no limit to the size of engines, the cars were wonderfully powerful.[1] And, which really gave point to the race, it was attracting the attention of Ford in America.

During the mid-'fifties, the Automobile Manufacturers' Association of the U.S.A. produced an agreement which banned its members from taking part in motor sport. A big car-maker obviously has to treat his image carefully. On the one hand, he wants his product to suggest a lively performance; on the other, he wants people to think of it as safe and reliable.

With the growing toll of road accidents, the American emphasis had switched to safety.

For the five years following the 'no sport' treaty, nothing happened. But then Ford began to have misgivings. Market research had shown that, among the younger generation, the company's reputation for manufacturing powerful and reliable engines was rapidly diminishing.

However much the more cautious elements may regret it, there is one certain way in which anyone in the automotive business can brush up his image with the youngsters: by taking part in motor racing, and by giving his successes the utmost publicity.

Henry Ford II, grandson of the founder, was only too well aware of this. Consequently, in 1962, Mr. Ford announced that he proposed to withdraw from the Automobile Manufacturers' Association agreement. For the first time in well over forty years, Ford were going back into motor racing.

[1] Ferrari never exceeded 5 litres in this respect.

In the following year, Ford's plans were made even more clear. A spokesman gave it out that they proposed to concentrate on sports car racing. They intended to conquer a realm which, ever since the sport began, had been dominated by European manufacturers. There were, of course, innumerable difficulties. By no means the least of them was that nobody in America had any experience of this kind of operation.

Ford's solution took things right into the heart of enemy territory. The first attack was based on the principle that, if you can't join them, *buy* them. Quietly Ford made a bid for Ferrari. Within the walls of his stronghold at Maranello, Enzo Ferrari considered the offer and rejected it.

The action moved to England. Here it was more successful. Eric Broadly, designer of the Lola, was approached by Ford and retained for two years to build and develop a special car. It was to be called a 'Ford Prototype'.

Henry Ford's goal was to win at Le Mans. This was the ultimate prize, the race which everyone wants to win, the victory which produces the biggest pay-off in terms of publicity. It took Ford three years to accomplish it.

Initially, the cars were raced by a firm known as Ford Advanced Vehicles, which was set up at Slough, England, by John Wyer, with support from the Ford Motor Company of America. Later, Carroll Shelby, Alan Mann, and Holman and Moody took over the running of the cars. All of them were, in one way or another, concerned with the development and tuning of Ford special power units. Shelby operated from California and Holman and Moody from Carolina. Alan Mann is British.

It was not until 1967, the last year of the Big Fords at Le Mans, that the cars were entered by the Ford Motor Company (U.S.A.).

In the 1965 race, a posse of prototypes put up the most fantastic speeds, making it abundantly clear that Ford had all the power anyone could desire. If this had been complemented by an equally high degree of reliability, there'd have been rejoicings in Detroit. Unfortunately, it wasn't. By midnight, all the Ford prototypes were out of the race, and a jubilant Ferrari had his sixth victory.

1966 was clearly intended to be The Year. From America there came to Le Mans a massive mobile workshop with 27 tons of spare parts and components—plus a team of mechanics, technicians, executives and goodness knows who else. The list of Ford drivers shone with such famous names as Bruce McLaren, Graham Hill, Ronnie Bucknum and Ken Miles. Henry Ford II was there in person, and made a lap of the circuit in a Ford Mustang before the race began.

At 4 p.m. on the Sunday afternoon, three Fords, their headlights blazing in triumph, drove up to the chequered flag in pouring rain. It was rather like a fine piece of formation driving. The victory which the team had so assiduously sought was theirs. And so were second and third places. At first it looked as if Ken Miles and Denis Hulme had won, but then it turned out that the New Zealanders, McLaren and Chris Amon, had beaten them by a matter of yards.

In the 1967 24-Hour Race, there were six cars entered by the Ford Motor company (U.S.A.) with fourteen drivers. Among them were Dan Gurney, A. J. Foyt Jnr. (who arrived straight from his triumph in that year's Indianapolis '500'), and Mario Andretti (the U.S.A.C. National Champion).

Dan Gurney and Foyt won.

Ford strategy at Le Mans in 1966 and 1967 was an adaptation of military science. You take the most powerful weapons, and you make sure that you have the most troops. If you are big enough, you may literally wear out the opposition, for you can afford to set such a fearful pace that they are bound to fall out. As their cars retire, so probably do yours. But, since you have more reserves than anyone else, you are likely to win.

Furthermore, the big Ford prototypes packed 7-litre engines, and those extra litres undoubtedly helped to conquer the smaller, 5-litre, Ferraris.

At the end of 1967, the Automobile Club de l'Ouest re-thought the Le Mans regulations for the umpteenth time. They put a 3-litre limit on prototypes and a 5-litre limit on sports cars. The days of the big bangers at Le Mans were over—at any rate, until the next time.

An American who never won at Le Mans was a young Texan named Jim Hall. Hall had highly original cars, equipped with automatic transmission, which he called 'Chaparrals' (from a bird which is commonly seen in Texas, and which is also known as the 'Road Runner'. It doesn't fly, but it travels very fast on the ground. Furthermore, it raises its tail feathers to act as an airbrake.)

Of the Le Mans 24-Hour Race, Hall once said to me: 'It's a very long race. It gives the machinery a great beating. It is very dangerous because it's so crowded. There are well over a 100 drivers involved, and they can't all be outstanding ones. The slow and medium speed cars are dangerous, though there are some poor drivers on the fast cars, too. It's a damn impressive race. If you want to win a race, I can't think of a better one to win.'

Hall, who inherited a fortune from oil, bought his engines from General Motors and built his cars at an establishment he maintains in Midland, Texas. The first Chaparrals were constructed in 1962. He told me: 'First of all, we decided to build a car. Then we looked at all the others. We based ours on a Formula 1 design. We decided that Colin Champan knew more about suspension than anyone else, and so we borrowed some ideas from him. The first car was based strictly on the Lotus. But we also went and looked at what the space-age firms were doing, and this led to our using fibreglass for the body. Without, perhaps, fully realising it, we were working towards automatic transmission right from the start—when we realised how light the car was going to be.

'We began to wonder why four gears were necessary, and why normal transmission was necessary. By fitting automatic transmission, we thought we'd flatten out a few of the bumps you get in the performance curves and stop the wheels from spinning so much at the back. The first car only weighed 1,200 lb.'

So the Chaparrals had automatic transmission and, so far as one could tell, were none the worse for it. A device which was a feature of the later cars was referred to in the Press by all manner of names. Hall preferred to call it, simply, 'The Wing'. 'It was near the centre of gravity,' he told me, 'and it kept the whole car down. Not just the rear, the *whole* car. In its operational position, it produced wind resistance and slowed the vehicle. To overcome this, there was a pedal which controlled it. When the pedal was pushed down, it depressed the wing and enabled the car to enter and leave corners quickly. At other times, the wing was in a horizontal position, and didn't act as an airbrake.'

For the sake of the record, the Mercedes-Benz cars which competed in the 1955 Le Mans race were fitted with airbrakes. In this case, however, they rose up vertically out of the body.

Hall's Chaparrals never won at Le Mans—perhaps because he couldn't afford to do things on the Ford scale, and hadn't enough of them. They were fitted with huge 7-litre engines; consequently, when they revamped the Le Mans regulations at the end of 1967, these cars were barred from taking part. However, they have since been able to compete in the Cam-Am series in Canada and the U.S.A., where the limits are much more generous.

Between 1959 and 1967, the red cars of Italy (in other words Ferrari) were responsible for winning the World Championship of Drivers twice: in 1961 (Phil Hill) and in 1964 (John Surtees). In the former year, they came first in four Grands Prix, of which two were won by Phil Hill. In 1964, they only won two of these races, each time with Surtees at the wheel.

There are occasions when one wonders whether the F.I.A. system of points scoring will ever be a completely fair way of deciding the championship. Undoubtedly the two greatest drivers in the past decade have been Stirling Moss and Jim Clark. Moss, in spite of fourteen victories in seven years, never won the World Championship. Clark, who won twenty-five *grandes épreuves* in six years (and beat Fangio's record) was only champion twice.

If one takes Moss's fourteen, one finds that Jack Brabham has won exactly the same number of races, and yet has been World Champion three times. On several occasions, the reigning champion has not necessarily been the driver who won the most races. The classic case, as already described, was 1958, when both Moss and Brooks won more events than Hawthorn. In 1964, Jim Clark won three Grands Prix against Surtees's two; and in 1967, Clark won four out of the eleven qualifying events, whilst Denis Hulme, who won the championship, was only victorious in two.

One of the more interesting features of Formula 1 motor racing in recent years has been the extent to which its fortunes have been in the hands of the smaller firms. It would, for example, be impossible to compare Lotus quantitively to Ford, or Cooper to British Leyland. The two giants in the small complex have been B.R.M., which is an offshoot of the giant Rubery Owen Organisation, and Honda. The rest have been relatively small outfits, most of them operating from factories on the outskirts of London. These and Lotus (which has its works in Norfolk) have been the most successful.[1] Since it was introduced in 1958, Lotus has won the Formula 1 Constructors' Championship three times; the Cooper Car Company and Jack Brabham have each won it twice, whilst B.R.M. has only won it once, and Honda hasn't won it at all. On the other occasions it was won by Vanwall and Ferrari.

With the increasing technical complexity of racing cars, it is obvious that these small outfits couldn't afford to go it alone. Help has come in the way of subsidies from the oil companies and the tyre and component manufacturers—though, since the end of 1967, the handouts have been drastically reduced.

---

[1] Though one has to remember that these teams do not build their own engines. Since 1967, Ford has been the great provider.

At about lunchtime on Easter Monday, 1962, Stirling Moss was standing beside a snackbar counter at Goodwood, drinking coffee with a small group of friends. Presently he sauntered away to take part in the day's Formula 1 race. Less than an hour later, he was unconscious in hospital, with his life hanging in the balance. Something, it was never discovered what, went wrong on one of the corners. Moss eventually recovered, but never raced again.

On April 7th, 1968, two events took place on the same day. One was the B.O.A.C. '500' race for sports cars and sports prototypes at Brands Hatch. The other was a Formula 2 event at Hockenheim in Germany. It was touch and go whether Jim Clark and Graham Hill, the Lotus drivers, would race at Brands Hatch or Hockenheim. Colin Chapman wanted them for the F2 race; Ford of Great Britain wanted them to drive a new sports car in the long-distance event. In the end, it was agreed that they should go to Germany (the Lotus cars were, in any case, powered by Ford-Cosworth engines).

That afternoon, the B.B.C. interrupted its programme to announce that Jim Clark had been killed. While he was negotiating a bend, his Lotus had suddenly gone out of control, left the road, shot into woods which bordered the track, and crashed into a tree. At first, nobody could believe it. Clark was the impeccable driver. He had been involved in crashes before, but he had always walked away from them. Now some footling failure (it may have been a tyre) had cost him his life.

His genius was proof against most things, but not this. If it was a puncture, it couldn't have happened at a worse time. The track was wet and the corner was fast. Nobody was better able to get himself out of trouble than Clark, but this unholy combination of circumstances was too much—even for him.

Clark's death shook the motor-racing world more than it cared to admit. Drivers felt that, if this could happen to him, nobody's life was sacrosanct. Large crowds attended his funeral at the little church at Duns in Berwickshire. Perhaps the finest gesture was that of the Lotus mechanics who, at their own expense, chartered a DC3 to fly up for it.

Many people said that Jim Clark was the greatest—greater than Moss, greater than Ascari, greater even than Fangio. And now he was dead. Few people have been mourned as he was mourned.

It is difficult to envy a modern racing driver for the life he leads. As recently as ten years ago, the stars only had to contend with about twenty events a year. Now, the figure is at least double. In those days, they had time to relax between meetings, to have other interests, to carry out the duties which, apart from racing, are the trappings of fame. When Tony Brooks was making his name, he was also completing his training as a dentist. Mike Hawthorn ran a garage, and ran it very well. Ascari was head of a business concerned with fuel. Others, of course, simply had fun. But fun is certainly not to be sneered at, and precious little of it finds its way into the life of the super-dedicated modern racing driver.

Perhaps the important thing about former aces is that they had time to be fully rounded, three-dimensional people. The modern star inhabits a narrow, rather dark, little world comprised of jet planes, circuits, racing cars, and hotels. He is a man with a fixed idea: living only to take part in events which, for such are the odds against it, he probably won't win and may not even finish.

The shape of his life is circular: revolving regularly year after year, to the same places on much the same dates. The only thing which can break the circle or produce, as it were, a tangent, is injury or death.

Drivers never talk about death. Whether or not they think about it is another matter. Hardly anybody knows the answer, for they are not given to discussing these things. Very little, indeed, is known about what, precisely, makes a great driver work.

A few years ago, a psychologist carried out an experiment in which a number of top drivers were compared with ordinary people. The idea was to perform some comparatively simple actions (such as arranging various shapes in certain patterns) in the face of as many distractions as the organisers could think up.

The concentration of the ordinary people soon began to fall off. They started to make little mistakes, and then bigger ones. The drivers, however, never faltered. They went on, carrying out their set tasks, apparently oblivious to all the racket which was going on around them.

Concentration is like a beam of light. The more intense it is, the more narrow it becomes. Just possibly, this may explain the kind of existence which top racing drivers seem content to lead. But so much else is unexplained. If you ask them why they do it, they answer in such unsatisfactory terms as 'because I like it', or 'because it's the only thing I'm good at', or 'because I have to keep on challenging myself'. Cynical outsiders say that they do it for the money, which has never struck me as a satisfactory explanation. A few have private means and don't need the stuff in any case. As for the rest, they may reach the big money and hold it for a while, but the price is exorbitant, and nobody in his right mind would equate motor racing with financial stability.

In this book, I have tried to tell the story of eighty years of motor racing. Basically, it has always been a question of who could go faster than the rest. The rules, the cars, the people have changed. From time to time, the very continuation of the sport in any shape or form has been threatened. Nevertheless, motor racing has always gone on. Wars may have interrupted it, but, during these years, there has always been a handful of enthusiasts who spent every moment of their leisure planning cars and races for when the fighting stopped. There is something indestructible about motor racing. One could make all kinds of guesses about the forms it will take during the next eight decades—turbine cars, jet cars, and all that sort of thing. But the one certain prediction is that, for as long as there are cars, there will be racing. Each generation will produce its small élite so that, whenever one driver retires or is killed, there will be another to get in a car and take his place. Death is the eternal dark intruder on the motor-racing scene. But, in a realm where people somehow manage not to think too much about it, death never gets in the way.